RETHINKING PENSION REFORM

This book presents a unique academic and practical perspective on managing pension funds to clarify the global debate on social security. The authors establish the basic choices in designing any system to help policy makers develop a system that achieves all their objectives. They examine reforms in Latin America to highlight flaws, and to estimate the true cost of these reforms and factors that affect these costs. The authors go on to discuss how the United States and Spain can implement robust systems incorporating many of the ideal features. The success of reforms depends on financial innovation to mitigate key risks, and some innovations are discussed that also demonstrate how pension reform choices affect the achievement of retirement objectives. Finally, the authors examine some proposed hybrid options to show how the beneficial features of these hybrids can be captured through good design in a single fund.

The late Franco Modigliani was Institute Professor Emeritus and Senior Lecturer in Economics, Finance, and Accounting at MIT and received the Nobel Memorial Prize in Economic Science in 1985 for his pioneering work in analyzing the functioning of financial markets and the behavior of household savers. Much of his writing relates to social security, capital markets, money supply, the euro, and unemployment. He wrote and edited numerous books, including *The Debate over Stabilization Policy* (Cambridge University Press, 1986) and the autobiographical *Adventures of an Economist*. Professor Modigliani's professional papers are collected in five volumes, published between 1980 and 1989.

Arun Muralidhar is Managing Director of FX Concepts, Inc., a private currency management firm, and Chairman of M^{cube} Investment Technologies LLC, a firm that assists pension funds in managing assets through innovative technologies. Before holding these positions, Dr. Muralidhar served as Head of Research in the Investment Department and as a member of the Investment Committee of the World Bank in Washington, D.C., and subsequently as Managing Director and Head of Currency Research at J. P. Morgan Investment Management. He is the author of *Innovations in Pension Fund Management* (2003) and articles in leading journals in finance, including the *Journal of Portfolio Management*, *Financial Analysts Journal*, *Journal of Risk*, *Derivatives Quarterly*, and the *Journal of Asset Management*. He received his Ph.D. in 1992 from MIT, where he studied under Professor Modigliani.

Rethinking Pension Reform

FRANCO MODIGLIANI
Massachusetts Institute of Technology

ARUN MURALIDHAR
FX Concepts, Inc.
M^{cube} Investment Technologies, LLC

CAMBRIDGE
UNIVERSITY PRESS

CAMBRIDGE UNIVERSITY PRESS
Cambridge, New York, Melbourne, Madrid, Cape Town, Singapore, São Paulo

Cambridge University Press
40 West 20th Street, New York, NY 10011-4211, USA

www.cambridge.org
Information on this title: www.cambridge.org/9780521834117

First published 2004
First paperback edition 2005

Printed in the United States of America

A catalog record for this publication is available from the British Library.

Library of Congress Cataloging in Publication Data
Modigliani, Franco.
Rethinking pension reform / Franco Modigliani, Arun Muralidhar.
p. cm.
Includes bibliographical references and index.
ISBN 0-521-83411-2 (hardback)
1. Pension trusts. 2. Social security. 3. Pension trusts – Cross-cultural studies.
I. Muralidhar, Arun S. II. Title.
HD7105.4.M63 2004
331.25′22 – dc22 2003068726

ISBN-13 978-0-521-83411-7 hardback
ISBN-10 0-521-83411-2 hardback

ISBN-13 978-0-521-67653-3 paperback
ISBN-10 0-521-67653-3 paperback

Contents

Preface

An important issue sweeping the globe is the immediate impact of worldwide population aging on the provision of old age pensions. Recognition of the trend in aging has spurred an extensive debate on measures to ensure the provision of postretirement livelihood for elderly citizens (*Economist* 2002, Chand and Jaeger 1996). This subject has led to a new breed of specialists in pension reform who advocate various proposals based on their political, social, or economic biases. As a result, there is a heated debate on pension reform involving extreme positions that are often supported by parties with vested interests. Widely divergent views in the debate have, unfortunately, blurred the distinction between differences based on values and political leanings and those based on differences in economic analysis (NASI 1999, ACSS 1997, Barr 2000). In addition, two distinct issues to be considered with respect to any proposed reform are (a) what the system should look like for the future, and (b) how one should achieve that system if it is different from the current model given present economic and political realities (the transition problem). Analysts have strong and differing views on both these issues (ACSS 1997, Schieber and Shoven 1999).

The problem of pension reform has acquired new urgency. Many countries adopted an innovative scheme for financing pensions. First proposed by Chancellor Otto von Bismarck in the nineteenth century and then adopted by many countries in the 1930s, this scheme is called "pay-as-you-go" (PAYGO). Traditional pension systems were "funded"; that is, pensions were paid out of the capital accumulated from the contributions of participants, employers, or both through the duration of the participants' working life. Under the PAYGO method, pensions are paid out of the current contributions of active members.

Why have so many countries opted for PAYGO? The simple reason is, in a funded system, the pension is paid out of the accumulated capital stock of each retiree's account. Therefore, only those who have contributed for their entire working life will receive a full pension. Participants who are close to retirement and did not contribute to the pension system receive nothing. Under PAYGO, however, current workers' contributions are used to pay full pensions to all workers from day one as if they had contributed in full throughout their working life. For this reason, when a universal mandatory pension system is begun, PAYGO provides the most appealing solution. The decision to use PAYGO is, in effect, a transfer to pensioners who, without having contributed, receive a pension at the expense of future generations that lose the capital accumulation of a funded system (generally without understanding the implications of the choice).

The PAYGO scheme can, in principle, be sustained indefinitely, if several conditions hold (Samuelson 1975). To begin with, the development of taxable wages that are taxed at a fixed contribution rate (we are assuming they are fixed) must be sufficient to pay the pensions. Pension payments, however, are influenced by the number of retirees and the promises made to them (which, over time, became more generous). The rate of taxable income growth depends on population, productivity, and wage growth. Problems arise when revenue and benefits are not balanced. In fact, some analysts feel that economic growth allows nations to run one of the most remarkable Ponzi schemes around.

Such problems have arisen in most public pension systems relying on PAYGO financing (i.e., in most parts of the world). These systems, generally identified as social security schemes, are heading for insolvency in several countries. Given current contribution levels, these systems will be unable, in most cases, to pay promised benefits in the foreseeable future unless they undergo drastic changes. This is the unavoidable consequence of two factors: (i) the ratio of contributing workers to pensioners receiving benefits will decline dramatically in the coming decades (in some cases, this level has dropped from forty workers per retiree to two to three workers per retiree), and (ii) the estimates for productivity growth are being scaled down. Challenging demographics of declining population growth and increasing longevity have a serious impact on the population pyramid.

Blahous (2000) has reported that, in the United States, in 1940, the average male lived 61.4 years and the average female 65.7 years. In 2000, this average climbed to 73.6 years for males and 79.5 years for females. Given this improvement in longevity, there is urgent need for speedy action on pension reform. If PAYGO is to be maintained, countries face a choice of highly undesirable alternatives, namely, (i) to raise taxes, (ii) to cut benefits, or (iii) some combination of the two. The problems are not immediate, and procrastinating is possible without immediate consequences. However, the longer the solution is postponed, the higher will be the costs to be borne by future generations. A profusion of proposals on social security reform have been offered in the United States and other countries by individuals, academicians, politicians, consultants, lobby groups, and international development agencies. Many, however, have confused social security with private arrangements for the provision of retirement wealth. Currently, several popular proposals have taken the direction followed by Chile.

Chile was one of the first countries to reform its pension system in 1981 by moving away from PAYGO to a total, or partial, return to some form of funded system (Pinera 1997). This shift was based primarily on the premise that investing accumulated assets in income-yielding assets would provide a significantly higher return than the implicit return offered by PAYGO, which is the long-run growth rate of wages.

This transition was effected by requiring individuals to redirect their contributions to individual accounts invested in financial assets managed by private firms. The system would eventually eliminate the role of social security and the public sector, and for that reason has come to be known as the "privatization of social security." This approach soon became the standard and was replicated in numerous other developing countries – often at the urging or coercion of agencies such as the World Bank. Many academicians and politicians in developed countries, such as the United States, favor this approach (Ferrara 1982). The Chilean model, however, suffers from very serious flaws, which can be corrected by better design. Countries such as Australia and Hungary have opted for systems whereby collective arrangements attempt to mitigate the problems in individual account models. In addition, several countries are in a position to make the transition from systems on the verge of bankruptcy to a more robust system that protects retirees from (i) retiring poor, (ii) bearing unnecessary risk, or (iii) being forced to make decisions on investment matters in which they have little or no expertise.

In attempting to clarify the global debate on social security, we focus on some analytical issues relating to the debate and go on to propose a reform framework. Chapter 1 provides definitions of key terms and examples of different pension systems and reforms around the world. Chapter 2 establishes the basic choices available to policy makers in designing a system for their country. These principles are meant to guide them in their attempt to develop the system most likely to achieve the many objectives of any public pension system. However, several countries are not starting with a clean slate and have to consider their current systems, the political and economic realities of their countries, and the likelihood of a feasible transition to the optimal social security system. It is useful to articulate the Ideal Model or *tabula rasa*, and to address separately whether initial conditions make the shift socially desirable, which is a distinction highlighted by Orszag and Stiglitz (2001). In examining some current reforms in Latin America, Chapter 3 highlights their flaws. Chapter 4 provides a framework to estimate the true cost of these reforms and factors that affect these costs. This sets the stage for Chapters 5 and 6, which discuss how countries on the brink of undertaking reforms, such as the United States and Spain, can implement robust systems incorporating many of the ideal features. Because the dynamics of any transition determines whether any reform will be broadly accepted or rejected, we consider several possible transition scenarios to highlight complex trade-offs inherent in any transition to a new system. These analyses attempt to address concerns relating to intergenerational equity (i.e., whether or not certain generations or cohorts are disadvantaged compared with others). The success of these reforms is unlikely unless there is significant innovation in financial markets to provide products that allow for the mitigation of certain key risks. Some of these innovations are discussed in Chapter 7. The main contribution of Chapter 7 is to show how the existence of a DB and a DC plan is critical for the success of pension reform. Finally, there is a general consensus that no one system can satisfy the goals of a reform program; hence, we examine some proposed hybrid options and show how the beneficial features of these hybrids can be captured through good design in a single structure (Chapter 8). Chapter 8 also introduces variable contributions as a mechanism for managing the risk associated with ensuring guaranteed replacement rates.

Previous research has demonstrated that this topic is multifaceted, and we do not profess to address all of them. Several analysts have examined the impact of changing benefits to save pension systems. Some analysts have looked at manipulating the retirement age, changing the basis for inflation indexation, adjusting benefit calculations, and suitably modifying survivor spouse pensions (e.g., Diamond and Orszag 2002, World Bank 1994). Others have explored issues relating to whether certain groups, such as minorities or divorced spouses, should be favored as in NASI (1999) or whether systems truly redistribute wealth the way they are supposed to. We address the former set of issues briefly in the context of Spain's reform proposal (Chapter 6). Initially, we develop a simple benefit structure that could be more effective for future generations and solve many of the existing problems. Later chapters on transition issues treat benefits as a given, for our solution is relatively independent and flexible in relation to benefit structures (as demonstrated in Chapters 5 and 6). In short, our work is directed to solving the problem of financing benefits rather than inquiring whether the benefits are appropriate. Although others emphasize political issues (Blahous 2000), we address the issue of political risk without supporting any particular political stance. We consider situations in the United States and Spain, but with the aim of being more global we emphasize the analytical framework. Finally, we consider specific financial innovations in the hope that our research will provide another clue to solving social security crises worldwide. Given the polarity of the debate, we anticipate as much criticism as support of our position. Our purpose will be served if the analytical framework we provide furthers the rigorous analysis of reform options.

Acknowledgments

Franco and I had talked about working together on a paper ever since I earned my Ph.D. in 1992, but my job trading derivatives and even managing pension assets for the World Bank did not lend itself to a rigorous academic collaboration – especially of the quality required by Franco. In the spring of 1998, I was asked to join a World Bank mission to China to talk about effective management of pension assets to Chinese government officials. I had made a similar trip to Jordan in 1996 but had not digested the magnitude of the problem affecting these countries. On the bus ride from Shangai to Hang Zhou (where the conference was to be held), I overheard my World Bank colleagues, who advised countries on pension reform, criticize defined benefit (DB) plans in favor of defined contribution (DC) plans without their ever having had the experience of managing or evaluating the risks of either. Needless to say, my training under Franco did not allow me to tolerate this, and, at the conference, I publicly disagreed with their recommendations, leading one of my colleagues to suggest that I was a "technocrat" and knew nothing about pension reform or savings. I was accompanied by a wonderfully smart young colleague – Ronald van der Wouden – who was kind enough to spend his free time in China to help me develop the guaranteed return, defined benefit concept. On the way back to Washington, D.C., I had a heated argument with another World Bank colleague and ran the risk of being thrown off the plane and even out of the business class lounge at Narita Airport. This experience showed that I had been trained well by Franco!

After being accused of having no understanding of macroeconomics and savings, I called Franco for assistance. He, at the time, was trying to convince the Italians that they were going down the wrong path in reforming their pension system. We finally met up in Martha's Vineyard in the summer of 1998, and I laid out the reason why I felt DB dominates DC when participation is mandatory (as my poor wife, Shaila, sat patiently through this discussion). Once Franco grasped the essence, there was no stopping him in generating one creative idea after the next to support DB plans. The chapter exploring the taxonomy of pension reform issues (Chapter 2) was developed over a dinner in Washington, D.C., in the fall of 1998 as Franco mapped out on a napkin the ideas he planned to present at a World Bank conference for Latin American reforms the following morning (and Shaila and I worked feverishly all night to develop the graphs and tables for his presentation). That conference was also the genesis for Chapter 3 (the critique of the Latin American reforms), as we met a number of key policy makers from the region and got a firsthand account of how decisions had been made in the reform process. Chapter 4 is the result of the infamous China trip during which Ronnie took a half-baked idea and demonstrated through his models why we were on the right track. Chapter 5 represents a labor of love, for we started a variation of this paper in late 1998 and never really finished it because the United States always gave us something new to work on – either a revised actuarial study, a change in government or government finances, or a new proposal by the incumbent administration. However, it was work on this paper that was the seed for Franco's brilliant concept of the swap between the U.S. Treasury and the Social Security Administration. Chapter 6 owes its origin to a brilliant student of Franco's – Pedro Sainz de Baranda – undertaking a Herculean effort to pull together a credible proposal for Spain. We have taken his work and adapted it to our framework, and we are deeply indebted to him for expanding the scope of our approach by including benefit reforms. Chapter 7 has a bit of a tainted history. I wrote this paper in 1998–99 in response to a prize offer by the Institute of International Finance (IIF) because I needed to prove that I had decent research capabilities for my green card application. I was first informed that I was a prize winner and had to be in Washington, D.C., for the award ceremony in a few weeks, only to be told a few days later that a big mistake had been made and the prize had been revoked (and no first prize was to be awarded!). Franco, outraged at this behavior, called several of his friends who were on the IIF committee to protest such an unfair decision – if for no other reason than that the IIF never told me why the prize had been withdrawn or whether the approach was wrong. So this chapter makes its appearance here with less fanfare. Once again, Ronnie and I had spent time mulling this over in the context of the World Bank's own pension reform plan – with the World Bank smartly choosing to keep a DB plan as the anchor. We were trying to find a way to help participants until it dawned on me that we could take a few liberties with economic theory to create the "Two-Pension Fund Separation" theorem. Chapter 8 is really the cornerstone of the book, and Franco and I troubled Ronnie no end (in between his wedding preparations) to make our intuition work with the simulations. It took another trip to Martha's Vineyard in July 2003 to come full circle and tie up all the loose ends.

This book is the result of many years of work on this topic by us, and we have benefitted significantly not only from those who collaborated with us on these topics, but also from those who were patient and considerate with their time in trying to educate us on the many facets of social security. In the former category, we thank Ronald van der Wouden, Pedro Sainz de Baranda, Maria Luisa Ceprini, and Kemal Asad-Syed. In the latter category, we express our deepest gratitude to Steve Goss, Chief Actuary of the Social Security Administration, for his generous, patient advice in an area where his knowledge is vastly superior to ours. We acknowledge the inspiration we received from Martin Feldstein's many publications demonstrating the power of compound interest. We are indebted to Peter Diamond, Alicia Munnell, and Alan Greenspan, who read earlier drafts of chapters and gave encouragement by noting some hopeful progress. Thanks also to Andrew Abel, Albert Ando, Shadrach Appana, Mel Aronson, Mukul Asher, Daniel Barr, Nicholas Barr, Fennell Betson, David Blake, Alan Blinder, Barry Bluestone, Zvi Bodie, Barry Burr, Michael Clowes, Douglas Elmendorf, Cagatay Ergenekon, Stanley Fischer, Sheldon Friedman, Arnoldo Hax, Roger Hickey, Larry Kotlikoff, Assar Lindbeck, Perry Mehrling, Lawrence Meyers, Olivia Mitchell, Leah Modigliani, the late Senator Daniel Patrick Moynihan, Sanjay Muralidhar, Rudy Penner, Pete Peterson, Tom Phillips, Monika Quiesser, Stephen Roach, Dallas Salisbury, Louise Sheiner, Allen Sinai, Gene Sperling, R. Thilainathan, Laura Tyson, Masaharu Usuki, Jaime Villasenor, and Paul Volcker. We also thank Mavis Robertson, Fiona Reynolds, Richard Grant, and Ralph Willis for sharing their experiences on the Australian super-annuation schemes. In addition, we are grateful to participants of the World Bank's Annual Conference on Development Economics (1999) for helpful comments.

We also thank Neetu Bhatia, Thomas Lissey, and Cybele Suarez for their dedicated assistance. Shaila Muralidhar and Denis Fernandes made a valiant effort to edit the document between our many changes. Thanks to Jamil Baz for introducing us to Scott Parris of Cambridge University Press and to Scott and his team for taking a mangled document and converting it into a readable book. Thanks also to our common friend, the late Kenneth McLeod (Stanford University Press), for his constant encouragement – he is sorely missed.

Serena Modigliani receives our unlimited thanks for putting up with all our idiosyncrasies, including fighting Franco when he wanted a computer brought to his hospital room and providing a reality check whenever we thought we had won the battle. She finally forced us to wrap up the project in July 2003. All errors are our own, and we apologize if we have missed mentioning someone.

August 2003

Disclaimer

The views expressed in this book by the authors and collaborators are their personal views and not those of the organizations they work for.

A Tribute to Franco

This book would not be complete without a tribute to Franco Modigliani, my co-author, mentor, and friend, who passed away in the final stages of preparing the manuscript for publication. I had promised his wife, Serena, that we would finish the book by August 1, 2003, as the work had dragged on for some time. After sending the completed draft to the publishers, I promptly left for the forests of Scandinavia. Two days later, Franco called me to say that he was not happy with Chapter 5 because we had left the reader with the impression that our solution to the social security crisis was arbitrary. So, "we" agreed to include an analytical appendix (Appendix 5.5) advocating our solution. My prior inclination had been to leave this and other work on variable contributions to a second edition. But Franco disagreed, and he worked tirelessly on this Appendix until its completion. On September 20, 2003 we agreed on all the changes to Appendix 5.5 save one, which was not included because Franco could not remember what it was. I re-sent the draft to the publisher and tried to call Franco on September 24 to see if I could track down that final change. As he had stirred the pot on Mr. Berlusconi getting a humanitarian award, he was impossible to reach and, on September 25, Franco moved on to bigger and better things. Therefore, I leave the blemish in Appendix 5.5 for someone else to find.

The next day, I dug out all the papers on the book – dating back over six years – to find a cartoon that Franco had sent me from *The New Yorker Magazine* (June 1999). It was his favorite, and he always got a big chuckle out of it. It shows a man alone on a small island with a helicopter hovering overheard. The punch line is, "Forget about me – save Social Security!" That to me is what this book is about, and I enclose the cartoon for others to enjoy. Franco often confided in me that saving social security globally was very dear to him because this was one of the few pieces of work that could improve people's lives. It really troubled him that politicians would allow the enrichment of the wealthy at the cost of the poor. I trust that all his brilliant ideas, now recorded in this book, will help achieve that goal for current and future generations.

So, I dedicate this book to Franco and Serena – two people whose wisdom, kindness, generosity, honesty, righteousness, and humor have touched many lives. We are all better human beings from that interaction. I also want to thank my family, friends, and the Seths – without them I may never have met Franco and Serena!

A.S.M.
February 2004

"Forget about me—save Social Security."

RETHINKING PENSION REFORM

1

A Primer on Pension Reform

DEFINITION OF TERMS[1]

Pension reform evokes certain primary questions: What is a pension system? Why must it exist? And, what does the balance sheet of a pension system look like? The primary purpose of a pension system is to help households achieve an allocation of life resources by smoothing consumption over life, as postulated in the life-cycle hypothesis (LCH). This is achieved by transferring resources from working life to postretirement, when income dries up.[2] Before debating the appropriate form of pension plan, it is worthwhile to record the reasons for the existence of pension plans. There is a plethora of literature on the subject, and researchers have undertaken a wide range of empirical studies (World Bank 1994). For example, Logue and Rader (1997) have suggested that, from a corporate perspective, plans must be set up for insurance against uncertainty about retirement income, to create recruitment and retention incentives, and to formulate a tax-efficient means of saving. These conclusions may be restated under three main headings for country and corporate plans.

First, redistribution and social insurance are particularly valid for public systems. This is equivalent to undertaking a social obligation to ensure that all citizens, especially the old, have the requisite resources to meet their basic needs. However, the primary reason for the state to provide this arrangement is the belief that many citizens are myopic and do not accumulate adequate resources for retirement (Samuelson 1975, Aaron and Reischauer 1998). An extension of this paternalistic view is the opinion that many segments of society may not be sophisticated enough to set up appropriate arrangements. In short, these systems are established to prevent the state from having to support a large segment of retirees. Some experts argue that

---

[1] Adapted from Muralidhar (2001).
[2] Modigliani and Ando (1954) and Modigliani and Brumberg (1963).

the pension scheme of the United States is a social insurance scheme, not a savings scheme (Blahous 2000). Pension schemes can also be a redistribution mechanism for transferring resources from the well-to-do to the poorer segments of society that cannot afford to accumulate adequate reserves. Although redistribution features are not a prerequisite for a pension scheme, they differentiate a pension scheme from a "social security" scheme. Generally, schemes with redistribution tend to provide, or should provide, a basic (rather than a generous) minimum pension payment.

Second, private savings must be encouraged. As economic theory demonstrates, countries need savings for capital formation, and individuals need savings to support themselves in the nonearning phase of their lives. Using a variety of incentives (such as tax credits and deferrals) and mandated contribution rules, governments encourage citizens to increase their rate of saving. The greater the need for such savings, the higher the contribution rate and, potentially, the benefit.

Third, the desired behavior has to be induced. At a macro level, a pension scheme allows individuals to adopt a life-cycle model of consumption, thus protecting myopic and unsophisticated individuals (Modigliani and Ando 1963). This involves saving during working life to provide for postretirement. At the corporate level, pensions are a deferred wage payable only if the employee exhibits desirable characteristics, such as integrity and honesty. In addition, companies are able to induce the desired behavior by offering matching contributions to ensure that employees retire without anxiety. Pensions can be structured to attract employees to join an organization, stay longer (typical corporate DB), have job flexibility (cash balance plan), and so on. On the one hand, Blahous (2000) has suggested that social security schemes should encourage work rather than early retirement. On the other hand, the basic philosophy of a funded pension scheme is to set aside funds today and invest them appropriately to support future consumption (liability) – even in early retirement.

Pension systems can be broadly categorized by the benefits they promise and the way they finance that promise. There is, essentially, a choice between two types of pension plans: defined benefit (DB) and defined contribution (DC). Financing methods, generally described as "pay-as-you-go" (PAYGO) and funded, are briefly dealt with in the following sections.

DEFINED BENEFIT PENSION PLANS

The essence of a DB pension plan is that it provides a "defined benefit" – a *prespecified annuity* either in absolute currency or as a fraction of a measure of salary (for example, a defined percentage of the final salary or an average of some past years of salary). The guaranteed pension benefit could be in either real or nominal terms.

In DB pension plans, participants, sponsors, or both make contributions that could change over time. The ratio of annuity or benefit to a measure of salary is known as the "replacement rate." The participant may be unaware of any relationship between contributions and benefits. However, the administrators of the system and pension finance experts know there is a unique "budget constraint" that links contributions, returns, and benefits to a given replacement rate (Asad-Syed, Muralidhar, and van der Wouden 1998). This relationship is highlighted in equation 1.1 and discussed in detail in the appendix to this chapter. DB plans rely on an inter- and intragenerational pooling of investment and liability risk, which is called the social allocation of risk by Bateman, Kingston, and Piggott (2001).

DEFINED CONTRIBUTION PENSION PLANS

In DC pension schemes, participants, sponsors, or both make *prespecified contributions*. The plan specifies contributions either in absolute currency or as a fraction of a measure of salary (e.g., 10,000 U.S. dollars annually or 5 percent of annual pretax salary). These contributions may also be partially or totally voluntary. Participants invest contributions in assets. The final pension is uncertain (prior to retirement) because it depends entirely on asset performance of the accumulated contributions. Accordingly, two individuals with identical contributions but different investment portfolios can receive widely divergent pensions. Further, two individuals with identical contribution histories can receive widely divergent pensions over different time periods.[3]

An important point is, even in DC plans, it is possible for contributions to change over time. This could happen because of changes in tax laws (either for mandated or voluntary schemes) or if existing contributions provide an insufficient or excessive replacement rate. This leads us to make a very important distinction between a DB plan and a DC plan:

> The essential characteristic of a DB plan is that the terminal outcome is defined (a target replacement rate to be paid to participants is articulated by a sponsor), whereas a DC plan is one in which the terminal outcome is variable.

Traditionally, corporate DB pension formulas define annuities based on the number of years of service multiplied by some accrual factor. Implicitly, the product of these two factors is the replacement rate. The problem with this statement of benefits is that the inclusion of years of service in the formula creates nonlinear growth in

---

[3] Bader (1995), Bodie et al. (1988), and Blake (2000) provide a more detailed description of DB and DC plans.

pensions as one ages, leading individuals to stay with the pension-providing institution because the cost of leaving increases over time. This creates a perverse incentive
to stay. This simple definition of benefits highlights one of the negative aspects of DB
plans, which has put all DB plans in a bad light! Godoy and Valdes-Prieto (1997) have
provided a general condemnation of all DB plans by suggesting that "[t]he defined
benefit approach exposes workers to the risk of a low final wage on which benefits
are based and must pay an implicit fee to the agents that provide the guarantee on
investment returns." (p. 70) This condemnation is unwarranted because a DB plan is
only a promise to provide a guaranteed replacement rate, and there is no need to use
the preceding formula to do so. One can see the relationship between contributions
and returns in this simple equation:

> *Nominal contributions over working life, compounded at the expected return on*
> *assets (with or without volatility) = Expected final wealth at retirement = Expected*
> *present value of desired annuity as of the retirement date (which can be related to*
> *the replacement rate)*   (1.1)

Nominal contributions are equal to the contribution rate multiplied by the nominal
wage. For simplicity, assume the contribution rate is fixed (we will return to this
assumption in Chapter 8). When returns are volatile, this equation characterizes
a DC plan. If the volatility of returns is eliminated, either through an investment
strategy or a guarantee, then final wealth and the present value of the annuity at
retirement becomes a function of salary growth. In other words, if the rate of return
is guaranteed, the replacement rate, which is the ratio of pension annuity to some
measure of salary (last year or average of last 35 years) can be guaranteed, given
salary growth. This equation can, therefore, also characterize DB plans. An example
in Chapter 3 shows the simple and explicit relationship between contributions,
investment returns, and pensions for given salary growth (see appendix to this
chapter for technical details). Previous pension reform research has not recognized
that good pension design can create a close link between DB and DC plans.

FUNDING METHODS

There are several ways to fund DB or DC plans. Presently, social security systems are
overwhelmingly PAYGO, DB schemes in which current participants are required to
make contributions used to pay the benefits of retirees. In a pure PAYGO, there is no
accumulation of funds because all contributions are disbursed to service pensions.
However, corporate or occupational DB or DC schemes tend to be funded (partially
and fully). Funding requires an accumulation of funds before retirement to service
future liabilities. Funds are invested in either marketable or nonmarketable assets.

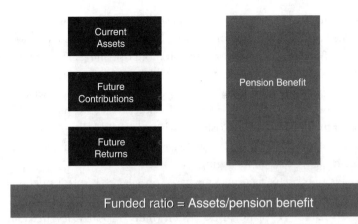

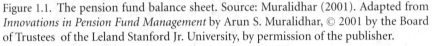

Figure 1.1. The pension fund balance sheet. Source: Muralidhar (2001). Adapted from *Innovations in Pension Fund Management* by Arun S. Muralidhar, © 2001 by the Board of Trustees of the Leland Stanford Jr. University, by permission of the publisher.

As a result, some combination of contributions and asset returns is used to service pensions. Some researchers (e.g., Logue and Rader 1997) have suggested that DC plans are always fully funded. This comment is true in the sense that the pension is entirely paid out of whatever capital has been accumulated, but it can be misinterpreted to suggest that the sponsor is indifferent to the size of the pension. Many researchers incorrectly assume that both sponsors and retirees are indifferent to the annuity paid out in DC plans. It is critical, even in a DC plan, for participants to have a target replacement rate (though it is not guaranteed) and to select their contribution, investment policy, or both to achieve that target. As a result, other researchers (Muralidhar and Van der Wouden 1998b) have suggested that DC plans are underfunded if the assets in the plan are insufficient to deliver a target replacement rate. Regardless of the funding method, a pension fund balance sheet can be distilled down as shown in Figure 1.1, for which different funding methods place greater emphasis on contributions or accumulated assets and asset returns to pay benefits. Similarly, reform can focus on changes to (i) benefits, (ii) contribution policy, and (iii) investment policy. Any, or all, of these may require changes in the institutional arrangements of the current social security system of a country.

COMPARING DB AND DC PENSION PLANS

DB plans spread investment risk across a large number of individuals of different ages and over different time horizons. These plans pool risk within a cohort and across cohorts. The plan sponsor, who generally bears the investment risk of the plan, has a much longer time frame and a much higher risk-bearing capacity than individuals in the plan. In other words, in a DC plan the time horizon is the life of one individual, whereas in DB plans the time horizon is much longer (if not infinite). For these reasons, DB plans on average can take on more risk and generate higher returns, and their asset allocation policy tends to take longer to change than can individual plans (see also Orszag and Stiglitz 2001). However, by pooling assets, DB plans incur lower costs for managing assets.[4] On the other hand, DC plans enable individuals to tailor their portfolio to the risk they wish to bear and allow for a better matching to their preferences. Individuals participate in all the gains and losses of their plan but incur higher costs in managing their assets.[5]

DB plans provide stable retirement income based on salary; DC plans offer less predictable retirement incomes owing to their dependence on investment performance. By their very nature, DB plans are less flexible (individuals have less freedom over their contributions) and are unresponsive to meeting the cash flow needs of individuals before and after retirement.

DB plans provide insurance for longevity. The possibility that the money will run out before the individual dies is largely nonexistent unless the sponsor defaults and there is no insurance coverage. Country schemes do not require insurance because the state is the sponsor and has the ability to tax citizens. In the United States, insurance for corporate plans is usually provided by agencies such as the Pension Benefit Guarantee Corporation (PBGC). However, individuals who contribute during their entire lifetime and die soon after retirement do not have the opportunity to bequeath a pool of funds to their heirs. DC plans do not provision for insurance, and annuities can be expensive to purchase. Often, it is difficult to access inflation-indexed life annuities in DC plans. However, bequeathing monies to heirs in the event of premature death is possible only in DC plans though DB plans offer survivor benefits.

A variant of the DC plan is the Provident Fund (PF) scheme, which is popular in Commonwealth countries. Under this scheme, individual contributions are pooled for investment and participants are credited an annual dividend, which is usually the rate of return on the assets. PFs also have some of the generational risk-sharing attributes of DB plans. In some cases, returns are smoothed over many periods to ensure that no one cohort is impacted by poor performance. However, this can create problems if the realized returns fall consistently, for the smoothing technique may result in promises exceeding available funds. If they are structured appropriately, PFs could be more optimal than individual DC plans from a macro investment

---

[4]   Blake (2000) has examined other noninvestment-related differences such as portability loss and cost of annuities. This paper finds that in the United Kingdom, total contributions into DC schemes tend to be much lower than those into DB schemes.

[5]   Blake (2000) states that "[a] DB scheme is invested in a portfolio containing: the underlying assets (and so, in part, a DC scheme) *plus* a put option *minus* a call option on these assets."

TABLE 1.1 Investment characteristics of defined benefit and defined contribution pension

Defined benefits	Defined contributions
1) Provide stable benefits	1) Allow for matching of cash flows with needs
2) Plan sponser bears risk	2) Individual bears risk
3) Pool investment risk	3) Individual has choice in investments
4) Provide insurance against longevity	4) Allow for bequeathing of wealth
A combination of DB and DC may be more advantageous	

Source: Muralidhar (2001). Reprinted with permission from Muralidhar (2001).

perspective. The two main disadvantages of PFs are that (i) individuals bearing the investment risk are usually disconnected from the decision makers, and (ii) participants are unable to choose their investment policies and, therefore, have no control over the level of risk taken. The latter disadvantage can be addressed, to some extent, by offering a series of subfunds within a PF framework with each subfund offering a different risk profile (also called "life-cycle funds" targeting cohorts of different ages).

Table 1.1 summarizes the comparison of DB and DC plans. Clearly, a mix of the investment characteristics of DB and DC plans would satisfy a larger group of individuals than would any one type of plan. Innovative new plans that incorporate the beneficial characteristics of each type of plan can achieve the same objective. Some corporations in the United States provide a cash balance alternative requiring the plan sponsor to guarantee a rate of return on investments (either a fixed or variable rate). If the contribution rate and return are fixed, the replacement rate of the participant is also guaranteed for given salary growth. With a variable rate of return (for example, U.S. Treasury 10-year rate + 3 percent) the replacement rate is variable. This plan was designed to ensure a more linear and steady accrual of pension rights, which were not skewed to emphasize the last few years of service disproportionately.

It is important to note that choosing between DB and DC plans also has noninvestment implications. For example, DC plans require a well-educated, financially literate group to use the freedom of choice to ensure adequate replacement rates at retirement. DB plans have to be supported by strong governance structures to ensure that sufficient funds are soundly invested to meet future liabilities. The relative mix of DB and DC plans is likely to be country and individual specific (discussed in detail in Chapter 7).

Reformers have thus been led to suggest either multiple systems within a country or a single system with facets of both systems. The most notable example of a multipillar system is the World Bank's three-pillar system (a mandatory PAYGO DB, a mandatory funded DC sponsored by the state or employers, and a voluntary DC). Bodie, Marcus, and Merton (1988) have argued for a hybrid minimum floor plan, where the DB is the floor. Our own proposal exploits many of these preferences.[6] (These issues are discussed in detail later in the chapter and in Chapter 8.)

INDIVIDUAL VERSUS POOLED ARRANGEMENTS

A fair amount of the debate focuses on individual choice versus group arrangements. We therefore highlight the issues that may arise from these debates and articulate some of the trade-offs. Individual choice is most commonly raised in the context of portfolio selection, whereas pooled arrangements are generally discussed in the context of risk sharing in DB plans. The case for individual investment arrangements is predicated on allowing individuals the choice to select their desired portfolio and bestow inalienable property rights on their savings. Pooled DB arrangements imply lower costs but may be susceptible to government manipulation because governments can control these assets. However, it is possible for pooled arrangements to be made in DC-type structures: the most notable is a PF or U.S. Thrift Savings Plan (TSP) in which the investment function is pooled but the individual bears the market risk.[7] Alternatively, Bateman, Kingston, and Piggott (2001) have pointed out that, in Australia, where mandated saving is made through employers, cost savings can be achieved by pooling through the employer (similar to TSP).

The second area where these issues are discussed is in the context of pensions: individual arrangements for annuities tend to be more costly and generally may not provide individuals with sufficient insurance because the market may be incomplete (e.g., no life annuities, no protection against inflation or anxiety about adverse selection). However, there is a tendency to regard pooled arrangements as more susceptible to political risks such as changing of benefits (Diamond 1997b). Hence, the trade-off in designing systems is that policymakers have to decide between individual or pooled arrangements and to explicitly trade off choice and political risk versus risk sharing and lower cost.

---

[6] Further, Muralidhar and van der Wouden (1998a) recommend that countries implement contributory defined benefit (CDB) plans in which the participant's contributions grow at a guaranteed real rate of return (guaranteed by the government). This plan engenders many of the advantages of DC plans (e.g., funded individual accounts, the possibility of borrowing) and at the same time provides insurance through the guarantee. They also suggest that individuals should complement such plans by investing additional funds in DC plans for supplementary savings. The corporate analog to the CDB plan is the cash balance plan.

[7] In the TSP, individuals choose desired funds from a menu of options, but then all choices are aggregated and invested to reduce cost.

EXAMPLES OF PENSION SYSTEMS

This section examines pension systems for countries and companies and provides some background on the different characteristics they engender.[8] The pension systems reviewed include the U.S. Social Security system, the Chilean and Mexican models, the Italian Supplementary System, the Hungarian and Malaysian models, and the U.S. 401(K).

Social Security System in the United States[9]

Established in the 1930s, the Social Security system is a mandated, public, DB system with very wide, compulsory participation. Few groups are permitted to opt out. The average pension benefit represents a replacement rate of approximately 50 percent of the best 35 years of salary history. Some adjustment is made to redistribute pensions to poorer participants; hence, individual replacement rates may differ from the average.[10] To this end, the replacement rate offered to those with a poor income history is higher than for those with a higher income. Benefits are paid until death, include substantial indexation to inflation (since 1972), and are extended to survivors. The system was designed along the lines of a PAYGO system with current contributors largely financing pension payments. Today, the Social Security system is not a pure PAYGO system, for it was recognized in the mid-1970s that, with prevailing contributions, the system was unavoidably heading toward insolvency. As a result, the Greenspan Commission in 1982–83 recommended a sharp rise in contributions, which would permit building up a reserve – the so-called Trust Fund – to cover future shortages. Unfortunately, that reform is insufficient and new reforms are needed to avoid insolvency in the twenty-first century. There is no individual choice in this system.

Chilean DC Model

The Chilean model, implemented in 1981, involves gradual phasing out of the PAYGO plan and replacement by a mandatory DC plan. New workers can participate only in the DC plan, whereas participants in the PAYGO plan can choose between the old and new plan. Assets are managed by private companies (called Administradora de

---

[8] For information on the U.K. pension system refer to Disney (1998); on European pension reform refer to Mantel and Bowers (1999); and on the Japanese system refer to Usuki (2002).

[9] For more details, see Diamond (1996a) and Blahous (2000), Chapter 5.

[10] As of 1999, monthly pension is 96 percent of the first $505, 32 percent of the next earnings up to $3043, and 15 percent for earnings above this level.

Fondos de Pensiones or AFPs) chosen by the participant from a list approved by the government. Individuals largely bear the risk of investment performance.[11] There are some guarantees in the Chilean system, including (i) a low social assistance benefit to those not covered by the mandatory plan, (ii) a state-guaranteed minimum pension of approximately 25 percent of the average wage if contributions are made for at least 20 years, (iii) a minimum profitability rate guaranteed for each pension fund relative to the average for the country, and (iv) state-guaranteed annuity payments if the insurance company fails (World Bank 1994). Variations of the Chilean scheme adopted in other parts of Latin America – in Argentina, Colombia, and Peru – offer a choice in the second pillar between a privately managed DC system and a public PAYGO DB system (Mitchell and Barreto 1997). However, individuals are permitted to make voluntary contributions to their funds to allow for early retirement (Godoy and Valdes-Prieto 1997).

401(K) Plans and Individual Retirement Accounts (IRAs) in the United States

These schemes are most prevalent in the United States and are most commonly referenced when discussing funded DC plans. Under the 401(K) schemes, both employers and employees contribute to these funds from pretax income. Participants are free to choose investment strategies from within a set of chosen private providers who manage the assets for the participants. They are allowed to borrow from their account, within limits and at their discretion, but must repay under established rules.

Under the IRA, individuals set up the plan directly if they meet certain eligibility criteria. Participants have sufficient choice in the structure (i) to select their asset allocation (a mix of bonds and equities; international and domestic assets) and (ii) to select preferred manager(s) from a short list of managers and mutual funds. Participants either have full discretion over asset allocation and fund selection (self-directed plans) or can delegate the responsibility to the service provider. Withdrawal of funds is permitted to finance certain activities, but if these monies are not returned before retirement, the participant incurs a tax event because the IRA is no longer a tax-deferred saving. The pension is the annuity that can be purchased from service providers given the accumulation at retirement.

In both systems, participants have some discretion over the level of contributions, but there are limitations on maximum contributions. These caps on contributions exist because such savings are tax deferred. However, the caps have changed over time, allowing participants to change the amount they contribute to these plans.

---

[11] This, in some way, serves the role of the first pillar in the World Bank framework.

Italian Scheme (and Australian Superannuation Schemes)

Italy has long relied on a PAYGO scheme supplemented by a severance pay fund, which are both noted for their oppressiveness (Modigliani and Ceprini 1998). Mandated pension contributions account for more than 40 percent of workers' pay. An interesting facet is that the benefits are based on the *realized* rate of income growth, giving the scheme a DC flavor. Most recently, Italy has been experimenting with a reform that allows workers to shift their severance pay fund contributions to individual accounts in common funds of their profession. These investments are for an initial period, after which workers are permitted to switch to the mutual fund of another profession or to funds that are broader. Hence, despite being privately managed individual accounts, there is a limited choice of investment vehicles and a somewhat arbitrary grouping of participants by profession (rather than age, income, or risk-bearing capacity).

Although Australia has corporate DB plans, in the Australian version of DC plans employers are directed to provide the plans, but superannuation companies can compete for participants. As a result, there are superannuation schemes at the company or industry level, but private firms can set up master trusts to offer accounts to individuals (Bateman et al. 2001). Australia is an interesting example, for there is little by way of investment restrictions or guarantees, which contrasts with the system in Hungary. A big risk in these systems is that the asset allocation applied to participants may not be appropriate because investment strategies are applied to broad groupings based on age (and do not account for wealth, consumption patterns, or desired annuity of individual participants). Scheiwe (2001) provides an interesting critique of the Australian model.

Mandatory Provident Funds

Under these schemes, prevalent in countries formerly under the Commonwealth (such as India and Malaysia), individuals contribute to the system, which then aggregates funds in a central pool. Such schemes are generally offered to private sector employees (Asher 1998, Thillainathan 2002). The pooled fund is then invested in different assets, and the participants earn dividends on their contributions, which are essentially equal to the returns of the investment strategy. In some countries, dividends are smoothed over a few years of returns to reduce volatility, which leaves open the possibility that the system will be "underfunded" if a series of negative returns occurs. It is not clear how such deficits will be covered. In Malaysia, a minimum guarantee of 2.5 percent is offered to participants. Participants have individual accounts but no choice. Generally, participants are allowed to borrow against these funds to purchase houses or make other investments that are deemed socially useful.

Bateman and Piggott (1997) have provided evidence to suggest that pooling has kept costs low, but the perverse incentive structure inherent in such funds may have led to decent returns for Malaysia albeit lower than those offered by the market.

Mexico

There are many similarities between the pension schemes in Mexico and Chile, except that Mexicans, who were under the old PAYGO DB and switched to the DC plan, have been offered (at retirement) the choice to get a pension based either on their actual accumulation or an assumed equivalent participation in the old DB (i.e., what the accumulation would have been if they had earned the PAYGO internal rate of return). Hence, the DC component of Mexico's reform can be viewed as being similar to that of Chile's with an explicit retirement guarantee for current participants. Future participants are given a minimum pension linked to the minimum wage at the time of retirement, as in the Chilean scheme. At retirement, participants can choose either to purchase an annuity from a private vendor or receive programmed withdrawals from the fund manager. The annual amount is based on the balance, including interest, divided by life expectancy. The annuity from the private vendor cannot be less than the minimum pension guarantee (Sales-Sarrapy, Solis-Soberon, and Villagomez-Amezcua 1996).

Hungary[12]

Hungary offers an interesting twist to the three-pillar model. Pension reform initiated in 1997 created a system with a mandatory PAYGO DB, a mandatory-funded second pillar (which is DC in broad structure), and a voluntary DC third pillar. The second pillar is the responsibility of nonprofit mutual funds, wherein contributing members are also owners of the fund. The fund organizations create the appropriate oversight structure and staff key positions with professionals. These organizations then have the freedom to delegate any of the responsibilities (from administration to asset management) to for-profit third parties. The appointment of a master custodian, though, is mandatory. Guarantees for the mandatory DC component are provided by a central guarantee fund (GF), and a minimum pension of 25 percent of the first-pillar pension is offered to eligible participants. The pension funds pay the GF an insurance premium equal to 0.3–0.5 percent of member's contributions and, although the government provides the ultimate backstop, the GF is expected to cover

---

[12] This section derives extensively from Parniczky (1998).

all payments through the internal reserve created by the collection of premiums. A series of regulations recommend portfolio diversification and other matters relating to prudent investment of assets, including the need to link assets with liabilities. In addition, the pension fund is required to offer a minimum return guarantee through an internal reserve fund, suggesting an element of smoothing of earned returns versus returns credited to member accounts. Payments to the first pillar are largely from employers, whereas payments to the second pillar are largely from employees. Employees in service before 1997 had the choice of not contributing to the second pillar, but new entrants have no such choice.

SUMMARY

The recent profusion of proposals on how to reform social security arrangements in the United States and other countries has inevitably confused the subject with private arrangements for the provision of retirement wealth. "Privatization" of social security is loosely defined and is often a misnomer. It has also been suggested that plans must be either defined benefit (DB) or defined contribution (DC) or be similar to models in the United States or Chile. This chapter has defined certain key terms and provided examples of different pension schemes and reforms around the world. It has raised an important distinction between DB and DC plans, namely, that the pension outcome in DB plans is defined and guaranteed, whereas DC plans have variable pension outcomes. This distinction is important because contributions need not be fixed in DB and DC plans. The remainder of the book will leverage this chapter to show that the optimal structure can be created through only two pillars that combine the best aspects of DB and DC schemes, PAYGO and funded schemes and individual accounts with pooled investment of assets.

APPENDIX 1.1. The Link between Contributions, Expected Returns, and Replacement Rates

This section, adapted from Asad-Syed, Muralidhar, and van der Wouden (1998), develops the notion that a guaranteed return on contributions provides a one-to-one relationship between contributions and replacement rates.

The following formulas are used to calculate the periodic benefit payments that an annuity can provide given a certain amount of wealth. The major assumptions are that annuity payments are made at the beginning of each period and all variables are deterministic.

If ExpR = ExpI, then

YearlyBenefit

$$
= \left[\frac{(1 + ExpI)^{(1 - \# Years)}}{\begin{array}{l}(1 + ExpR)^{(1 - \# Years)} + (1 + ExpI)^{(1 - \# Years)} \cdot (1 + ExpR)^{(2 - \# Years)} \\ \qquad \cdot \left(\dfrac{(1 + ExpI)^{(\# Years)} - (1 + ExpR)^{(\# Years)}}{(ExpI - ExpR)} \right) \end{array}} \right]
$$

$$
\times \, EndBal. \tag{A1.1.1}
$$

If ExpR = ExpI, then

$$
YearlyBenefit = \frac{EndBal}{\# \, Years}, \tag{A1.1.2}
$$

where

    EndBal is the total present value of the annuity (BALANCE NEEDED AT RETIREMENT),

    ExpR is the assumed return in the annuity calculation (EXPECTED RETURN),

    ExpI is the increase in the benefit payments of the annuity (EXPECTED BENEFIT INFLATION), and

    #Years is the number of benefit payments the annuity provides (LIFE EXPECTANCY).

YearlyBenefit in formulas (A1.1.1) and (A1.1.2) provides the amount of the first payment of the annuity. If the EXPECTED BENEFIT INFLATION is zero, all further payments of the annuity are of the same value. If the EXPECTED BENEFIT INFLATION is larger than zero, the benefit payments increase periodically with this percentage. The replacement rate is now represented by the ratio of this *YearlyBenefit* amount to the final or average career salary of the participant.

    The following formulas are used to calculate the amount of wealth the participant has accumulated at retirement:

If CapR ≠ SalGrowth, then

EndWealth

$$
= \left[\frac{\begin{array}{l} StartSal \cdot ContriRate \cdot \left((1 + SalGrowth)^{(\# Periods)} - (1 + CapR)^{(\# Periods)} \right) \\ \qquad + \, IniWealth \cdot (SalGrowth - CapR)(1 + CapR)^{(\# Periods)} \end{array}}{(SalGrowth - CapR)} \right].
$$

$$
\tag{A1.1.3}
$$

If $CapR = SalGrowth$, then

$EndWealth$

$$= StartSal \cdot ContriRate \cdot (\# \, Periods \cdot (1 + CapR)^{(\# \, Periods)})$$
$$+ IniWealth \cdot (1 + CapR)^{(\# \, Periods)}, \qquad\qquad (A1.1.4)$$

where

  $IniWealth$ is the wealth the participant starts with when they begin contributing to the savings scheme (INITIAL ACCOUNT BALANCE);

  $CapR$ is the expected investment return on the contributions made to the savings scheme by the participant (EXPECTED RETURN ON CONTRIBUTIONS),

  $SalGrowth$ is the expected salary growth of the participant during their career (EXPECTED SALARY INCREASE),

  $\#Periods$ is the number of periods the participants make contributions to the savings scheme (the difference between RETIREMENT AGE and CURRENT AGE),

  $StartSal$ is the starting salary of the participant when he or she starts contributing to the savings scheme (CURRENT SALARY), and

  $ContriRate$ is the fixed contribution rate of the participant, a percentage of the participant's salary that is saved in each period (CONTRIBUTION RATE).

Define $EndWealth$ to be the amount accumulated by the participant at the time of retirement. This can be used as input for the annuity payment formulas (A1.1.1 and A1.1.2), which determine the yearly benefit stream the participant can afford to buy with this total $EndWealth$ amount.

The next set of formulas determines the savings rate (contributions rate) of the participant, which provides a predetermined expected amount of wealth at retirement.

If $CapR \neq SalGrowth$, then

$ContriRate$

$$= \left[\frac{(CapR - SalGrowth) \cdot (IniWealth \cdot (1 + CapR)^{(\# \, Periods)} - EndWealth)}{StartSal \cdot (1 + CapR) \cdot ((1 + SalGrowth)^{(\# \, Periods)} - (1 + CapR)^{(\# \, Periods)})} \right]$$
$$(A1.1.5)$$

If $CapR = SalGrowth$, then

$$ContriRate = \frac{EndWealth - IniWealth \cdot (1 + CapR)^{(\# \, Periods)}}{StartSal \cdot \# \, Periods \cdot (1 + CapR)^{(\# \, Periods)}}. \qquad (A1.1.6)$$

Formulas (A1.1.5) and (A1.1.6) produce a percentage that represents the amount the participant has to contribute in each period as a percentage of salary to achieve the targeted *EndWealth*.

As is evident from the preceding formulas, selecting a replacement rate for given demographic parameters (such as number of years of employment, life expectancy) and economic variables (salary growth, postretirement inflation, return on the postretirement annuity) is equivalent to selecting a contribution rate and rate of return on investments, and vice versa. In other words, one can target a replacement rate and then select an optimal contribution rate if there is some assurance about returns. Therefore, guaranteeing a rate of return on investments for a given contribution rate and other parameters effectively ensures a guaranteed replacement rate. Hence, a DB scheme can be assured if the return on assets can be guaranteed.

2

A Taxonomy of Pension Reform Issues

INTRODUCTION

The existing confusion over privatization, and what it implies, makes it important to clarify the meaning of social security and the "desirable properties" it should strive to achieve. This chapter establishes the basic principles by which a social security system may be evaluated. It reviews some basic pension concepts and highlights the desirable characteristics of any social security system by explicitly stating the trade-offs in the selection of different social security design aspects. It creates a yardstick by which any social security system can be measured and provides a simple format that will help decision makers analyze the merits and demerits of any proposal. Finally, for a given set of desirable macro- and microeconomic properties, this chapter offers an "Ideal Model" and compares it with other models implemented around the world. A transition from the current systems in the United States and Spain to an implementable version of the "ideal" system is explored in Chapters 5 and 6, respectively. This chapter concludes with suggestions for simple modifications to improve the design of currently implemented reforms.

SOCIAL SECURITY: DEFINITION, DESIRABLE PROPERTIES, AND DESIGN FEATURES

SOCIAL SECURITY

The proposition that social security must be provided by the government is a funda-mental aspect of old age support that has begun to get clouded in reform discussions. In essence, unless one takes a libertarian view, it is the role of the government to ensure that people do not reach old age poor (Aaron and Reischauer 1998, and

This chapter expands on Modigliani and Muralidhar (1998).

Diamond 1995). Admittedly, what constitutes being "poor" is debatable, but there can be little argument that the government must provide for old poor people either by offering a guarantee or by ensuring a basic quality of life to all citizens. The increasing populace of old poor people requires governments to increase the provision of housing, shelter, and medical care. If not, the existence of the elderly poor will lower the quality of life for the young as well. Several proposals that recommend "privatizing" social security disregard this fundamental principle in order to insulate retirement savings from profligate governments or to cater to the notion that everyone should have free choice in their retirement savings options. Yet, ultimately, the government has to act, and individuals have to pay higher taxes.

In some countries, social security is integrated with disability, survivor insurance, and old age medical programs. We focus on the pension aspects of social security, but the principles we apply to pension systems in this book can be extended to other programs in which stochastic liabilities have to be serviced (Muralidhar 2001).

Once it is accepted that governments must provide social security, however small the pension, it is important to create a menu of macro- and microeconomic "desirable properties" for the social security system.[1] No single plan can achieve all these properties, but a yardstick is provided against which the program can be evaluated. For example, in Blahous (2000) three desirable properties are distilled: (i) providing social insurance and relating contributions to benefits, (ii) increasing the incentives to work, and (iii) reducing inequities across demographic groups. Some analysts have considered capital market development to be a beneficial feature of pension reforms. We suggest capital market improvements as secondary to the goal of ensuring adequate old age pensions, though efficient capital markets are critical to the long-term success of pension reform. Alternatively, some members of the Advisory Council on Social Security (ACSS) and Ball and Bethel (1997) have listed nine principles as critical for Social Security: it has to be universal; an earned right; wage-related; contributory and self-financed; redistributive; not means-tested; wage-indexed; inflation-protected; and compulsory (ACSS 1997). Even though, in the end, our desirable properties may be subjective, we have listed them.

Macroproperties

Research indicates, although individuals across countries may exhibit identical savings behavior over their lifetime, a country with high growth rates tends to exhibit

---

[1] Muralidhar and van der Wouden (1998a) provide a similar list of desirable properties of second pillars. The discussion in this chapter constitutes the basics of the entire social security component.

high savings rates (Modigliani and Brumberg 1963). According to the "virtuous cycle of savings and growth," higher long-term savings are likely to finance long-term investments critical to growth in a country.

In addition, where national savings can be safeguarded against misuse by the incumbent government and the option to set aside funds for retirement is offered to the majority of the population, welfare improves and inequalities in wealth are kept in check.

We now detail the major desirable macro properties.

CONTRIBUTION TO NATIONAL SAVINGS. A high rate of national savings is critical to sustain growth in a country. However, a pure PAYGO social security scheme makes no systematic contribution to national savings. For the individual, contributions represent a forced saving and are not used to finance investment but, instead, are used to pay pensions, thereby financing the consumption of the retired. In contrast, contributions in a fully funded system are invested in earning assets and increase national savings and wealth as long as they exceed outlays for the payment of benefits (Hemming 1998). This occurs as long as the pension system grows – essentially, during its formative stage until it reaches maturity, or as long as the (real) wage bill rises. In fact, pension wealth and savings behave like national wealth and savings in the life-cycle hypothesis (LCH) model. Under a PAYGO system, notably, growth does not increase the capital stock but is used to improve the benefits-to-contribution ratio.

This negative effect on capital formation was not considered a source of concern when the system was introduced and might even have been viewed as desirable at the time because of the concern with oversaving. Diamond (1997b) has pointed out that, although a partially funded system is not uncommon and is potentially a good idea (because it may help to protect the system from variations in government budget), the downside is that it may give governments the incentive to "dissave" if the funds can be accessed easily. However, as long as any surplus is loaned to the government or invested in government debt, as in the United States, the beneficiaries are as protected as any other creditor. Debt to social security is (or should be) no different from any other debt.

SUSTAINABILITY. A scheme can be made sustainable as long as outflows are reasonably well linked to inflows, as demonstrated in Figure 1.1. Sustainability is also ensured when there is a residual insurer of the last resort with adequate resources and the ability to smooth intertemporal volatility. PAYGO schemes begin to fail when demographic profiles change. They also suffer from the inability to diversify risks internationally.[2] These risks include demographics, economic growth, and as-set market performance. For a sustainable social security system to function in the United States and other countries, contributions will have to rise, or benefits will have to fall dramatically by the middle of this century.

Defined benefit (DB) plans have a built-in intergenerational pooling of the afore-mentioned risks. Well-designed DB plans can withstand short-term shocks. As long as its sponsor (i.e., the government) does not have limited liability, a DB plan can be made sustainable through a combination of variable benefits, contributions, and investment policies. But once variability is allowed in benefits, the system can no longer be labeled "defined benefits." On the other hand, DC plans are sustainable, for pension payments are linked directly to capital accumulation. However, sustainabil-ity must be distinguished from the level of pension payments because a DC scheme may provide highly uncertain and extremely low pensions.

INSULATED FROM POLITICAL RISK – INDISCRIMINATE USE OF FUNDS BY GOV-ERNMENTS. In designing any system, it is important to insulate any accumulation from profligate governments and thereby ensure that citizens have confidence in the system and do not try to evade participation. The history of pensions is littered with examples of governments, in both developed and developing countries, utilizing monies set aside for old age to finance deficits or so-called development projects. In certain African and Asian countries, investment of Provident Fund assets is restricted by governments, allowing them the freedom to access scarce resources at low cost. Argentina recently tried to convert U.S. dollar assets into Argentine pesos at a dis-advantageous rate to lower its debt, resulting in serious implications for retirement wealth (Ciampi 2002). Developed countries, too, have not escaped the clutches of politicians. Social Security surpluses in the United States have been used to acquire government debt, possibly facilitating the continuation of deficits. Diamond (1997b) has argued that political risk can be either "bad," whereby monies are squandered, or "good," wherein benefits are increased to achieve political gains; but both can result in a social security crisis.

The possibility of such manipulation of pension money has led institutions, such as the World Bank, to recommend individual account DC schemes with privately man-aged assets,[3] for the government cannot appropriate property rights to these assets. Diamond (1997b) has acknowledged such insulation in DC schemes because there is no guaranteed benefit, but he argues against allowing property rights under a DB scheme inasmuch as the government bears all the risk in the DB scheme. Orszag and

---

[2] Refer to Mehrling (1998).
[3] See James (1998).

Stiglitz (2001) have questioned the World Bank's assumption that a corrupt government under the old system can somehow be converted into a benevolent government under the new, privatized alternative. Later in the chapter, we explain and demonstrate that individual accounts need not necessarily imply a DC scheme or private asset management and that insulation against political risk can be ensured by explicit guarantees, financial innovation, and the establishment of institutions with appropriate governance structures (e.g., the Investment Boards in Canada and Ireland), or all of these solutions. Chapter 3 demonstrates how DC plans need not be insulated from political risk if they are subjected to stringent and misguided regulation.

UNIVERSAL AVAILABILITY. This is the least controversial of the properties. Clearly, universally available schemes, and those that include participants in the informal sector, are likely to reduce inequalities. Universally available schemes can be broadly subcategorized as mandatory or voluntary. It is generally believed that individuals tend to be myopic with regard to retirement savings (Aaron and Reischauer 1998). Thus, it is deemed advantageous to society to create a mandated scheme that is available to all citizens. Chile, Italy, Mexico, and the United States have mandated universally available systems. The U.S. 401(K) plan, however, is voluntary and not universally available.

CERTAINTY OF OUTCOME (IN REAL OR NOMINAL TERMS). Final outcomes are influenced by salary growth over working life, the contribution and accrual rates (or return on investments), and whether payouts are promised in real or nominal terms. In addition, benefits can be paid either in lump sum amounts at retirement or as an annuity over some or all of one's retired life. Diamond (1997a) has made a persuasive argument about why social security should not be a DC plan because it lacks a certainty of outcomes. Some of these arguments relate to unresolved questions (especially in developing countries with underdeveloped financial markets) on how annuities will be offered and purchased in countries without private annuity markets. The best outcome would be a definite, real benefit until death because it provides clarity on the size of the pension and insurance against two key risks, namely, inflation and longevity. Some experts argue that inflation adjustment is inadequate and prefer insurance against a decline in the standard of living, thereby linking the real aspect to standard-of-living indices (Bodie and Merton 1992). However, with so many stochastic variables and risks, complete insurance may not be feasible. For example, systems may have to protect against low salary growth (for few instruments are available in the market that can hedge against this risk) by some form of minimum pension. This safeguard is needed because a pension system may protect against several risks, but if the base pension amount is too low owing to a poor rate of wage growth, retirees face the risk of sinking into poverty when competing against inflation or increases in the cost of living. Some countries have considered innovative ways to protect the purchasing power of pensions against inflation. Toward this end, regulators in some Latin American countries wanted to offer a choice between peso or U.S. dollar pensions, but this was hard to implement as the Argentine example has shown.

It is not obvious to many reformers that, for a given contribution rate and salary growth rate, a guaranteed nominal return on assets can be used to ensure a nominal value of terminal wealth. This is a simple mathematical identity, as shown in Chapter 1 (equation 1.1) and demonstrated in greater detail in the appendix to this chapter. In Chapter 8 we demonstrate how the terminal outcome can be guaranteed, even when realized returns are volatile, by allowing variable contributions. In fact, Orszag and Stiglitz (2001) have emphasized that a DB plan can be seen as a DC plan with certain options. In the "Ideal Model," the portfolio of options encompasses put and call options on the return of a market portfolio struck at the guaranteed rate. Effectively, participants buy puts to protect against underperformance relative to a guaranteed rate, and they sell calls to give up any upside relative to this rate (Blake 1994).

Further, one may be given either a definite annuity or a definite lump sum amount from which an uncertain annuity may be purchased. The annuity, if purchased at retirement, will be uncertain because of prevailing interest rates and future demographic assumptions. On the assumption that the number of years from retirement until death is known, an individual would be indifferent to a choice between a definite or an uncertain annuity at retirement as long as the cost of the annuity is the individual's certainty equivalent.[4] In unpooled arrangements, the premium for guaranteeing individuals a definite outcome is likely to be higher than the certainty equivalent.[5] This is so because providers charge those who seek longer term annuities more than the average in anticipation that these participants know they are likely to live longer than the average. In a pooled arrangement, the provider of insurance (annuity or pension) has a fair chance of achieving the average if there are a large number of participants in the pool. Further, when real benefits need to be offered, as in the case of countries with moderate to high inflation rates (not adequately reflected in the contract interest rates), the absence of appropriate capital markets to hedge inflation risks results in an unavailability of such products, prohibitive costs in the

---

[4] A certainty equivalent is equal to an amount that would make one indifferent between a certain and an uncertain outcome.

[5] This is one of the basic principles of insurance, and mandatory occupational health insurance schemes have substantially lower premiums than if individuals acquired their own insurance. In addition to the adverse selection problem, in a mandatory pooled arrangement, self-insurance reduces the residual risk to the insurer.

private market, or both. Cavanaugh (1996, 103–104) has crystallized the discussion by highlighting the fact that "risk is more easily borne if it is widely distributed. Also, Social Security is a social insurance system in which the government guarantees a level of benefits, and these benefits can be provided at a lower cost if the investment risk is retained by the fund rather than shifted to the individual."

When death is uncertain, a final issue is whether terminal wealth at retirement should be spread over a fixed term or over life. Once again, individual arrangements with insurers to hedge against longevity risk are likely to be more costly than pooled arrangements. The greater the uncertainty (generally when there are poor data or small samples), the greater the cost differential between pooled and unpooled arrangements.

HIGH RETURN PERMITS A HIGH BENEFIT-TO-CONTRIBUTION RATIO. As with any pension scheme, the after-fee return on accumulated reserves is critical, as shown in Figure 1.1. In the traditional U.S. Social Security system, individuals receive low implied returns for their respective contributions because of the factors implicit in this calculation of returns. The returns in a PAYGO system are equal to the sum of population growth and productivity. Aaron (1966) has shown that, when the rate of return on assets exceeds the sum of population and productivity growth, funded systems are preferred over PAYGO systems (in the steady state). The current global forecast suggests that a combination of these two factors will probably lead to low implied returns (Table 2.1). As a result, the required contributions tend to be high. However, it is possible that there are short periods when PAYGO is preferred to funding, and the superiority of one system over another may change over time. We address the implications of such a possibility in Chapter 8. Switching between systems may not be feasible, but there are alternative ways to take maximum advantage of the preference for dynamic shifts in systems.

Offering low returns on contributions is unsustainable and likely to lead to evasion by participants. Sometimes, redistribution causes the returns credited to one's account to be much lower than realized returns, and this seepage can be harmful. Systems with higher ratios, such as 401(K)s and the Chilean system, where investment returns are directly credited to the individual account, potentially have less seepage and thereby may lead to greater participation. Individual account schemes, if credited appropriately with asset returns achieved, are likely to have high ratios if the assets are invested appropriately.[6] In effect, pension schemes with high ratios are those with low redistributive elements and administrative costs, and vice versa.

---

[6] In some Provident Fund systems, administrators smooth dividends by reporting dividends different from achieved returns in an attempt to reduce public outcries. These can lead to perverse results.

TABLE 2.1 Testing the viability of pension systems in different countries

Country	Growth rate in working population[a] (%)	Growth rate in labor productivity[b] (%)	Real rate of return on pension fund assets[c] (%)	Growth rate in retired populations[d] (%)	Unfunded pension scheme viable[e]		Funded pension scheme viable[f]		Funded scheme superior to unfunded scheme[g]
					If real pension growth is in line with productivity?	If real pension growth is zero?	If real pension growth is in line with productivity?	If real pension growth is zero?	
United Kingdom	0.0	2.1	6.3	0.7	No	Yes	Yes	Yes	Yes
Germany	−0.7	2.5	5.5	0.8	No	Yes	Yes	Yes	Yes
Netherlands	−0.3	2.1	4.3	1.2	No	Yes	Yes	Yes	Yes
Sweden	0.1	1.8	2.8	0.6	No	Yes	Yes	Yes	Yes
Denmark	−0.3	1.9	5.8	0.5	No	Yes	Yes	Yes	Yes
Switzerland	−0.2	1.5	2.2	1.1	No	Yes	Yes	Yes	Yes
United States	0.4	1.6	3.9	1.4	No	Yes	Yes	Yes	Yes
Canada	0.4	2.6	4.1	1.7	No	Yes	Yes	Yes	Yes
Japan	−0.6	4.1	2.9	1.4	No	Yes	Yes	Yes	Yes
Australia	0.5	1.8	4.2	1.9	No	Yes	Yes	Yes	Yes

[a] Projected annual average growth rate in working populations aged 15 to 64 between 1990 and 2050 (*Source: World Population Prospects: The 1994 Revision*, United Nations, 1995).

[b] Annual average growth rate in real GDP per capita between 1967 and 1990 assumed to hold over the period 1990–2050 (*Source:* Penn-World Tables, http://www.nber.org/pwt56.html).

[c] Annual average real return between 1967 and 1990 assumed to hold over the period 1990–2050 (*Source:* Davis 1995, Table 6.15).

[d] Projected annual average growth in populations over the age of 65 between 1990 and 2050 (*Source: World Population Prospects: The 1994 Revision*, United Nations, 1995).

[e] Unfunded pension schemes are viable if the sum of the growth rates in the working population and in labor productivity exceeds the sum of the growth rates in the retired population and in real pensions.

[f] Funded pension schemes are viable if the real return on pension assets exceeds the growth rate in real pensions.

[g] Funded schemes are superior to unfunded schemes if the real return on pension exceeds the sum of the growth rate in the working population and in labor productivity.

Source: Reprinted with permission from Blake, David (2000), "Does It Matter What Type of Pension You Have?" *The Economic Journal*, February, 46–81.

There is a perception that merely investing in the stock market can raise returns. Although this is possibly true over a longer horizon, there are periods during which this is not necessarily the case. Further, the greater the return on an asset, the greater its variability and the risk that a particular return may not be achieved. This risk may be mitigated through guarantees or spreading the risk over many generations, as in a traditional DB plan (Geneakopolous, Mitchell, and Zeldes 1999).

Microproperties

Viewed broadly, pension funds or social security arrangements are a form of "smoothing" of consumption over the lifetime of an individual.[7] They are necessary because individuals earn income over a limited time span but have to finance outflows over their entire lifetime. Several researchers have argued that the labor supply decision is another way to achieve this smoothing.[8] Workers can, to a limited extent, increase their supply of labor in future periods if there is inadequate wealth accumulation, or vice versa. However, this is no longer feasible when the individual reaches retirement. In a pensions framework, the flexible labor supply decision (the marginal rate of substitution between labor and leisure) is the equivalent of a flexible contribution policy or dynamic taxes on wages (Muralidhar 2001). We return to this aspect in Chapter 8.

There are other choices. The greater the choice between types of vehicles available to individuals for accumulation of wealth, the better off they will be. The choice could be, at a minimum, in the selection of assets, amount contributed, terminal wealth or targeted replacement rate, and temporary withdrawals during the accumulation phase. If all this can be achieved at a low cost without compromising the level of pensions, *or its risk level*, individuals and society will be better off.

This section considers some key microeconomic properties.

SMOOTHING OF CONSUMPTION AND INVESTMENT. Under the LCH, individuals save in order to finance dissaving during retirement. However, some volatility in consumption and investment patterns (e.g., financing homes, high medical costs, and children's education) has to be assumed during the course of one's working life. Good design allows for individuals to finance such volatile patterns without

---

[7] Refer to Modigliani and Brumberg (1963).
[8] See, for example, Bodie, Merton, and Samuelson (1992) and Krishnamurthi, Muralidhar, and van der Wouden (1998a).

necessarily squeezing accustomed standards of living or cannibalizing postretirement consumption and is invaluable for providing a hedge against one's own consumption and investment needs. Home loans against Provident Fund balances are common, and some public pension plans in the United States offer home equity loans against DB balances.

Another alternative proposed by one of the authors (which is soon to be implemented) is to issue a credit card against one's accumulated balances. With appropriate repayment and default prevention provisions, this addition could have significant value for the individual. Unfortunately, some politicians in the United States have been trying to block this option – a consequence of serving business interests at the expense of representing the interests of voters.

Diamond (1997b) has suggested that allowing early access to funds is a bad idea, for it allows governments to permit such withdrawals as a substitute for government-provided benefits. As a result, there is significant risk to the overall social security system – especially if these funds are not replaced prior to retirement of the participants.

CHOICE OF REPLACEMENT RATE, CONTRIBUTION RATE, AND PORTFOLIO (MATCH RISK PREFERENCE). The mix of contribution policy and investment policy, for a given salary growth path, dictates the replacement rate, as demonstrated in Figure 1.1. The assumption that individuals in a country may have one desired replacement rate or risk preference is restrictive but is embedded in reform design. For example, in reforms implemented in Latin America, mandated investment portfolios, especially those that are 100-percent invested in government bonds, may imply a risk-aversion that may not favor the young and the wealthy. Further, in pooled arrangements (Australia and Hungary), individuals may have a choice of fund companies but not necessarily a choice of products within the fund (Bateman et al. 2001). Mandated contributions also have this adverse feature. Some individuals may prefer to save more through higher contributions but would have to seek out voluntary private schemes that can be more expensive. Good design need not necessitate such options, and Australia and Chile allow voluntary contributions to their funds in addition to government-mandated amounts. The greater the freedom, the greater the welfare of participants.

One additional feature, which we review briefly in Chapter 6 in the context of Spain, is to allow workers to continue to be active beyond the mandatory retirement age, exempt this employment from social security contributions, and have participants receive a pension proportionate to their inactive time (if they remain as part-time workers). This flexibility is valuable in allowing individuals to determine the optimal mix of retirement and work-related income.

LOW COST OF MANAGEMENT. Low cost of administering programs and investing funds leaves more money for pensions through higher after-fee returns. In the United States, it is estimated that individual accounts could cost 1 percent of returns, and the pooled variant, as in the Thrift Savings Plan (TSP), could cost as little as 0.10 percent (Blahous 2000). Therefore, from a pure cost perspective, the pooled arrangement may be preferred (Seidman 1999). Hungary may have created a structure whereby the bargaining power of participants is enhanced through their enrollment in pension funds. Kotlikoff and Sachs (1998) have attempted to mitigate costs in their version of the privatized plan by requiring all firms to offer an identical diversified portfolio (a global market capitalization weighted index), but competition for clients would clearly cause fund managers to incur high marketing costs (Aaron 1997). Clearly, pooled arrangements offer a much better cost structure than individual-based schemes. Further, where regulation is myopic and investment managers can deduct marketing and advertising expenses from gross returns of the portfolio, the replacement rate for affiliates is likely to be low. This practice is widespread in Latin America. Chapter 3 addresses the pitfalls of not focusing on after-fee returns and provides ways to address these adverse cost structures. Lower fees imply higher after-fee returns, which in turn lead to higher replacement rates.

DESIGN FEATURES

Several aspects of pension reform need to be identified and addressed to realize the desirable properties. It is difficult to achieve the best outcome for each of the aforementioned properties, but it is possible to achieve many of them through optimal design (Vittas 1996). This section highlights some of the key aspects of pension design and demonstrates a combination of different features that could closely replicate the best solution.

CONTRIBUTIONS. The issue is whether contributions should be mandatory or voluntary. If they are mandatory, should the level be (i) determined and fixed, (ii) variable and dictated by the state, or (iii) contributed "voluntarily" by individuals in a range around a prespecified rate? Most schemes mandate a fixed contribution rate into the social security system and suggest that individuals who wish to save more may do so in voluntary schemes. The U.S. Social Security scheme maintains a mandated contribution that, in principle, can be – and has been – changed. However, where there are no redistributive distortions, it is possible, as in Australia and Chile, to have a mandated range of contributions. Typically, in voluntary contribution schemes, one finds the possibility of a range of contributions (e.g., 401(K) plans) because most countries have not allowed a range around a basic, mandated contribution. Voluntary systems, however, tend to put a cap on how much can be contributed, which is often dictated by tax considerations, because this saving is a form of tax deferral.

CONTRIBUTORS. Debates have raged over whether employers or employees should pay the contributions to social security. In the long run, employees bear the cost of the contribution anyhow, so we make the radical recommendation that only employees should contribute. Effectively, to reflect the "overhead" associated with contributions, the employer adjusts the final real wage. This prevents the wasteful, protracted bargaining by labor unions to get employers to increase their contributions to pensions. There is evidence (e.g., in Europe) that the illusion of the employer, rather than the employee, paying for the benefits has labor pushing for unreasonably high benefits. In industries in which labor has sufficient power to get the employer to bear the cost, labor is capable of demanding salaries that compensate for the cost of contributions. Also, if employees contribute, the case for property rights for these pensions is much clearer.

ACCUMULATION. Conventional wisdom seems to have drifted toward funded schemes and away from PAYGO schemes. This is because research has shown that PAYGO pension systems discourage national savings and embody strong redistributive elements across generations. However, within funded schemes there are fully funded and partially funded options. As a result of the strong views of the regulatory body in countries such as the Netherlands, there is a bias for corporate plans to be fully funded. More recently, corporate funds in Japan and the United States have begun to face the problems of being partially funded or underfunded.

Under DB-funded schemes, the following relationship holds in steady state:

$$c^* + (r - \rho)A_{t-1}^* = p^*, \tag{2.1}$$

where c^* is the contribution rate, r is the nominal return on investments, ρ is the growth of income and is equal to population growth and productivity growth ($r - \rho$ is the net return defined as the gross rate of return received from investments and reduced by adjustments for growth in population and productivity), A^* is the steady-state asset to wage ratio and p^* is the pension cost relative to the wage bill or the cost ratio. Given this relationship, in Chapter 3 we examine some of the dynamics of the system.

A key benefit of accumulation, when the implied rate of return on PAYGO is less than the return from assets, is that contributions are lower and the volatility of contributions (caused by changes in parameters) is also lower (Chapter 3). Blake (2000) has highlighted the countries in which PAYGO is dominated by funding (Table 2.1). Feldstein (1996) and others have made similar arguments, but most proposals have considered only the level of contributions and not their likely variability. Lower taxes and volatility of these taxes are likely to lead to greater predictability of after-tax income, less labor market distortions, less evasion, and greater welfare (Diamond 1994, Corsetti and Schmidt-Hebbel 1997).[9] There is a bias to believing that, if conditions for funding to dominate PAYGO are met, the system would need to be converted to a fully funded system. However, for long-term liabilities, a partially funded system in which current funding covers present liabilities may be sustainable as long as future returns and contributions make up the deficit (see also Samuelson 1975). There may also be a case for mixed systems based on the impact of the funded system on the capital markets (Chapter 8). Once again, these systems need to be designed appropriately to ensure that unfunded liabilities are serviced without extensive volatility to contributions.

TERMINAL OUTCOME. The pension debate is polarized between DB and DC outcomes at retirement, and this focus overlooks the fact that DB schemes include substantial salary growth and inflation risk (wage or price) and DC schemes are subject to the enormous risk of low replacement rates from investment volatility. Though the DB scheme may guarantee a replacement rate relative to final earnings, this does not ensure a particular standard of living. However, within a social security system in which the government attempts to prevent old age poverty, it is reasonable to assume that predictable benefits are beneficial to participants and governments. As highlighted in Chapter 1, one can distinguish between terminal outcomes that are guaranteed or defined (generally DB schemes with a target replacement rate) and those that are variable (DC schemes).

ASSET MANAGEMENT. Most people assume that pooling (of assets) has the advantage of lowering management costs only. In fact, pooling liabilities is also beneficial because it lowers the cost of providing life annuities through the law of large numbers and diversification. Pooling of annuity risk is achieved through a DB structure (Chapter 4). Nevertheless, pension reform proposals are replete with recommendations

---

[9] Many have argued that the transition to a funded scheme cannot be Pareto improving because the transition requires additional savings today for lower contributions in the future. However, these analyses have ignored the fact that the lower volatility of contributions could lead to welfare improvements.

that countries implement privately managed, individual account, DC schemes.[10] These recommendations fail to recognize the possibility of maintaining "individual accounts" from an accounting perspective, managing assets through private managers with a pooled DB scheme, and achieving a much lower welfare cost in offering the same expected target replacement rate.[11] The money may mingle, although the accounts are kept separate. Yet, Seidman (1999) makes the case for pooling of risk but negates the possibility of individual accounts. A critical aspect of a DB scheme is that it is an insurance scheme; hence, pooling assets (and liabilities), especially when the system is mandated, allows for a much more efficient risk posture for the group of citizens as a whole. Hence, pooled structures are preferable not only from a cost perspective but also from risk-bearing, risk-sharing, and risk-taking perspectives. However, pooled structures within DC schemes, such as those in Provident Funds or possibly in Hungary, are able to incorporate some risk sharing to the extent that returns are smoothed over time and minimum returns are offered. One may therefore conclude that it is important to distinguish between accounting and investment arrangements in a discussion on pooling.

INVESTMENT MANAGEMENT ARRANGEMENTS. Assets can be managed either by the private sector or the government and with little or no discretion or with complete discretion. The trade-off is, when assets are managed privately, costs are likely to be high, and governments would need to limit discretion to manage agency risk (Muralidhar 2001). Such management requires informed oversight by governments. It also presupposes the belief that active management adds value over passive, indexed portfolios. When governments take over the asset management function, they can either perform the investment functions internally with complete discretion or hire external managers and monitor their performance. There is no evidence to suggest that external managers working for state-run pension funds in the United States have fared better than internal managers (Mitchell and Hsin 1997). Seidman (1999), whose proposal is considered later, argues that funded social security can be managed using private firms to manage a diversified portfolio of assets. Ball (1978) proposes that social security funds be passively managed in a pooled arrangement. Such an arrangement can be advantageous with good governance because, in addition to reducing issues of oversight and lowering cost, it erases the possibility of active involvement of governments in debates on the appropriateness of corporate governance. Blahous (2000) would not consider this an efficient arrangement. Those

[10] See James (1998).
[11] See Muralidhar and van der Wouden (1998b).

opposed to government-endorsed bodies overseeing assets fear that large sums of money under the control of political bodies could lead to renationalizing of private companies. The threat of renationalization of privatized companies through government ownership of equity is negated if the social security system is legally set up to ensure that the equity is owned by individuals but managed on their behalf by the oversight body. In the "Ideal Model," we introduce an innovation to allow for investments in equities and protect against political risk.

GOVERNMENT INCENTIVES (ENTRY AND EXIT). The issue is that governments may either try to increase savings by mandate through compulsory arrangements or to induce such behavior through incentives. The most interesting incentive is to consider tax credits on (i) contributions, (ii) returns on investment, or (iii) the amount withdrawn at retirement. The alternatives range from taxation of retirement savings (all flows taxed) to retirement savings being tax advantaged (one of the flows being tax exempt) or completely tax exempt. Most countries fall into the second category. For example, in the United States, contributions to 401(K) plans are deductible from income for income tax purposes, but the benefits are taxed; Social Security contributions of an individual are taxed, whereas the benefits exemption is means tested. In Italy, contributions are not taxed, and in Chile, contributions and earnings are exempt, but the benefits are taxed. In pension reform parlance, this is called an EET (or exempt, exempt, taxed) scheme and has been adopted by several Latin American countries (Mitchell and Barreto 1997). However, Australia appears to tax all three: benefits, contributions, and earnings (Bateman et al. 2001).

An interesting issue is the impact of these schemes on national savings (Corsetti and Schmidt Hebbel 1997). Often, increases in private savings from such tax incentives are offset by increases in government dissaving, resulting in no net impact on the country. Occasionally, there is a perverse effect whereby tax incentives lead to additional consumption rather than savings. Such increased consumption may occur when a tax incentive is given for some form of saving rather than for an *increase* in saving, which was probably the case with some of President Reagan's programs. The goal of any such incentive should be to reduce private and public consumption for a given amount of (maximum) income.

LIQUIDITY AND WITHDRAWABILITY. Many governments take the paternalistic view that monies set aside for pensions should not be tapped before retirement. However, individuals who set aside savings for retirement often incur debt to finance current investment or consumption. This debt is normally in the form of mortgage

TABLE 2.2 Obligations and benefits for different pension models

Design features / Pension models	1 Contribution Volunt.	Mandat. Fixed/variable	2 Accumulation Funded	PAYGO	3 Terminal outcome Defined benefits Real/nominal	Variable benefits	4 Asset management Indiv.	Pooled	5 Investment management Private Discretion Some/total	Govt.-mandated
Rational behavior-Life cycle	✓		✓			✓	✓		Total	
IRA	✓		✓			✓	✓		Some	
401(K)	✓		✓			✓	✓		Some	
Traditional SS		Variable		✓	Real			If assets exist		
Mandatory PF		Fixed	✓			✓		✓		
Chile-"Privatized SS"	✓	Fixed	✓			✓	✓			Limited
Mexico		Fixed	✓			✓	✓			Limited
Ideal SS	✓	Variable	✓	Some portion	Real			✓		

loans, educational loans, or credit card balances that carry commercial or premium rates of interest, often higher than any prospective return on their mandated savings. Institutions lend to individuals with the expectation of full compensation on the maturity of the loan.

An inefficiently regulated system (as in the existing system) permits individuals to save in one account and dissave in another – all of which could take place in the same account. The poor structure provides large rents for financial intermediaries to the detriment of the individual. Some pension schemes allow withdrawals for housing and other stated expenditures: the American 401(K) system allows borrowing from one's account without a specified motivation but requires repayment within stated terms. We do not know of any mandated public pension system that allows borrowing from one's pension credit balance to provide such security against one's changing consumption or investment needs. A good social security scheme should permit withdrawals with adequate provisions to ensure repayment or tax penalties for early pension withdrawal. In Mexico, participants can withdraw as much as 10 percent of their pension balance in case of partial disability or unemployment. However, unemployment can be invoked as a reason for withdrawal only if no withdrawals have been made in the previous 5 years (Sales-Sarrapy, Solis-Soberon et al. 1996).

Table 2.2 lists various design aspects and assigns different pension fund models to each aspect. Different models tap different design aspects.

BLE 2.2 (*continued*)

Design features	5 contd. Investment management			6 Contributors			7 Government incentives			8 Liquidity/ Withdrawability		
	Government			Employer	Employee	Govt.	Favorable tax treatment		Related to exit	None	Total or partial	
	Internal-Discretion	Indexed	External-Mngr.			Ensure final beneft					Invest.	Consumption
							Principal	Return				
ion els												
nal LCH					✓						Total	Total
					✓		✓	✓	✓		Total	Total
K)				✓	✓		✓	✓	✓		Partial	Partial
tional SS				✓	✓		Employer			✓		
datory PF	✓	✓	✓		✓			✓	✓		Partial	
-"Privatized SS"					✓		✓	✓			N/A	N/A
co					✓	If poor returns	✓	✓				Partial
SS		✓	✓		✓	If poor returns	✓	✓			Partial	Partial

s: Volunt. = voluntary; Mandat. = mandatory; Indiv. = individual; Govt. = government; Mngr. = manager; Invest. = investment. SS = social security;
= provident funds; IRA = individual retirement account.

THE "IDEAL MODEL" (COMPARISON WITH OTHER SCHEMES)

In this section we describe the "Ideal Model" and compare it with other schemes to highlight its welfare-improving characteristics. The Ideal Social Security Model relies on a DB scheme that involves elements of a DC scheme and has government sponsorship (Lindbeck and Perrson 2001).[12] Orszag and Stiglitz (2001) have argued that any ideal model is unlikely to be realized in practice but is yet worth identifying. However, the shift from existing models to the Ideal Model does not require a complete overhaul of existing arrangements[13] but rather a change in philosophy and the willingness of governments to be more responsible. The amount of pension benefits to be achieved from such a model should be modest, but it affords better scope for individuals to retire above the poverty line. In addition, voluntary savings are urged under a more "free-to-choose" arrangement. We recommend a two-pillar approach to retirement savings: the Ideal Model and a voluntary DC scheme. We show how this can be more beneficial to participants and countries than the World Bank's three-pillar system and, by eliminating one pillar, can lower the cost to society

---

[12] Ensuring that these arrangements are incentive-compatible is addressed in Muralidhar and van der Wouden (1998a). A similar statement has been made in Bodie et al. (1988) without specifics.

[13] Muralidhar and van der Wouden (1998a).

of implementing a sustainable and effective system. Chapter 7 demonstrates how this simple structure can allow people to achieve an optimal trade-off between desired pensions and the risk they are willing to incur.

THE IDEAL MODEL FOR SOCIAL SECURITY[14]

It is critical for the policy maker to estimate the replacement rate or terminal retirement wealth (or retirement annuity) required from a social security system. To achieve this replacement rate, policy makers have to estimate a reasonable contribution rate, and assumptions have to be made about expected salary growth rate (possibly by a cohort), number of years of participation, and expected returns on assets. The equation for this balance would be as follows:

Normal contribution over working life compounded at the expected return on assets (with volatility) = Expected final wealth at retirement = Expected present value of desired annuity or desired replacement rate. (2.2)

Our research indicates that policy makers in Latin American countries had not focused on this relationship – especially the linkages among variables during the early stages of their reforms. If this aspect is neglected, replacement rates are likely to be low because no variable can be targeted in isolation.

CONTRIBUTIONS. At a minimum, the contribution rate required to achieve the previous identity should be mandated and credited to the individual accounts. Chapter 8 recommends variable mandated contributions and shows how risks to the system can be managed more efficiently through variable contributions. At this stage, we recommend that poor individuals be allowed to contribute up to 5 percent above the mandated contribution level to enable them to target their own replacement rate. This does not cause major problems, for there is limited redistribution among individual accounts. The method adopts the positive features of the Australian and Chilean systems. By constraining the size of variable contributions, the size of assets under this scheme can be managed to prevent growth to unacceptable levels (see Chapters 5 and 8).

ACCUMULATION. The scheme should be funded – partially or fully. The greater the accumulation, the greater the funds available from the returns on the assets; hence, the lower the required contribution. Where there are no issues with fully funded

---

[14] Many other aspects of a similar scheme are addressed in greater detail in Muralidhar and van der Wouden (1998a,b). Also, they show why a well-planned system in which the government is required to top up any shortfalls immediately is likely to have lower political risk of manipulation.

systems crowding out private investors (we return to this in Chapters 5, 6, and 8), full funding is preferred because it would lead to lower contributions, and lower volatility of contributions relative to PAYGO (Chapter 3).

TERMINAL OUTCOME (AND THE GUARANTEED RATE OF RETURN SWAP). The terminal outcome is ideally a DB annuity based on accumulated balances in individual accounts that guarantees the real value of annuities until death. As demonstrated earlier, this is achieved through government guarantees of an annual real rate of return (net of costs) on all contributions and, hence, allows for individual accounts. This controls the second element or return volatility in equation 2.2. The guarantee can be made more transparent through the use of a swap contract between the social security agency and the treasury. As part of the swap, the treasury periodically pays the social security agency a guaranteed return and receives the returns from the invested portfolio. In effect, only net payments are made by the parties to the contract (i.e., guaranteed rate minus portfolio returns). The payments or receipts on the swap will need to be made in cash or marketable assets to ensure that social security is fully invested in the target portfolio. Chapter 5 explains in greater detail how such an arrangement would take place in the United States. The guaranteed rate swap also provides a hedge against political risk. If, by any chance, governments divert assets to low-yielding alternatives, they would immediately realize the cost of such a diversion through the swap, thereby making the cost transparent.

Intertemporal risk pooling is feasible inasmuch as the scheme is a DB one and the law of large numbers holds for the DB sponsor (i.e., a hedge against longevity risk of individuals[15]). Ideally, this guaranteed rate would give individuals the opportunity to receive the desired annuity from the DB scheme and is tied to market rates of return. However, given uncertainties in asset and labor markets and average longevity, governments may be permitted to change the offered guaranteed rate for future contributions. For example, a change in terminal payout may be made effective 10 years into the future, insulating against immediate increases in benefits to curry political favor with participants. In addition, these changes can be based on the balances in the swap account (i.e., the equivalent of a reserve fund), and guaranteed returns can be raised (lowered) if accumulation (debt) exceeds some threshold.

In Chapter 8, we demonstrate how the terminal guarantee can be ensured through variable contributions. When the average return of the portfolio is equal to or greater than the guaranteed rate, the government bears only the risk associated with the variability of actual returns. If the long-term average return falls below the guaranteed

---

[15] Note that the system is protected as long as the average life expectancy is accurate. However, should this change, a DB scheme will need to adjust its contribution rate or investment strategy.

rate, then the government incurs a debt that will be financed through additional taxes (which impacts participants). Chapter 8 evaluates the use of variable contributions to manage the risk of the long-term average rate falling below the guaranteed rate.

For individuals with low salary growth rates and adequate participation, the Ideal Model offers a real pension (i.e., a minimum floor). In poor countries, this also reduces the stigmatization experienced by individuals who are embarrassed to seek assistance from welfare programs. Appropriate schemes would have to be designed to penalize fraudulent claims.[16] The floor can be financed through (i) general budget revenues, (ii) an increment in the contribution rates for all participants, or (iii) a slight reduction in the rate of return applied to contributions (relative to the earned rate), that is, lower benefits or a lower promised replacement rate to the average participant. If options (ii) and (iii) are considered, redistribution enters the equation and marginally distorts the relationship between contributions and market returns. The benefit, however, still has a direct relationship to contributions, and can be easily monitored. As Diamond (1997b) notes, redistribution distorts the relationship between contributions and pensions, but we attempt to mitigate the distortion through our guaranteed return structure. We also favor the possibility of part-time work after the mandatory retirement age, with proportional adjustment of pensions (as in Spain).

WHO CONTRIBUTES? Individuals contribute to their own individual accounts. In addition, the government creates a sinking fund for any surplus receipts from the portfolio over the guaranteed rate. If the actual returns fall short of the guaranteed swap rate, the government will withdraw from the sinking fund the amount needed to fully fund the scheme, if the sinking fund has a surplus, thereby providing an additional source of funds. Chapter 5 explains the operation of such a reserve fund for the United States. When these surpluses are deemed to be long term, they can be used for a reduction in contributions, higher guaranteed rates, or one-time increases in accumulations in individual accounts and vice versa. However, these changes raise the issue of compromising intergenerational equity to achieve intergenerational sharing of risk (see Chapter 8).

ASSET MANAGEMENT AND INVESTMENT MANAGEMENT ARRANGEMENTS. Given the DB pension, it is critical that assets be pooled for investment. We favor passive, indexed management over a clearly defined asset mix policy (e.g., initially a market capitalization weighted benchmark) and market benchmarks over active, externally

---

[16] We would like to thank Shadrach Appana and Ronald van der Wouden for their help in developing this point.

managed assets (though the Canadian system permits active management). Active management can be enforced once the system is fully functional. The ideal portfolio would be appropriately diversified in local and international markets and constructed with due consideration to the local market environment. Whether these portfolios are managed by the public sector or the private sector is not an issue with us; what concerns us is that after-fee returns closely track the gross returns of the benchmark (i.e., within a few basis points). We, therefore, recommend that a blue-ribbon board be appointed to oversee the investments (Aaron and Reischauer 1998). Canada and Ireland have created such boards.[17] Mitchell and Hsin (1997) demonstrate the importance of good governance and board composition for fund performance.

A critical aspect of the individual account structure that we favor is a simple statement to participants that provides details on after-cost returns, potential re-placement rates, and an indication of reasonable action to be taken on voluntary savings. Currently, only one software package we know of can offer advice on in-vestment and savings patterns for voluntary savings.[18] Seidman (1999) has a similar proposal but, given the absence of individual accounts, the social security agency would provide participants with details on the size of the fund, overall income, and so on, which are details that would probably overwhelm the average participant.[19]

Our plan most closely resembles the one proposed by Seidman (1999). Though his proposal is focused on reforming Social Security in the United States, the model is general enough to be applied in other countries too. It requires maintaining current benefits (to a large degree) but creates a funding vehicle through mandated contributions to a common fund, which is to be managed by private firms selected through competitive bidding. Variability in returns is managed by a stabilization fund, which receives the excess of return over the promised return and draws on accumulated reserves when it falls short.

The key differences between the Seidman model and ours is the recognition that a DB plan is nothing but a guaranteed rate of return plan and that the swap mechanism not only ensures that social security is always appropriately funded but also that

---

[17] Such a board was also proposed by the Maintain Benefits (MB) plan proponents of the ACSS (1997).

[18] ORTEC Consultants in the Netherlands has a software (Optimized Personal Asset-Liability System or OPAL) that gives individuals advice on investment and savings behavior. Other software packages, which are designed for individuals, offer advice only on asset allocation, thus limiting their usefulness.

[19] In the United States, even though the system is PAYGO, individuals have a social security card and account, and can receive statements of their projected benefits. Blahous (2000) suggests that President Roosevelt initiated this structure to ensure control and that the system would never be canceled. In other words, the cards and account numbers were meant to prevent politicians from abandoning the system.

political risk in manipulating assets is minimized because it will have direct budgetary impact. Therefore, any attempt to direct investments to favored regions that has been shown to reduce returns (Mitchell and Hsin 1997) will show up as additional payments in the swap. Professor Seidman, in contrast, feels that political risk can be managed by excluding social security from official budget reports with a separate balance sheet to prevent the government from raiding funds. In addition, given the structure, Seidman's proposal is unable to create "individual" accounts because benefits are measured by the previous (more complex) formula, whereas our plan greatly simplifies this equation. Seidman (1999) attributed several of the features of his plan to Feldstein (1975), but Professor Feldstein has subsequently moved in the direction of recommending individual account DC plans for several reasons. (This is discussed in Chapter 5.) Most critically, neither Professor Feldstein nor Professor Seidman contemplates variable contributions, the value of which is demonstrated in Chapter 8.

GOVERNMENT INCENTIVES. Ideally, no government incentives are required because the base contribution is mandated (though variable, as discussed in Chapter 8), and voluntary contributions are included in accounts that guarantee a rate of return. However, if properly managed, making retirement savings tax advantaged can raise private savings and national savings.

LIQUIDITY. Individuals should be permitted to finance personal loans (e.g., education, downpayments on housing, and medical care), including credit and debit cards, using the balances in their account as collateral, subject to strict limitations on terms. Enforcement of this arrangement can be privatized, but individuals should have the same discretion to make these choices (i.e., without a paternalistic approval process) as they do with credit cards or mortgages. Borrowing against these retirement savings will be at the guaranteed rate, and thus individuals will be no worse off when they repay these borrowings to themselves. The accumulation in participants' accounts will be the same as if the contributions earned the guaranteed rate throughout working life. However, this rate is likely to be less onerous than commercial rates, thereby raising the overall wealth of participants.

DESIRABLE PROPERTIES

The Ideal Model resembles, in many ways, the cash balance plan with a "fixed" guaranteed rate of return. The Ideal Model could be called a contributory, funded, defined benefit plan (CFDB) to distinguish it from either standard PAYGO or corporate DB plans. Table 2.3 demonstrates how the Ideal Model goes a long way in achieving the

TABLE 2.3 Detailed desirable properties of major schemes

9

Pension models	Contrib. to savings	Smoothing	Sustainability	Certainty of replacement rate — Nominal	Real	Minimum	Variability of contrib.	Universal availability (Yes) Volun.	Mand.	Choice — Contrib. rate	Portfolio	Replace. rate	Mngt. cost (Gross-Net return)	Benefit to contribution ratio
Rational behavior- Life cycle	✓	✓	✓	No	No	No	Yes	✓		✓	✓	✓	High	Medium
IRA	✓	✓	✓	No	No	No	Ltd.	✓		Ltd.	✓	Ltd.	Med.	Medium
401(K)	✓	✓	✓	No	No	No	Ltd.			Ltd.	✓	Ltd.	Med.	Med./High
Traditional SS		Ltd.	✓	No	✓	✓	Possible		✓	No	No	No	Low	Low
Mandtory PF	✓	N/A	✓	No	No	✓	No		✓	No	No	No	Low	Med./High
Chile "PrivatizedSS"	✓	N/A	✓	No	No	✓	Possible		✓	Ltd.	Ltd.	Ltd.	High	Medium
Mexico	✓	Ltd.	✓	No	Old DB	✓	No		✓	No	Ltd.	Ltd.	High	Medium
Ideal SS	✓	✓	✓	No	✓	✓	Yes		✓	Ltd.	No	Ltd.	Low	High

Notes: Contrib. = contribution. Ltd. = limited; Mand. = mandatory; med. = medium; Mngt. = managemen; N/A = not available; Replace. = replacement; Volun. = voluntary.

"desirable properties" with few negative consequences. This is a realistic arrangement and is not very different from existing social security arrangements.

Comparison with Other Plans

The social security debate ranges from "do nothing or no reform" to a completely privatized system. We briefly describe how the Ideal Model compares with mandatory U.S. Social Security (reflective of the "do nothing approach") and the mandatory Chilean model (reflective of the "privatized" approach). Table 2.3 summarizes the comparison with the rational behavior, IRA, 401(K), traditional social security (SS), mandatory Provident Fund (PF), and the Chilean and Mexican plans by identifying the desirable features that can be achieved by the various reform approaches.

SOCIAL SECURITY IN THE UNITED STATES. The fundamental problem with the current system is that there is little contribution to national savings, and the redistributive elements could lead to evasion where possible. The system is unsustainable because of low growth of population and productivity, and smoothing is not feasible. (This is discussed in more detail in Chapter 5.) Social Security in the United States is not a pure PAYGO system because reserves were set aside in a reform of the system; however, we treat it as a PAYGO system in this analysis because the reserves will be consumed in a finite period of time. Finally, the lack of choice, particularly with regard to spending patterns, makes these social security schemes seriously defective.

CHILEAN DC MODEL. The Chilean model has the advantage of creating a self-financing and hence sustainable funding vehicle. It fails to facilitate smoothing, but minor adjustments can be made to permit borrowing against accumulated resources. However, the two biggest risks or costs of the Chilean-type model are (i) the uncertainty of final outcome which, in volatile asset markets, can lead to substantial poverty among many cohorts,[20] and (ii) the extremely high management fees given the absence of incentives for regulators to control them. Though researchers have documented the fees, a shortcoming of these analyses is that few have addressed the impact of an inadequate replacement rate (in turn, the cost to future generations). We address this in Chapter 3. Informed individuals in Chilean-type models would do well to evade these schemes because the "limited" choice is likely to affect them adversely.

---

[20] Estimates of how large these welfare costs can be are provided in Muralidhar and van der Wouden (1998b). See also Chapter 4.

SUMMARY

This chapter has attempted to clarify the debate on social security by placing the responsibility on the government, where it should be. By focusing on the "desirable properties" and design aspects, this taxonomy has attempted to demonstrate how an ideal model can be constructed to ensure that individuals across cohorts get a reasonable pension and are able to use the savings to smooth intertemporal consumption and investment. By comparing the Ideal Model with other models, the chapter has demonstrated how welfare-improving characteristics are relatively easy to implement – especially since pension reform is still in its infancy. However, it may not be feasible to implement all elements in all countries given the current state of social security systems. We discuss transition issues, and the impact on various aspects of the Ideal Model that can be implemented, in Chapters 5, 6, and 7. In most cases, the most politically sensitive aspect to adopt in the Ideal Model is the notion that benefits are equal to the contribution rate growing at a guaranteed rate of return even though this is similar to a more transparent, stable variant of the DC proposals. This follows because participants are skeptical about any changes to benefits. Hence, in discussing transition issues in Chapters 5 and 6, we take the current benefits as given and show how our recommendation can be used to create and make the transition to a new system with many of the desirable properties of the Ideal Model.

3

An Evaluation of Pension Reforms

THE CHILEAN REVOLUTION AND ITS CONQUEST OF LATIN AMERICA AND THE WORLD BANK

During the last two decades, a revolution has been sweeping across Latin America with countries pushing for a radical reform of the public pension systems. In essence, countries have made three fundamental and dramatic paradigm shifts from the inherited pay-as-you-go (PAYGO) system in an effort to imitate the so-called privatization of the Chilean scheme: they have moved from PAYGO systems to funded systems, from defined benefit (DB) schemes to defined contribution (DC) schemes, and from schemes with public management of any accumulated assets at moderate administrative cost (with certain inefficiencies) to private asset management at significantly higher costs. Countries such as Argentina, Colombia, and Peru have adopted a partial variant of the Chilean model by offering participants a choice: either an individual account, privately managed DC system or a public PAYGO DB system (Mitchell and Barreto 1997). Many countries in Asia and Eastern Europe are considering adopting some of these changes, and even the United States is discussing the creation of private retirement accounts as a supplement to, or replacement for, Social Security.

Many countries and reformers (e.g., the World Bank) have made the case for privatized schemes based on an inappropriate comparison. In seeing the potential shortcomings of a public PAYGO system, they have sought to change all aspects of the system. There appears to be a mixing of issues on four key points in the design of these proposed new systems. It seems that many reform discussions have fallen short by (a) not comparing DC plans with similar or equivalent DB plans, (b) not distinguishing between governance or the development of investment policy[1] and

---

[1] A common failing of just about every pension reform implemented to date in developing countries is that the investment policy is not clearly specified in one or more of the following categories:

the physical implementation of investment policy or selection of securities and investments, (c) blindly supporting private over public investment management,[2] and (d) not comparing passive versus active management in the presence of clearly defined market benchmarks. When countries consider implementing mandatory, privately (actively) managed DC plans, the proper alternative for comparison should be a mandatory, well-defined DB plan with the following features: (a) identical ex ante target replacement rates,[3] (b) funding with identical long-term contributions as in the DC structure, (c) centralized governance with privately managed investments (a model common and successful in occupational DB plans in developed markets),[4] and (d) the possibility of passive and active investment options relative to market benchmarks.[5] Such a comparison would make the case for DC plans less attractive. Some analysts have suggested that some of the adverse features of DC plans, namely, high administrative costs, difficulties in securing diversified portfolios, imperfections and high costs of annuities, and high transition costs, are reasons for caution (Asher 1998). Baker and Kar (2002), in a critique of the World Bank approach, demonstrate that the costs of administration, annuities, establishment of a regulatory body, and time spent by individuals are many multiples of the cost of running the U.S. Social Security system.

In Chapter 2, we provided a taxonomy of pension reform issues and suggested that countries embarking on pension reform with a clean slate would be better off adopting an individual account (with somewhat flexible contributions and the privilege of borrowing a regulated portion of the account balance) DB system insured through a

---

definition of asset classes, target allocation to asset class, permissible range of investment around target, and market benchmark for asset classes. The last failing is serious, for funds cannot be compared without a passive, neutral alternative. In many markets, passive investing is a difficult benchmark to beat on an after-fees basis.

[2] A debate carried out extensively in developed countries and referred to as the case for internal management (in public or private nonfinancial institutions) versus external management.

[3] Replacement rates can be specified in several different ways, including on the basis of final salary, average salary, and so on. We will not address this here. We emphasize ex ante targets, for it is difficult to have an ex post target that can be achieved with a high probability in either DB or DC without significant cost.

[4] This is only one permutation. Another could be centralized governance and investment management, which is not taken up here because we prefer to ignore the debate on whether internal management is better or worse than external management! There is no clear conclusion on this issue.

[5] The global capital market convention prescribes that passive investment refer to a nearly identical replication of a prespecified market benchmark in terms of security selection and the percentage allocation of total to a particular security. Active management would imply discretion delegated to the portfolio manager in security selection and percentage of total allocated to securities. There are degrees of active and passive that are not explored in this chapter. Refer to Muralidhar (2001).

guaranteed return on contributions. Assets would be pooled but managed passively by either the government or private asset managers. However, many countries have gone past this stage and implemented reforms. They have made two leaps required for reform: the establishment of a new system and the transition.

This chapter looks at major changes embedded in existing reforms and indicates fundamental flaws in their design. Some of these problems have been pointed out by other researchers (e.g., Diamond 1994); however, we address the same issues from a different perspective to show how potentially damaging they can be. To do so, we make the proposition that the role of any public pension system is to provide a reasonable annuity at retirement, such as some target replacement rate. The expected (fixed) long-term contribution rate is determined by estimating the ex ante replacement rate, the real return on investment, real salary growth, and demographic characteristics relating to the number of years of service and life expectancy and using the model in the appendix to Chapter 1.

In the evaluation of any scheme, one must ask what the target replacement rate is and how likely it is that the replacement rate will be achieved. Blahous (2000) suggests that, to evaluate a pension scheme, one must consider the rate of return and the replacement rate, for neither measure in isolation provides adequate information on the success of a scheme. In a funded scheme, for a given replacement rate (and growth of wages), the rate of return determines a unique, fixed, long-term contribution rate.[6] We will examine the sensitivity of the long-term contribution rate to various parameters under PAYGO and under the funded system to demonstrate the advantages of funding and look at the implications for replacement rates from moving to privately managed DC accounts.

The following are the key issues that we seek to highlight:

(i) In steady state, funded systems are preferable to PAYGO systems for reasonable assumptions on returns and real income growth. However, as these variables evolve, the dominance may not be as great as is sometimes suggested.

(ii) Where PAYGO systems have been replaced by funded schemes invested in equity, and the system deficit is financed by government debt (e.g., recognition bonds), government debt is being leveraged (i.e., government borrowing to buy equity to reap the risk premium). Similar problems arise when schemes invested solely in government bonds shift the investment strategy to investing in equities to get higher returns. For a transition to a reformed system to provide real benefits to a country, it must succeed in increasing national saving.

---

[6] In a multiperiod setting, it is possible to have different contribution paths (e.g., with variable contributions) that achieve this relationship.

(iii) The assertion that DC schemes are better than DB schemes is the result of an incorrect comparison.

(iv) Most countries have not set target or desirable replacement rates when determining mandatory contribution rates. This results in uncertain outcomes for participants. The average participant is not sophisticated enough to know what replacement rate they will achieve, and it does not appear that governments set the contribution rate based on an analysis of the relationship between a target replacement rate and the expected after-fee rate of return.

(v) For countries that have adopted DC schemes, there is likely to be considerable volatility in achieved replacement rates caused by volatility of asset returns across cohorts, leading to many cohorts retiring poor.

(vi) High administrative costs (especially as a percentage of salaries) leads to a substantial reduction in replacement rates.

(vii) Increased choice in DC plans is likely to require extensive regulation, and this regulation could allow governments to control asset allocations (e.g., require that some portion of the assets be invested in low-yielding government bonds to fund budget deficits). In other words, proponents of DC schemes have underestimated the political risk that these schemes imply.

This chapter addresses each of these issues in greater detail, provides examples of the design flaws, and, where possible, provides estimates of the costs that will be incurred in terms of budget impact, contribution rates, and replacement rates. To date, no other discussion on these topics has emphasized the impact on all these parameters. The purpose of this chapter is to highlight these implications of pension reform that may have been ignored in previous debates.

COMPARING FUNDED SCHEMES WITH PAYGO SCHEMES

In comparing funded schemes with PAYGO schemes, one needs to distinguish between the steady state and the transition. We demonstrate, in the next section, that the required long-term contribution under funding (assuming current projections) for given benefits is smaller and also less sensitive to possible unanticipated changes in relevant "exogenous" variables such as the rate of growth of population and productivity or life expectancy. The variability of required long-term contributions is rarely taken into consideration in the social security reform debate, but minimizing the variability of long-term contributions is a key objective in the management of corporate pension funds (Muralidhar 2001). If reformers recognize the importance of containing the variability of long-term contributions, it would enhance the case for funded schemes. In Chapter 8, we examine the benefit of short-term variability around a long-term average contribution.

Funded systems are less exposed to the threat of insolvency that plagues the PAYGO systems wherever they exist. These crises reflect the unforeseen current and prospective decline in the growth of real payrolls that reduces the implicit rate of return, causing the PAYGO systems to struggle because there will be fewer (or less affluent) young workers to collect from relative to the pensions promised to older retired people. Receipts will fall short of the benefits promised. With funded schemes, the funds available to pay pensions will basically be unaffected by growth-related changes in the "demographic structure" because the pension is not paid by the contributions of younger workers but from the capital accumulated by the pensioner. Changes in productivity growth (or life expectancy)[7] do require some changes in required long-term contributions, but only to a minor degree as compared with those required under a PAYGO system. The main determinant of the required long-term contribution is the long-run average real net return on the investment, that is, nominal return adjusted for inflation and real growth. But we demonstrate that even variations in this variable, within historically realistic limits, would not require drastic changes in the long-term contribution rate.

In addition, the funded system, in contrast to PAYGO, results in a large accumulation of assets and thus makes a valuable contribution to the national stock of capital, to national income, and to national saving as long as the pension system grows (in real terms). This rise in saving is especially valuable at a time when private saving is unusually low in countries such as the United States, creating worrisome problems with respect to the level of foreign indebtedness.

Finally, one should expect that lower long-term contributions required by a funded scheme would reduce the labor market distortions created by the current PAYGO systems, encouraging greater participation by the labor force and less evasion of contributions. There is evidence that the enormous social security payroll taxes levied in Europe – frequently two or three times as large as in the United States – bear some responsibility for the huge unemployment rate.

OVERVIEW OF LONG-TERM CONTRIBUTIONS REQUIRED UNDER A PAYGO SYSTEM VERSUS A FUNDED SYSTEM

Ignoring transition issues initially, we begin by reviewing the forces that determine the required long-term contribution rate in steady state for the two alternative

---

[7] Changes to these variables will impact the transition, as discussed in Chapters 5 and 6.

financing approaches: PAYGO and full funding.[8] For each financing method, the contribution rate depends on several parameters, which are reviewed in this section. Some of the parameters are "exogenous," that is, outside the direct control of policy makers. They include the following:

(i) The rate of growth of real income (ρ) and its two components (items ii and iii),

(ii) The growth of the labor force (n),

(iii) Productivity growth (q),

(iv) Longevity (e), and

(v) The rates of return on various financial assets (r) and their volatility.

The policy determined parameters include the following:

(i) The standard retirement age, which, together with longevity, determines the average duration of the pension annuity;

(ii) The portfolio in which the accumulated capital of the fund is invested (mostly important for a funded scheme because, under the pure PAYGO system, there is, in principle, no accumulated capital to invest); and

(iii) The so-called rate of replacement, or the ratio of the pension to some measure of income earned while working and contributing. The specification of the replacement rate involves detailing what measure of income should be used (e.g., terminal versus lifetime average) and how it is related to the years of contribution.

Define a_t to be assets in a funded system at time t and w_t to be the wage bill at time t. Also, define A_t to be the asset-to-wage ratio, c_t to be the contribution rate at time t (i.e., contributions divided by wages), and p_t to be the cost ratio. In a funded system, one can observe the following dynamics:

$$A_t = [a_{t-1}(1+r)]/[w_{t-1}(1+\rho)] + c_t - p_t, \text{ where } \rho = n + q. \quad (3.1)$$

As a result, A can be approximated by the following:

$$A_t = A_{t-1}(1 + r - \rho) + c_t - p_t. \quad (3.2)$$

Equation (3.2) can be rewritten as

$$A_t - A_{t-1} = A_{t-1}(r - \rho) + c_t - p_t. \quad (3.3)$$

---

[8] This section is based on hypothetical data to demonstrate the marked differences in contributions between the two approaches.

But when the pension system reaches a steady state, assets must grow at the same rate as the wage bill, that is, the growth of A_t must be zero, implying the following fundamental relationship:

$$c_t = p_t - A_{t-1}(r - \rho). \tag{3.4}$$

We will call this equation the "Golden SS Rule." The net return on the system's reserves helps pay a portion of the benefits provided the net return is positive or $r > \rho$, which is a necessary condition for funding to be preferred over the PAYGO system.

The effect of the major parameters on the required contribution rate under different financing schemes is illustrated in Tables 3.1A and 3.1B. It also supports our contention that, under realistic assumptions, a funded system is distinctly preferable to PAYGO both because it requires lower long-term contributions and insolvency poses less of a problem. The rate of return (r) in the tables is the real (gross) rate of return. However, there are situations, as shown in Tables 3.1A and 3.1B, in which PAYGO requires a lower contribution rate than funding, namely, when $r < \rho$.

For our calculations we assume a set of parameters, which we regard as plausible though they do not necessarily coincide with those relevant for the United States or any other country. They include 40 years of contributions and a replacement rate of 50 percent of life average income. (If we changed the assumptions on the replacement rate, all the contribution rates reported would change in proportion.) As for average length of life after retirement, we show the implications of two alternative assumptions: in the left portion of the tables we assume life expectancy of 16 years, whereas the right side of the table assumes life expectancy to be 18 years. It is further assumed, for the funded scheme shown in Table 3.1B, the assets of the fund are invested in the "indexed portfolio" of all marketable securities and swapped for the real interest rate indicated in the extreme left column.

The PAYGO Scheme

Table 3.1A shows an estimate of the ratio of current pensions to contemporaneous (taxable) wages or the so-called cost ratio for pensions for different parameter values. However, under a pure PAYGO financing scheme, because pension outlays must, by and large, be equal to current contributions, the cost ratio also measures the ratio of required contributions to wages or the "equilibrium contribution rate."

The main factor to note in Table 3.1A is the extreme sensitivity of the contribution rate to growth parameters of population (n) and productivity (q), and hence their sum (ρ). The required contribution rate declines with population growth (n) as per the well-known "age pyramid" effect. The lower the n, the higher the ratio

TABLES 3.1A and 3.1B Cost and contribution rates for alternative systems and selected scenarios (as a percentage of wages; some cells intentionally left blank)

Assumptions: working life = 40 years; average salary = 50% replacement

Table 3.1A: PAYGO

Cost ratio = Pay-as-you-go scheme contribution rates for different scenarios

Population growth	Retired life – 16 years				Retired life – 18 years			
	0%	1.00%	1.40%	2.00%	0%	1.00%	1.40%	2.00%
0%	20.00%	15.40%	13.40%	11.90%	22.50%	17.20%	N/A	N/A
1%	15.05%	11.70%	10.40%	9.00%	16.77%	N/A	N/A	N/A
2%	11.24%	8.80%	7.00%	N/A	12.41%	N/A	N/A	N/A

(Real productivity growth)

Table 3.1B: Funded

Cost ratio = Funded scheme contribution rates for different scenarios

Return on assets	Retired life – 16 years				Retired life – 18 years			
	0%	1.00%	1.40%	2%	0%	1.00%	1.40%	2%
0%	20.00%	20.11%	20.15%	20.23%	22.50%	22.62%	22.67%	22.75%
1%	15.05%	15.33%	15.45%	15.63%	16.77%	17.08%	17.21%	17.41%
2%	11.24%	11.60%	11.75%	11.97%	12.41%	12.81%	12.97%	13.22%
3%	8.33%	8.70%	8.86%	9.10%	9.12%	9.53%	9.70%	9.96%
4%	6.13%	6.48%	6.63%	6.86%	6.66%	7.04%	7.21%	7.46%
5%	4.49%	4.80%	4.93%	5.14%	4.84%	5.17%	5.32%	5.54%
6%	3.26%	3.53%	3.64%	3.82%	3.50%	3.78%	3.90%	4.09%
Approximity replacement on final salary	50%	41%	38%	34%	50%	41%	38%	34%

(Real productivity growth)

Note: N/A = not available.

of retired beneficiaries to the active workers that must support the former with their contribution and, hence, the higher the required contribution rate – and the quantitative effect is impressive. The effect of productivity growth is more complex, but it works in the same direction and is similar quantitatively. Thus, the required contribution depends essentially on the sum: $(n + q = \rho)$. It is seen from the table that a decline in ρ by two percentage points from 2 to 0 requires a rise in contribution of some 9 percentage points from 11 percent to 20 percent! But for many of the countries in Europe (e.g., Italy), the replacement rate is up to 80 percent of terminal income, which means around 100 percent of the average income, and therefore the figures in the table must be doubled (Modigliani and Ceprini 1998). In particular, with a productivity growth closer to 1.5 percent, and little population growth, the table suggests an equilibrium contribution of double the 20–25 percent level, which is close to what social security levies actually are in those countries.

In short, with PAYGO financing, the required contribution is very sensitive to small and very plausible changes in prospective growth. Therefore, that approach does not provide the basis for a stable pension system – one that is not continuously threatened by major crises such as the current system.

The Funded Scheme

Table 3.1B reports the contribution rate needed under a funded system. In a funded system, in steady state, outlays are financed by the sum of contributions and interest on accumulated assets. This is shown in equation (3.4). An interesting aspect of equation (3.4) is the opportunity to examine the dynamics of this equation to changes in n and q. These dynamics help us understand the implications of various variables in the funded system. We start first with population growth, which we know has no implication for the contribution rate.

$$dp/dn = 0 + (-A_{t-1}) + (r - \rho)dA/dn \tag{3.5}$$

$$\text{or } dA/dn = (1/(r - \rho))[dp/dn + A_{t-1}] \tag{3.6}$$

We know that the cost ratio is a declining function of population growth, which means, if population growth increases, there must be an appropriate adjustment in the asset–wage ratio. In general, A will be in the neighborhood of 2–3, and dp/dn (from Tables 3.1A and 3.1B) is in the order of 4–5. Hence dA/dn is also negative, suggesting that the asset–wage ratio must decline. The intuition behind this, from work by Modigliani and Brumberg (1980), is that wealth is largely an increasing function of age, and population growth increases the ratio of young to old. Therefore, with population growth, the wealth–income ratio tends to decline.

The more difficult scenario is the impact of productivity growth on the variables. We know that $dp/dq < 0$ and $dc/dq > 0$ from Tables 3.1A and 3.1B (as real wages increase, contribution rates need to increase to support the higher annuities required to sustain a given replacement rate).

$$dp/dq = dc/dq + (-A_{t-1}) + dr/dq(A_{t-1}) + (r - n - q)dA/dq \quad (3.7)$$

or

$$dA/dq = (1/(r - n - q))[dp/dq - dc/dq + (1 - dr/dq)(A_{t-1})]. \quad (3.8)$$

In general, dr/dq can be assumed to be greater than 0. Given the previous analysis of population growth, this suggests that dA/dq would also be less than 0.

A comparison of Table 3.1A with Table 3.1B reveals, in striking fashion, the much smaller required contribution for given benefits under the funded system.[9] The reason for the difference is, in the funded scheme, a large portion of the pensions is paid not from the cash contribution but from the interest on the accumulated wealth. Take, for instance, the case most favorable to the funded system in Table 3.1B: a zero growth of income, 6-percent rate of return on investment, and 18 years retirement. Here the PAYGO contribution is 22.5 percent versus only 3.5 percent for the funded system! Such a difference may seem impossibly large. The explanation, of course, is that, by the time the funded system reaches maturity, the social security trust funds (TFs) hold assets amounting to about 3.2 times wages, the return on which, at 6 percent, is sufficient to fill the gap.

To be sure, the preceding illustration is rather extreme, but the difference remains large even in more realistic cases. For instance, let us consider the case most similar to the long-run growth assumptions for the United States, corresponding to the so-called intermediate cost projections. The corresponding contribution required under PAYGO is shown by the shaded entry on the right side of Table 3.1A, namely, 17.2 percent (which is the 1999 estimate of the Old Age and Survivor cost ratio for pensions by the third quarter of this century). It is clear from the corresponding column of Table 3.1B that the required contribution for the funded system is less than 4 percent for a rate of return of 6 percent, and for a rate of return of 5 percent it is just over 5 percent or more than two-thirds lower. Even with a return as low as 4 percent (roughly 2 percent higher than the current real rate on U.S. Treasury

---

[9] Sections of Table 3.1A are intentionally left blank because they do not add to the analysis.

inflation-proof bonds), the equilibrium contribution is but 7 percent or less than half of the PAYGO contribution.

Tables 3.1A and 3.1B also highlight several other aspects in which a funded system dominates PAYGO financing (Feldstein 1997). We have already argued that, in a funded system, the required contribution is independent of (n). The data in Table 3.1B establish that the required contribution is also hardly affected by (q) and is in the opposite direction from that under PAYGO; namely, it declines if (q) declines (because of the resulting increase in the "adjusted" rate of return). Not surprisingly, the contribution is seen to increase with life expectancy (e), but the effect is surprisingly small. With a 5-percent return, a rise in (e) from 16 to 18 years, which is fairly large requires an increase in contribution of only about 0.35 percent, whereas under PAYGO the increase is close to 2 percent. But even that small effect can be erased by relying on the often-proposed remedy of somehow "indexing" the standard retirement age to life expectancy. Specifically, we suggest that the retirement age (i.e., the years of contribution) be linked to life expectancy in such a way that the increased contribution offsets the cost of the partially increased expected duration of the stream of pension payments. Of course, we would retain the present option to retire earlier than the standard but with a cut in the pension reflecting the smaller contribution and longer benefit period.

Further, Table 3.1B validates the claim in Chapters 1 and 2 that a fixed contribution rate, compounded at a guaranteed rate of return, can ensure a particular replacement rate for given demographic profiles and salary growth. In other words, Table 3.1B can be seen as representing the various possible combinations of fixed contributions and guaranteed returns to ensure a guaranteed replacement rate. Therefore, a guaranteed return plan for a fixed contribution rate is also a funded DB plan.

To summarize, the results of this section provide evidence for the claim set out in the summary that, on the grounds of the current cost-to-benefit ratio, of flexibility, and of stability of required contributions in respect of likely changes in exogenous parameters, the fully funded system is superior to PAYGO (in steady state). Further, this analysis gives three key conclusions:

(i) The cost ratio and the net returns depend on growth; hence, the dominance of funding over PAYGO may be overstated if one carelessly disregards the role of growth.

(ii) In the PAYGO system, a decline in the growth rate has a large impact on the required contribution (for given benefits), whereas with a funded system the effect is of a smaller magnitude (and opposite in sign) as a result of the accompanying increase in the asset–wage ratio (we will examine the impact of growth on nominal rates of return later).

(iii) If the asset–wage ratio rises, it may lead to a decline in r. This, in turn, may make the funded system less dominant. Under such scenarios, mixing systems may make sense, and we will examine the case for mixed systems in Chapter 8.

The more complex issue of the transition from a largely unfunded system, like the PAYGO, to a funded system, remains to be considered. Many fail to realize that the superiority of the steady state funded system is due to the capital accumulated in this system. The capital permits lower contributions and could make up for a future shortfall (i.e., less contributing young people can be offset by a higher return to capital or greater productivity), but only if the capital is accumulated first. This ignorance has led many uninformed people to the erroneous belief that the widespread crisis can be solved through building a funded system by requiring participants to redirect their contribution from social security to individual (or pooled) portfolios invested in the market. This is addressed in the next section.

Diamond (1998) argues that, because of transition costs, any professed efficiency gains are overstated (see also Samuelson 1975). Sinn (1999) argues that, in present value terms, there is nothing to be gained from a transition to a funded system even though it offers a permanently higher rate of return. The typical argument is that any reduction in contributions in the future comes at the cost of higher contributions today, and the present value of the two flows, properly discounted, coincides so that there is no net benefit but, instead, just an intertemporal transfer with unchanged expected benefits. On the other hand, Corsetti and Schmidt-Hebbel (1997) demonstrate that a transition from PAYGO to full funding could raise welfare by bringing more resources into the formal sector. Furthermore, even though there may not be a net benefit in moving from PAYGO to funding in a world of stationary growth and returns, this conclusion does not hold if there is a prospect of lower future growth, thereby requiring higher contributions or lower pensions. Again, although funding may result in lower individual contributions that may not be very different from the transition cost, it can produce net positive external effects through the lowering of long-term contribution volatility and reduction in labor market distortions. As a result, we are generally supportive of the shift towards funded systems (provided the appropriate relationship exists between returns and growth).

FINANCING THE TRANSITION FROM PAYGO SCHEMES WITH DEFICITS

The difficulty in transitioning from a PAYGO scheme to a funded system is that pension promises under PAYGO need to be serviced from current contributions during the transition period; hence, contributions cannot simply be transferred to the new funded scheme. Many countries have used budget surpluses or reduced benefits in an attempt to offset PAYGO deficits arising from transferring contributions to the new scheme. Chile, for example, used off-market recognition bonds to finance the promised pension but was helped in the maneuver by budget surpluses. Peru issued such bonds with a guaranteed 0-percent real rate (Mitchell and Barreto 1997). Others have even considered increasing taxes or maintaining the old scheme with partial contributions. In Mexico, this guarantee has been achieved by assuring transition participants that they will receive the higher of their PAYGO DB or DC pension. Countries with no surplus have been forced to issue debt to finance the residual pension obligations.

The most common form of debt used to cover previous obligations is the recognition bonds of the type issued by the Chileans. These are largely claims against the government that are nontraded except at retirement, are likely to carry an off-market interest rate,[10] and are typically issued to older participants.

In the United States, in an attempt to extend the life of the Social Security scheme, a proposal was put forth (Feldstein and Samwick 1997) to create personal retirement accounts with 2-percent contributions invested in a 60-percent equity – 40-percent bond investment. These contributions would be in addition to the 12.4-percent contributions to Social Security, were projected to earn a real 5.5 percent, and were to be facilitated by offering individuals dollar-for-dollar personal income tax credits for the amount they were to deposit in their personal accounts. The combination of this account and reduced pensions from Social Security, consistent with the smaller receipts due to factors such as aging, was supposed to extend Social Security indefinitely at the current 12.4-percent contribution rate. In good part, the plan relies on the expectation of extracting greater returns from the investment of reserves in market securities rather than in government debt, as is currently done with the reserves in the Trust Fund.

It was anticipated in 1997 that these credits could be financed from expected future budget surpluses (approximately 0.8 percent of gross domestic product). Research by Modigliani and Modigliani (1987) suggests that individuals would rather use surpluses to finance such transitions than pay higher taxes. However, these surpluses will not materialize because of a tax cut implemented by the Bush Administration and the economic slowdown since 2001; hence, the American government will eventually need to finance these tax credits with debt.

---

[10] In Chile, they carry a 4-percent real rate of interest, whereas other government bonds have paid substantially higher rates. The apparent reason for selecting a 4-percent real rate was that this is the rate required to achieve a 70-percent replacement rate. We thank Jonathan Callund for this information.

Corsetti and Schmidt-Hebbel (1997) evaluated debt-financed versus surplus- (or tax-) financed transitions and suggest that debt-financed transitions have only a marginal impact on national savings, the capital stock, and intergenerational distribution of welfare, although these results are in sharp contrast to the results reported in Modigliani (1966). Clearly, surplus- or tax- financed transitions benefit non-tax-paying future generations at the cost of those who are currently paying taxes. Valdes-Prieto (1997) would argue, unless growth effects or additional savings are triggered, welfare cannot be improved.

Increasing government debt to finance these transitions is a bad idea because it will not produce any new net saving; as the pension system accumulates reserves, it is matched by an equal growth of government debt, which at high levels leads to large debt service payments. As Alan Greenspan has pointed out, moving to funding is not a panacea if there are no additional savings (Blahous 2000 and Greenspan 1996). There are basic problems with any of these approaches as there is no net increase in savings (Orszag and Stiglitz 2001).[11]

To be sure, there is some possibility that government debt financing may provide a net increase in resources. For instance, in the Latin American reforms, government financing allows an equal buildup in reserves, which are invested in higher yielding assets (e.g., equities). It is hoped that over time these investments will return more than the cost incurred by the government. This mechanism partly underlies Feldstein and Samwick's (1997) proposal. Allowing the pension system to invest the contributions in equities while paying pensions through the buildup of government debt might produce some extra returns (equity premium), but this is equivalent to allowing the government to invest in a portfolio of risky assets levered by government borrowing. This drastically unsound practice is fraught with risks, and is equivalent to government acquisition of a highly levered equity portfolio, because it is entirely financed by government borrowing in the hope of earning the equity risk premium. In the privatized social security situation, one aspect is that government deficits finance the equity buildup in individual portfolios. In the end, because of its obligation to ensure retirement safety, the government bears the risk while having limited discretion on how the portfolio is actually invested. Not only has this not been perceived as an issue, but it has even been viewed as a positive. The International Monetary Fund (IMF) has apparently permitted such debt to exceed the ceiling they maintain for countries, and Moody's has improved its rating of Hungary after such a transition (James 1998).

---

[11] Increases in contributions have two ways of impacting national wealth: (i) directly through increased savings and (ii) a second-order effect through returns on these investments.

In a modified form of this proposal, a consumption tax has been suggested,[12] in addition to privately managed personal accounts, as a means of covering the PAYGO deficit. Had these contributions to the funded system been made from government surpluses, additional savings could have ensured a transition. (We demonstrate a more effective scheme in Chapter 5.) However, with such surpluses declining worldwide, the only option is to impose a tax to force additional savings, and it should be implemented so that there is no dissaving elsewhere.

In summary, additional resources are needed to attack the *real* source of the insolvency – namely, the decline in the growth rate – and this is the only way to move toward a funded system. Building up a funded component can help solve the crisis by increasing the amount of capital and output and, it is hoped, not appreciably reducing the productivity of capital. But where do these resources come from? Whether they are used to pay the pension or (identically) pay the contribution to the new fund, if they are financed by a deficit they solve nothing because it does not bring new savings; thus, this is a very unsound approach. It leverages the government portfolio at great risk, and does not add any resources, but merely redistributes the existing risk and capital income between the private and the public sectors. New savings can be captured only from tapping into budget surpluses or raising contributions. We propose an increase in savings through an increase in contributions invested in higher expected return (and risk) assets. In as much as these new contributions cannot be offset by tax credits, the proposed increase is similar to the tax proposed by Kotlikoff and Sachs (1998). As the size of the fund grows, it can be used to offset the growing PAYGO deficits (see Feldstein and Samwick 1997). A proposal along these lines has been made for the United States and Spain (see the discussion in Chapters 5 and 6[13]).

MOVING FROM DB TO DC SOCIAL SECURITY SCHEMES

Privatization was first introduced in Chile (aiming at total funding) followed by several Latin American and other developing countries (World Bank 1994, James and Vittas 1995). In the United States, the best known formulations of privatization aim at a mixed system with only partial funding and possibly an "opt-out" provision (e.g., President George W. Bush, Archer and Shaw 1999, Feldstein and Samwick 1998).

---

[12] See Kotlikoff and Sachs (1998). As long as current retirees also bear the cost, this arrangement would be fair, or else a reduction in benefits is an alternative form of taxation.

[13] See also Modigliani and Ceprini (1998) for Italy.

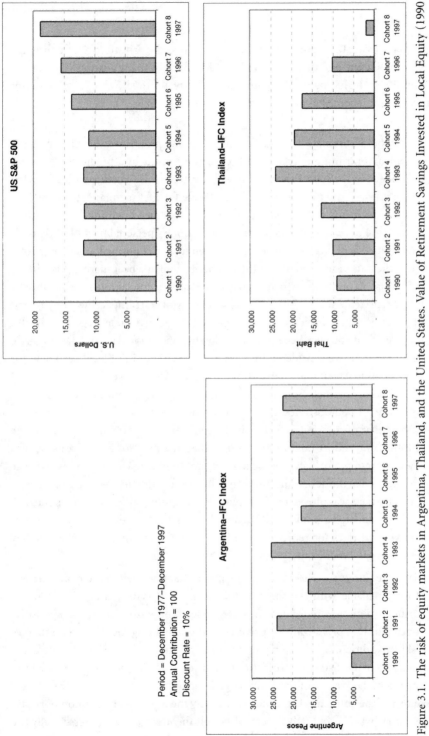

Figure 3.1. The risk of equity markets in Argentina, Thailand, and the United States. Value of Retirement Savings Invested in Local Equity (1990 terms).

In many cases, the argument for the switch is that the privatized alternative provides a higher rate of return. This has been debunked by many analysts (Orszag and Stiglitz 2001), including us. We maintain that "privatization" as the primary source of retirement income has at least four major shortcomings:

(i) It would eliminate the existing defined and progressive benefit structure in which contributions related to life earnings result in a predictable pension guaranteed by the state. Privatization would replace this structure with a "defined contribution" structure in which, in exchange for lifetime mandated contributions, participants do not get a predictable, guaranteed pension but a "lottery ticket" (the uncertain, erratic performance of one's personal portfolio). Participants' retirement income will depend on their luck in choosing the right portfolio and if the date of retirement is at the height of a bull or a bear market. Also, in the individual accounts structure proposed, luck plays a crucial role in achieving the target replacement rate. This is because when you start impacts where you end up when you bear investment risk. All else being constant, average final wealth for given contributions becomes a function of conception date and date of birth. As an example, we considered the case in which 100 units of local currency (for individuals in Argentina, Thailand, and the United States) were invested annually in local equity markets from 1976 onwards for cohorts retiring between 1990–97. As Figure 3.1 demonstrates, even for investments in the most developed market, such as that of the United States (investing in the S&P 500 index), there is the risk that one cohort might retire poorer than the next solely as a consequence of investment performance of the market (not fund managers). The case is more pronounced in the developing markets. The risk to retirement wealth from investing in markets was proved by the recent global equity market downturn. Burtless (1998) conducted a similar analysis and demonstrates the dramatic variability of replacement rates for retirees in the United States depending on whether they retired in the 1960s or the 1970s.

(ii) To require or even encourage people to gamble their retirement nest egg is irreconcilable with the spirit of the current DB system, which aims at ensuring a minimum retirement income. **Indeed, on close reflection, it must be concluded that privatization "privatizes" the only thing that should be shared: risk!** In addition, it has the highly undesirable effect of fostering manmade inequalities in the distribution of retirement income. Under the individual portfolio approach, the average of the returns of all portfolios must be close to the average return of the entire market, which is precisely the return on a common portfolio (Auerbach 1997). In a DB system, although the *average* return is essentially the same – except for the much higher management cost of individual portfolios (Diamond 1996b) – every participant secures that average. On the other hand, with individual portfolios the individual returns exhibit wide disparities even with identical contributions – some end up above average but they are offset by those that do worse, including those whose income is too low to bear such downside risk. The inequalities generated by privatization are especially repellent because they are artificial and serve no useful (e.g., incentive) function.

(iii) Individual portfolios will tend to increase the gap between the rich and the poor in two ways: (a) the rich will be in a position to gain more from the option because they have more investment experience, access to better advice and tools, and lower management costs. They can also better afford the risks inherent in equities and other more remunerative but riskier investments. The rich, thus, end up with a higher return on their retirement savings. According to Wolff (2002), in the United States, "[t]he contraction of traditional DB plans and their replacement with DC plans appears to have helped rich older Americans but hurt a large group of lower- and moderate-income households (p. 52)." In addition, research has demonstrated that, even in difficult investment periods (e.g., the year 2001), the wealthiest individuals have been able to preserve, and even grow, their capital as a result of access to good advice and products that may not be available to poorer individuals (Kaban 2002). (b) The pension based on an individual account would eliminate wealth redistribution as a fraction of the accumulation of the rich is now used to subsidize the pensions of the poor in systems such as the U.S. Social Security system. In other words, the rich are credited with a somewhat lower return than the poor. This provides a further inducement for the rich to exit Social Security and invest in their own portfolio. As they do so, the subsidy is taken away from the poor and returned to the rich. In the end, the poor will receive smaller pensions or will have to contribute more, whereas the pensions of the rich are enhanced.

(iv) Some of the privatization advocates understand the dangers posed by down-side risk – at least for the poor – and have suggested amendments that would ensure some minimum outcome (Feldstein 1996, Archer and Shaw 1999). For example, the two main possibilities include higher-than-required contributions under DB for a particular replacement rate and some optionality on pension outcome (i.e., government insurance against shortfall risk). But these remedies are highly unsatisfactory, for the first is disadvantageous to the participants, and the second would encourage excessive risk taking because the participants would retain any favorable outcome while unloading unfavorable ones onto Social Security. This free option is not only economically inefficient but also may be expected to substantially increase the contribution that must be charged to keep the system solvent (Muralidhar and van der Wouden 1998b). This is addressed in more detail in Chapter 4.

In all the reform discussions, there has been little mention of what the target replacement rate should be (and, in turn, a contribution rate and expected return for a given working life and retirement horizon) or why a predictable outcome should be rejected in favor of DC schemes. More often than not, subjective arguments are put forward in favor of DC schemes because they involve more individual choice (though not used in Sweden and Australia) and less political risk. The unfortunate aspect of these discussions is that no attempt is made to cost out the trade-off in terms of the replacement rates, contribution rates, and government debt of achieving these so-called advantages. We address political risk in the section entitled "Regulation and Political Risk" and explore the cost of choice in more detail in Chapter 4.

THE PROBLEM OF MOVING TO "PRIVATE" MANAGEMENT OF FUNDS

In this section, we discuss three issues: (i) the importance of clearly defined benchmarks and good governance, (ii) the ability of asset managers to beat passive benchmarks, and (iii) the high fees charged by private managers and their impact on reducing replacement rates. When these three are examined closely, the naive prescription for private management of assets is shown to be shallow.

IMPORTANCE OF BENCHMARKS AND GOOD GOVERNANCE

The fallacy propagated by institutions such as the World Bank is that private management of funds is more efficient than public management of funds. This claim is clarified in Figure 3.2 from World Bank (1994), which purports to show that public management of assets leads to poor returns.

This result has been debated by several analysts (Mitchell and Carr 1996, Mitchell and Hsin 1997). It is untrue that publicly managed funds (whether it involves governance or investment management) have lower real rates of return than privately managed funds.[14] Japanese pension funds, which are privately managed, are likely to yield results on the wrong side of this table as would publicly managed U.S. pension funds. A cursory examination of the tabulated data in Figure 3.2 is sufficient to show that the argument made by the World Bank (1994) suffers from a spurious correlation and an extremely biased data sample. Two critical issues that are ignored are the importance of separating the funds that have clearly specified investment

---

[14] A similar and stronger case is made in Minns (1996).

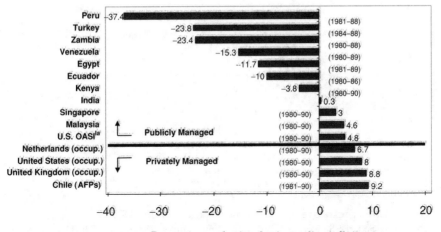

Figure 3.2. Comparing investment returns for public and private funds. Average annual investment returns for selected pension funds, 1980s. Source: World Bank (1994). Figure 3.7. Reprinted with permission from the World Bank.

policies and how much value has been added by funds relative to their benchmarks.[15] If this restatement were done, a completely different picture would emerge and would, it is hoped, put more emphasis on specification of investment policy (Mitchell and Hsin 1997). Extensive research has been conducted on the performance of public funds (Mitchell and Carr 1996, Mitchell and Hsin 1997, Munnell and Sunden 2000), and these papers demonstrate that a reasonable case can be made for the efficiency of public funds – especially where good governance exists.

Orszag and Stiglitz (2001) fault this analysis on a similar ground but state it differently. They feel that no adjustment is made for the risk taken to generate such returns, and one cannot conclude arbitrarily that welfare is reduced without examining the portfolio rebalancing actions of individuals to accommodate such allocations in their public pension. In other words, performance in the public pension is one part of a multipillar system; hence, a poor performance in one pillar could diversify risk in another.

ABILITY OF PRIVATE MANAGERS TO BEAT PASSIVE BENCHMARKS

A simple chart of the performance of 251 private asset managers relative to the S&P 500 index over a 10-year horizon (Figure 3.3) demonstrates that the average

---

[15] The problem with these analyses is identical to the problem described in Muralidhar and U (1997).

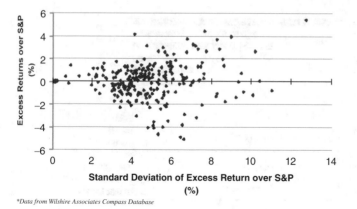

Data from Wilshire Associates Compass Database

Figure 3.3. Average excess returns of private managers is zero. U.S. equities manager performance vs S&P, 12/87 to 12/97 (251 managers). Source: Muralidhar (2001). Reprinted with permission from A. Muralidhar and R. Weary.

outperformance (before fees) of the entire group is zero with substantial risk.[16] Some managers beat the index, and others underperform, to give a simple average of the universe of 0-percent excess. In short, private asset management cannot guarantee returns higher than a publicly managed passive fund and, on average, even private managers with all their sophistication do not beat the passive (low-cost) alternative.

A critical area that has been overlooked in many of the reform discussions is that in many countries in the developing world assets were given to private firms with little or no prior experience in asset management. However, these moves were justified in an attempt to create a private fund management industry. What we do know is that the confidence in the level of a manager's skill is a function of performance relative to a passive benchmark and longevity of experience (Ambarish and Seigel 1996). Where no prior track record exists, in highly volatile asset markets it will take over 50 years of data to segregate the poorly performing funds from the truly skillful managers. In tests that we conducted on data for Mexican funds, it would require over 100 years of data to have even 75-percent confidence in a manager's skill. The required length of experience far exceeds the average life expectancy of participants!

IMPACT OF HIGH FEES

To add insult to injury, there is no dearth of analyses to show that private fund management has resulted in significant costs in Latin America. Initial estimates of

---

[16] The same seems to apply to investment-grade U.S. Fixed Income managers and non-U.S.-investments. See Muralidhar (2001).

TABLE 3.2 Difference between gross and net contributions (net of manager fees)

	Gross contributions (percent of wages)	Fees (percent of wages)	Net contributions (percent of wages)	"Seepage" = fees/gross (percent)
Argentina	7.5	2.45	5.05	32.7
Chile	10.0	2.36	7.74	23.6
Colombia	10.0	1.75	8.25	17.5
Mexico	12.0	2.75	9.25	22.9
Peru	8.0	2.45	6.55	30.6
Uruguay	7.5	2.05	5.45	27.3

these asset management costs are approximately 17–33 percent of total contributions (an estimate of 20 percent for Chile is given in Diamond 1996b). For comparison, we provide (in Table 3.2) asset management and administrative costs in Latin America that have been referenced from two sources.[17]

It is reasonable to ask why asset management companies charge such high upfront fees. The arguments normally put forward in support of these levels are that managers perform an additional service of administration and collection of contributions, require the fees to sustain their marketing efforts, and utilize the fees for start-up related costs. Indeed, proponents of such arguments would postulate that the asset management component of these fees is relatively low.

The most troubling aspect is that high fees, relative to the low cost of passive management, result in enormous reductions in the replacement rate for individuals. Using the simple model from the appendix to Chapter 1 to estimate replacement rates, we provide estimates of the impact of these cost structures in Latin America on projected replacement rates. For simplicity, we assume the following for all countries:

Annual inflation (salary, benefit, and asset) = 5 percent
Real salary growth   = 3 percent (nominal = 8 percent)
Real asset returns   = 6 percent (nominal = 11 percent)
Years of service   = 40 years
Life expectancy (post-retirement)   = 10 years

Benefits are indexed to inflation.

The results for different countries are provided in Table 3.3.

---

[17] Guerrard (1998). These numbers are similar, if not identical, to those provided to us by Monika Quessier. Rather than focus only on the numbers, we are more interested that countries adopt the method proposed here.

TABLE 3.3 Impact of manager fees on replacement rates

	Replacement on final salary (%)	Replacement on final salary (%)	Loss on final salary replacement rate (%)
Argentina	70	47	23
Chile	93	72	21
Colombia	93	79	24
Mexico	112	86	26
Peru	75	63	12
Uruguay	70	51	19

What this simple table suggests is, with the exception of Peru, individuals receive an effective replacement rate approximately 20 percent less (on final salary) than projected on a gross basis. This is a very significant result, for in many countries it is anticipated that the first and second pillars will provide a replacement rate of approximately 70 percent. Because of administrative costs, this loss can be made up only by three harmful changes: (i) increasing savings elsewhere (or reducing present consumption), (ii) achieving higher real returns (which come with higher risk), and (iii) extending working life and reducing retired life. These are adverse outcomes and will be required because of poor design and the absence of emphasis on after-fee returns. Bateman et al. (2001) report that fees are likely to reduce retirement accumulation by 8 to 16 percent in Australia, which is clearly lower than in the Latin American countries. This reflects the lower costs associated with pooling assets with private managers and potentially better initial conditions. We recommend that countries require fund management companies to report after-fee returns and assess the impact of these returns on the expected replacement rate for different cohorts.

REGULATION AND POLITICAL RISK

There is a naive presumption that DC plans with private management of assets reduce political risk, but we show this need not be the case. The reforms in developing countries are taking place in an environment in which the average population is poor, ill-educated, and clearly financially naive. Pension reform conferences are breeding grounds for stories on how the selection of fund managers is based on the skirt length of the sales representative or the quality of the toaster provided! There is a high likelihood that individual citizens do not understand the importance of developing a coherent investment policy to achieve some replacement rate target (which is also likely to be dynamic with age and wealth), nor do they understand the interrelatedness of contribution policy and investment policy in achieving such targets[18], let alone have the ability to distinguish between good and bad managers.[19] It is critical to accept that developing an investment policy or an asset allocation rule is as important, if not more so, for individuals in DC plans as it is for sponsors of DB plans. Research has shown that 90 percent of variability of returns, or reduction of asset-liability risks of pension funds, are derived from the investment policy and the balance from investment management (Brinson, Singer, and Beebower 1991; Muralidhar 2001). As a result, it is important to have strong regulation, but this can be used by politicians to abuse the system.

The three major forms of political and regulatory risk that participants are exposed to relate to contributions, investment returns, and benefits. For example, mandatory contributions can be raised by politicians and regulators if it appears that returns are too low, and there may be no financial penalty for such actions. In addition, considerable attention has been given to the poor management of assets or diversion to nonprofitable activities in DB plans. The same could happen in DC plans. Another related investment risk is that returns credited to participants may be different from those earned, and this is the case in many Provident Funds. However, under privatized schemes, fraud is a key risk, for the managers of investment management firms can divert funds or defraud investors because benchmarks are not clearly articulated. The third risk relates to changing the terms of the benefits ex post, (and this can be an outright reduction of the benefit), a change in inflation indexation, an extension of participation terms, or limits on the number of years for which the benefit is paid. We examine the first two, emphasizing the risk related to investments because this is a key risk in DC plans. The third is generally a risk unique to DB plans and has been addressed in the design of the Ideal Model (i.e., individual accounts with a guaranteed return on contributions).

RISK RELATING TO CONTRIBUTIONS

Participants in the DC plan are also exposed to the risk that the government could raise the mandatory contribution rates should it appear that insufficient funds are being accumulated in individual accounts. Low levels of accumulation could result from poor forecasting, poor asset performance, or the disinclination of previous governments to raise contribution rates. Because there is no explicit ex ante target

---

[18] Casual observation by the authors would affirm the view that most pension funds, even in OECD countries, are not familiar with the workings of dual-policy optimization.

[19] A somewhat related anecdote is that of poor and less educated individuals in the United States being more likely to participate in the lottery. See Chinoy and Babington (1998).

replacement rate in a typical DC plan, participants do not clearly comprehend what they can expect to receive and how it is to be achieved. The government bears no monetary cost in raising contributions even though it could be unpopular. In the Ideal Model, political risk is managed because, for a given replacement rate, the effective rate of return credited to participants must be lowered if the contribution rate is to be raised. Given the relationship between the contribution rate, replacement rate, and guaranteed return, a rise in the contribution rate implies either a higher replacement rate for a given return or a reduction in the return if the replacement rate is unchanged. No such mechanism can be implemented in the classic DC plan.

RISK RELATING TO INVESTMENTS

Fraud

Participants are vulnerable to fraud, as custody arrangements, performance, and risk reporting standards are not standardized and are, therefore, not uniform for all fund managers.[20] With front-end fees and the incentives of regulators not totally aligned with those of participants, developing countries have inefficient contracts between citizens, fund managers, and regulators.

The risk of financial panic to capital market development, should one of these financial institutions fail, is also significant. Governments also have to recruit and train the regulators, and it is likely, as the regulators become more sophisticated, the demand for such talent from the private sector will lead to high turnover, which can ultimately be controlled only by increasing salaries. For example, the National Commission for the Retirement Savings System (CONSAR), the regulator in Mexico, had extremely talented staff and has experienced such turnover.

These shortcomings have not escaped the reforming countries and have given rise to attempts to protect individuals, the financial system, and the government to whatever extent possible.[21] In brief, strong regulation of these funds is called for and in many cases has been implemented.[22] Fund managers are required in some cases to coinvest in their own funds to ensure a personal incentive to maximize the value of the respective funds. In some countries, the performance of a manager has to be within a specified band around the average performance to ensure that investments are "in line" with others. For example, in Chile, no Administradora de Fondos de

[20] The regulator of investment funds in Mexico, CONSAR, has done outstanding research in this regard but has yet to implement national standards.

[21] Refer to Grandolini and Cerda (1997) on how this is being dealt with in the case of Mexico. See also Shah (1997).

[22] Bateman et al. (2001) and Reisen and Williamson (1997) provide an international comparison of asset regulations.

Pensiones (AFP) was permitted to earn 2 percent more or less than the average of the AFPs (Mitchell and Barreto 1997).

Although regulators monitor performance and are more capable of evaluating it than individuals, they face no monetary penalty (it is not clear if they face nonmonetary penalties) should an investment manager renege on his or her commitments and defraud the group of participants by appropriating funds and declaring the fund bankrupt. Coinvestment is one measure that mitigates the risk of inappropriate investment of assets by managers, but even coinvestment is not sufficient to prevent fraud because the amount of capital invested by the owners is probably too small relative to outside assets. In a DB plan, pooling with centralized governance under a blue-ribbon board (and appropriate custody arrangements) can create better incentives for effective monitoring.

Poor Performance of Markets and Private Managers

In many cases, restrictions are being relaxed to include international assets for diversification, thereby lowering the risk to local market performance. Where countries have recognized that weak performance of markets or private funds expose citizens to the risk of low replacement rates, they have either offered minimum guarantees on pension payments (as in the case of Mexico) or mandated minimum rates of return to hedge market risk. In addition, countries have forced investment performance to be within a corridor created by some averaging of the performance of all funds (as in Chile) to hedge against managers underperforming peers (returns less than the passive portfolio).[23]

Unfortunately, these involve giving away options on investment performance, as in Mexico, or mimicking a DB in an inefficient way. Some researchers have proposed that individuals should be given access to purchase options close to retirement and thereby lock in historical asset returns as a way of minimizing asset–liability risk at retirement. If the purpose of these plans were to provide a DB-like payout, it seems obvious that the best structure would be a good DB plan.

Absence of Good Advice on Asset Allocation or Private Managers

Under the current design implemented in various countries, an individual has no way of knowing what replacement rate or final wealth they are likely to achieve

---

[23] In the absence of prespecified market benchmarks, these weighted average performance bands serve as a benchmark. However, a true benchmark or market index is one that has certain investment characteristics (like duration, market cap, etc.), is easy to replicate because the rules are known up-front, is maintained by a credible independent institution (e.g., IFC, local stock exchanges), and is relatively inexpensive to trade.

during their lifetime (i.e., expected value and distribution) and who, if anyone, will provide advice on whether the contribution or investment policy is appropriate or in need of modification. Research is only gradually beginning to let individuals know what outcome they might achieve (Leibowitz et al. 2002), but even these techniques cannot provide advice on what decisions should be taken by participants concerning contributions or investments to correct potential problems of low replacement rates.

Further, there is no clear established process by which individuals with little or no financial expertise can get unbiased information about the selection of managers.[24] In developed countries, fund-ranking agencies like Morningstar have been created, and, despite the problems in these ranking systems, it is reasonable to hope that a similar industry will flourish in developing markets as well. However, research has shown why the services of these agencies are inefficient for a broad audience – because they prespecify the objectives of individuals, failing to recognize that a broad group of participants may have diverse sets of objectives and that rankings may be different based on objectives (Muralidhar and Muralidhar 2001). One regulator in particular, CONSAR in Mexico, has taken steps to assist in the process of developing a uniform, publicly available methodology and would, in our opinion, be best suited to do so given the theoretical absence of any conflicts of interest.

Insufficient Choice

Individuals do not control investment policy for their funds, which is often mandated by regulators, but the individual is expected to bear the risk of a possibly incorrect investment policy. In effect, the risk taker (i.e., the regulator who establishes investment policy) is completely delinked from the risk bearer (i.e., the individual who could retire poor), creating additional incentive problems.[25] The restrictions on deviating from the average performance lead to insufficient choice because all managers effectively offer the same portfolio and possibly causes the fund managers to waste undue resources on marketing costs to demonstrate their "superiority."

More important, in countries that have mandated DC plans with 100 percent or substantial government bond asset portfolios, the shift from the PAYGO DB to DC has not had any net impact on government debt and the way it is financed. This shift

---

[24] We ignore the aspect of selecting "good" performing managers over "bad" managers, for this is more art than science. Further, there is reason to believe, supported by research, that it is extremely difficult to separate luck from skill. See Ambarish and Seigel (1996) and Muralidhar (2001, Chapter 10).

[25] This is the case in a pure Provident Fund.

has only privatized the purchase and sale of this debt. Valdes-Prieto (1997) attempts to examine the cost of such constraints.

Bad Regulation (Political Manipulation)

Unfortunately, the political economy problems in the PAYGO or funded DB plans are not entirely alleviated by the privately managed DC schemes. Although it is true that the private sector is more actively involved in the pension system, thereby reducing the opportunities for corrupt politicians to take advantage of these funds and distribute surpluses, the government, in effect, continues to guarantee a ready market for its debt and its profligacy. This occurs because the regulators controlling the asset allocation of the funds are government employees and are influenced by the same political considerations they were subject to before the reforms.[26] Especially where the mandated allocations include government debt, the government continues to exercise full control over the investment funds under the guise of privatizing who buys and sells the debt (Fontaine 1997). Godoy and Valdes-Prieto (1997) highlight the dangers of regulators exercising their political influence over fund managers to achieve political ends, including influencing the way these funds vote on shareholder issues. However, many seem convinced that DC schemes have lessened the ability of governments to manipulate these funds.[27] As Orszag and Stiglitz (2001) point out, in a critique of the World Bank's approach – why should governments that are so corrupt as not to be trusted with public funds become so benevolent that they set up a system that reduces their control and changes their behavior? We conclude that malfeasance can be as dangerous under individual account schemes as under public DB schemes and ways to prevent this include good design, governance, and transparent benchmarks.

SUMMARY

This chapter has focused on potential flaws in pension design and reforms with the aim of encouraging countries that have already implemented reforms to correct them quickly and of cautioning countries contemplating reform not to repeat these errors. The first conclusion is that, once a steady state has been reached, funding is

[26] It is trivial to note that allowing funds to invest in securities other than government bonds does not alleviate this risk. The government does not need a 100-percent allocation to government bonds to achieve this result.

[27] It will take a very simple game-theory model to show how governments will change allocations over time if they wish to continue to "take from the till."

generally preferable to PAYGO because of lower long-term contributions as well as lower volatility of required long-term contributions. However, the transition from an unfunded to a funded system requires an accumulation of capital that cannot be achieved by simply transferring contributions. When there is a government surplus, it can be used to generate the accumulation; otherwise, higher contributions or taxes are required. Many countries have instead financed the transition through government budget deficits. But this is a very unsound approach. It amounts to the government's acquiring a highly leveraged portfolio at great risks. It does not add any resources but merely redistributes existing risk and capital income between the private and the public sectors. For this shift to be beneficial, additional savings are required.

Second, the reliance of DC schemes on individual portfolios invested in market instruments leads to (a) significant benefits to rich participants at the cost of poor participants, (b) very uncertain replacement rates, and (c) high welfare costs of implementing DC schemes relative to equivalent DB schemes. It is also not clear that external private management, with much discretion, is preferred to in-house public management. Probably the three most critical issues for achieving appropriate investment returns are relying on clear benchmarks, utilizing indexed products, and having the oversight of a blue-ribbon board. Privatized DC schemes typically lack these factors. Further, the existing costs of managing individual "privatized" accounts are enormous. In addition to being excessive, they finance activities beyond pure asset management (e.g., investment start-up costs and advertising). The problem is that regulators have not focused their attention on after-fee returns. When performance is adjusted for management fees, replacement rates are greatly reduced. Thus, paradoxically, private management requires extensive regulation, but then regulation of DC schemes can be used by bad politicians to achieve political ends. To depoliticize this process requires an independent blue-ribbon board, and it is easier for such a board to monitor one portfolio in a DB plan than all the individual accounts for all cohorts in a DC plan. In the end, if regulators and policy makers do not pay attention to ensuring that individuals get a decent replacement rate with a high degree of certainty, pension reform will lead to widespread old age poverty and the transfer of wealth from the poor to the asset management industry. These were the outcomes that pension reform was supposed to guard against but that, in reality, poorly thought out and badly designed reforms are threatening to turn into a prescription for disaster.

4

Welfare Costs of Defined Contribution Schemes

With Ronald J. P. van der Wouden

It is evident that countries in the process of reforming their pension systems have leaned toward implementing mandatory, individual account, defined contribution (DC) schemes that are privately managed to partially or entirely replace their PAYGO DB schemes. In the United States, the discussions are increasingly drifting in the same direction with President Bush. The recently appointed Bush Commission on Social Security advocates some version of a privatized Social Security scheme. The chronic problem of mandated DC schemes is that individuals bear the investment risk, and they are the least capable economic unit to do so. Therefore, with variability of investment returns, individuals could retire with an annuity below a basic target level.

Chapter 2, and Muralidhar and Van der Wouden (1998a), recommend an alternative model, which we will refer to as a contributory, funded, defined benefit plan (CFDB). A CFDB plan is a funded scheme whereby the government ensures the benefit through a guaranteed real rate of return on fixed contributions. This scheme has all the attractive properties of a DC scheme while capturing the risk-sharing and insurance benefits of a defined benefit (DB) scheme. In Muralidhar and Van der Wouden (1998a), the authors provide a "gedanken" experiment to demonstrate how a CFDB would be welfare-improving over the currently implemented DC alternative, with less political risk and better incentives for regulation, when the system is mandatory. That paper provided the structure and institutional requirements for such a model, to protect against a large fraction of the population retiring poor. We have proposed a variant of this model and have argued for converting social security to a funded DB scheme with lower contributions and greater stability in contributions (Chapter 1). We achieve the guaranteed rate of return by requiring the treasury to enter into a swap with the Social Security Administration (SSA) to exchange the returns of a market portfolio for a guaranteed rate of return.

When a country implements a social security scheme, the goal is to ensure that citizens do not retire as paupers. Hence, if individuals retire poor, the government will need to provide welfare programs to alleviate the situation. Turner and Rajnes

(2002) provide a rich list of examples of guarantees in different countries (see also Pennachi 1997). For example, in Brazil, DC plans are required to provide a guaranteed annual real rate of return of 6 percent. In Germany, pension funds must guarantee a minimum pension equal to the nominal value of all contributions, or effectively a 0-percent return. However, some industry funds offer higher return guarantees of 3.5 percent. There are similar rules in Belgium and Switzerland (Payne 2002). Provident Funds often offer guarantees: Malaysia and New Zealand offer a minimum annual nominal rate of return of 4 percent.

As highlighted in Godoy and Valdes-Prieto (1997), the state is assigned the obligation of ensuring social security in many cases. In some countries such as Denmark, citizens have the right to demand such assistance. Walliser (2002) declares that guarantees are neither free nor cheap, and we attempt to estimate the cost of such guarantees. We assume that the guarantees are debt financed and that governments should, therefore, seek to minimize the cost of guarantees in the design of pension schemes. The cost estimated here is often ignored in reform discussions. The one cost of pension reform we are unable to measure is the cost to individuals from a reduced choice in investment options in the CFDB relative to a DC scheme. This is one of the stated benefits of privatized schemes, namely, that individuals value choice, and privatization is therefore good (with rarely any discussion of whether a construction or railroad worker would benefit from being asked to make a choice in an area in which he or she has no expertise when this could be delegated to experts at a low cost). By highlighting costs of privatized DC options, we attempt to provide a threshold of advantages that a privatized DC should cross before it is chosen over funded DB options. In Chapter 7, we will return to this problem to demonstrate that the "freedom of choice" is overstated and not utilized. We show that the absence of any DB options, even with complete choice to participants (of classic investment products), will lead to lower welfare for participants.

The literature on this topic is reviewed in Orszag and Stiglitz (2001) to demonstrate that some form of guarantee, explicit or implicit, exists in most second-pillar reforms, and, as highlighted in Diamond and Valdes-Prieto (1994), it is difficult to exclude implicit guarantees, especially since contributions are mandated. Moreover, Walliser (2002) points out that guarantees can come in two forms: contingent payments (based on income, means tests, or minimum returns) and noncontingent payments such as flat pensions.

Previous research has not examined the cost of such guarantees or the factors that will affect the cost to governments. In this chapter, we demonstrate the conditions under which the CFDB (or more generally, a well-designed, funded DB scheme) outperforms a funded DC scheme and highlight the sensitivity of the welfare gains to various economic parameters.

These two pension schemes are compared from two different angles:

1. Comparison from the perspective of the country: This analysis will be conducted by comparing the expected debt[1] for the country when the country implements either a DC type of structure or a CFDB pension scheme. The difference between the expected debts is defined as the "welfare gain" of implementing the CFDB scheme rather than a DC type of scheme.
2. Comparison from the perspective of the individual (or participants) in the country: In this analysis, we monitor the participants and compare the expected amount by which their wealth is below a target defined as the retirement wealth needed to achieve a minimum standard of living.

Not surprisingly, because DB plans in general, and the CFDB plan in particular, are able to pool risk across participants in a cohort and across cohorts (i.e., with different characteristics, and over time), the welfare gains from a country level and from the participants' point of view are substantial. Some researchers mistakenly propose that the way to minimize old age poverty, or the probability that participants retire with an annuity below a target in DC schemes, is to raise contribution rates (Feldstein and Ranguelova 2001). These researchers do not realize that the cost of a higher contribution need not be borne in a DB scheme. Higher contributions for the same replacement rate imply reduced consumption for participants, and this cannot be welfare indifferent.

The analyses in this chapter focus on the welfare cost impact (i.e., government debt to minimize retirement poverty) of demographic structures and the investment environment in either a country or a region. We demonstrate the impact of pooling participants in a country with different characteristics. It appears that by pooling more participants, who have different participation periods in the retirement plan, the CFDB scheme outperforms the DC scheme. This result is very interesting not only for countries in general but also for regions consisting of multiple countries in the process of reforming their pension systems. Regions are able to benefit from economies of scale and the regional diversity of the participants being pooled. Such risk diversification lowers the cost of providing guaranteed pensions or life annuities. This result contrasts with the work of Valdes-Prieto (1997), which examines the benefit for funded systems from being able to access international assets and thereby diversify merely asset risk. Consequently, regions such as Euroland, the

---

[1] Notice that any type of pension scheme has an expected debt. The expected debt in a scheme that provides a certain guaranteed benefit is explicit (i.e., DB-type schemes and DC or Provident Fund schemes with guaranteed returns), whereas the expected debt in a scheme that does not ensure a guaranteed benefit payment (i.e., DC-type schemes) is implicit.

Caribbean Islands, and the Pacific Islands will benefit the most from implementing a CFDB type of pension rather than trying to implement individual country-level schemes.

We also focus on the impact of the investment policy of retirement accounts. We conduct these exercises to demonstrate the impact of investment choice on welfare. This impact is important for countries such as the United States, but especially so for developing countries in which the volatility of asset returns is higher than in developed countries and the need for investment diversification is greater. It appears, for countries with very high volatility of investment portfolios, the welfare gains of moving away from the individual account DC structure to the CFDB are enormous. It also appears, because the pension plan has access to greater diversification opportunities, the CFDB plan is able to benefit more than the DC option. This result is particularly important for reformers designing pension schemes because, at present, many countries may not even benefit from diversifying locally but are likely to benefit substantially from international diversification.[2]

The results in this chapter are based on the assumptions that the participants covered by social security (i) make a mandated, fixed, annual contribution until retirement[3]; (ii) have to provide their own retirement annuity; and (iii) retire at a mandated age. However, one of the favorable consequences of the CFDB structure is that, when the plan provides the annuity payments and the retirement age is flexible, the participation periods of the participants will be even more diverse. Both these extensions favor the CFDB over the DC pension scheme.[4]

The following points briefly summarize the CFDB model as described in Chapter 2 and Muralidhar and van der Wouden (1998a):

1. Individuals make contributions to a public CFDB scheme that will be operated by the Social Security Administration (SSA).
2. Assets are pooled and invested in marketable securities such as equities and bonds.
3. Individual records of contributions and terminal wealth are maintained.
4. All participants in the CFDB plan are assured their benefit through a guaranteed real (or nominal) rate of return on the fixed annual contributions. (The "fixed contribution" assumption is relaxed in Chapter 8.)

---

[2] Kelley, Martins, and Carlson (1998) and Srinivas and Yermo (1999).

[3] The CFDB model can also be set up to allow (i) contributions from employers only and (ii) the participant to adjust contributions on an annual basis. Flexible contributions are preferred to fixed contributions. This is explored in Chapter 8.

[4] See also Bodie et al. (1988).

5. There will be centralized governance by the SSA; asset management can be decentralized or public, and assets can be actively or passively invested. A swap with the treasury ensures the guaranteed rate.

To illustrate the key results, we will use a Monte Carlo simulation model because it provides a simple method for modeling the economic environment of any pension plan. This is in contrast to other approaches that review the guarantee as an option and try to price it as such (Lachance and Mitchell 2002). The problem of pricing options on replacement rates, using the standard options pricing theory, is that asset-liability markets are incomplete (Muralidhar 2001, Chapter 6); hence, a true price cannot be revealed in these models. Before describing the model and illustrating the results, we devote a section to the general importance and use of targets. This part is not given the attention it deserves in existing pension reform recommendations, but it will play a crucial role (in any pension system) in defining and achieving the objectives and in describing the risk.

THE IMPORTANCE OF TARGETS

Any pension or fund management exercise can be seen as an asset-liability problem, for wealth is set aside to service some liabilities or future annuities (i.e., wealth for wealth's sake is irrelevant). The pension fund balance sheet demonstrated in Chapter 1 highlights this perspective.

Setting targets is critical to define the objectives and risk in any pension management process. If there are no targets, there are no goals, and, eventually, the underlying objective function is uncertain. In addition, the targets have to be very clearly specified to measure the degree to which objectives have been achieved and to facilitate the possible achievement of these objectives in the future.[5]

However, setting the right objectives for pension funds is, from a practical point of view, an extensive process. Pension funds, in particular, are affected by the wishes and requirements of different groups. Each group, such as employees, retirees, or sponsors of the pension fund, has its own vested interests and wants to serve the individuals it represents. Further, it is often the case that these objectives are based on emotional rather than economic considerations,[6] which makes it difficult to capture all the objectives in a simple mathematical formula (Muralidhar 2001, Chapter 3).

---

[5] See Muralidhar (2001).
[6] For example, a decision to have asset performance equal to or greater than that of peers often leads to suboptimal asset-liability allocations.

To identify the appropriate policy for managing retirement wealth, participants or organizations must define their objectives. Under a DC scheme, participants have to define their own investment policy, the contributions they are willing to make to the extent that they are not mandated (which requires a trade-off between consumption today versus the future), and the investment risk they are willing to bear to achieve a reasonable amount of wealth at retirement.

Three essential characteristics need to be embedded in a target. First, it has to be transparent and clear. Clarity and transparency facilitate monitoring for all the parties involved. This is critical in getting broad acceptance and for the measurement of actual performance against a target. Second, a target has to be set on an ex ante basis, which means that any individual or organization has to determine, before retirement (e.g., at the time of pension plan enrollment), the annuity aimed for at retirement. The third feature, and the most critical one, is that, at any intermediate period before retirement or termination of a plan, it should be possible to test the adequacy of the current position in reaching the ex ante target eventually. Simply put, participants must be able to see whether their current financial position is adequate to ensure their chosen minimum standard of living during retirement. The ability to set intermediate targets, which can be extracted from the final target, is critical to a successful pension strategy.[7]

The management of a corporate pension plan has to deal with these intermediate targets daily.[8] The main concern of this group is to manage the assets of the plan so that they are sufficient in every period to cover the liabilities, or else "top-up" contributions will need to be made by the sponsor. These decisions are usually made on the basis that all current (and potentially future) obligations for existing staff need to be covered. In some variations, corporations even provision for future staff. In principle, a DB fund can have current assets (at points in time before termination of the fund) less than the estimated liabilities and still service existing beneficiaries. In brief, as long as current assets exceed current liabilities there is no cash flow problem because current retirees can be paid from the contributions and accumulations of current employees.

In a DC scheme, each participant has to manage his or her own pension fund on a regular basis to ensure a certain amount of wealth at retirement. If in either the DB or the DC scheme the total assets are not sufficient to meet all targeted future obligations, the plan runs a "funding" deficit. There has been a tendency to treat DC plans as always being fully funded in that the pension annuity depends on accumulated wealth that is uncertain. However, we maintain that if the DC pension

---

[7] See also Krishnamurthi, Muralidhar, and van der Wouden (1998a) and Leibowitz et al. (2002).
[8] Boender, van Aalst, and Heemskerk (1997).

annuity falls below a target level, then the DC plan is underfunded (Muralidhar 2001, Chapter 2, and Leibowitz et al. 2002). Although the overseers of a pension plan always aim to avoid these situations, with the uncertainty of assets returns, inflation, and so on, it is impossible to be 100-percent sure that such situations will not occur. On the other hand, it is possible to construct strategies (Chapter 8) that will, with a high likelihood, achieve the targets (i.e., with a reasonably low probability that these deficits will not occur). Consequently, setting the right targets ensures clarity of the risk a plan is able to bear.[9]

THE FRAMEWORK FOR ANALYSIS

This section provides the background on the CFDB and DC plans that sets the stage for presenting the results. The results are presented from three perspectives:

1. That of the individual participant in the pension plan (or a DC perspective);
2. That of the entire CFDB plan; and
3. A comparison between the CFDB and DC schemes.

INDIVIDUAL PERSPECTIVE

In the DC (and the CFDB) pension plans, individuals have to decide the level of retirement wealth they would like to target. They must make a trade-off between pre- and postretirement consumption. This, in effect, is smoothing to ensure a retirement consumption bearing a reasonably "comfortable relation" to active life consumption adjusted for the number of resident family members and other factors. As a result, this target wealth must be related to the participant's future career path, both as a source of future contributions and as a basis for selecting retired consumption, thus enabling each individual to target, on an ex ante basis, a specific replacement rate, which can be expressed in terms of either final or average career income.[10]

To calculate this target retirement wealth, each individual or institution has to make assumptions on the following variables:

1. Expected real salary growth, and wage and price inflation;
2. Expected asset returns (pre- and postretirement);
3. Retirement age;

---

[9] On the one hand, a plan can be an organization that manages retirement wealth; on the other, it can be an individual managing personal pension assets.

[10] It is important to realize that setting a wealth target is equivalent to targeting a replacement rate. The wealth target should be the present value (at retirement) of the desired retirement annuity.

4. Pre- and postretirement life expectancy (in defined contributions), unless the individual is entitled to, and satisfied by, a life annuity;

5. Target retirement income;

6. Whether the target is inflation-adjusted (as is rational in dealing with a long-term horizon) or not; and

7. Mandatory or voluntary contribution rate.

It is important to recognize, if the individual targets a replacement rate for given assumptions on variables 1 to 6 listed above, there will be a unique fixed contribution rate consistent with other variables. On the other hand, a given contribution rate predetermines, under the preceding assumptions, a unique expected replacement rate (in terms of expected future income) or target wealth upon retirement.[11] These are simple identities, and the appendix to Chapter 1 and simulations in Chapter 3 demonstrate the interrelationship. The duality of the problem is critical and is often unrecognized in pension reform design. The impact of the variability of parameters is dealt with in Chapter 8.

In addition, an important element that is not on the list is the investment policy or mix of assets that optimally achieves the target retirement wealth of the participants. The entity setting the investment policy and the bearer of the investment risk are different in the CFDB and DC pension plans. In the "pure" DC plan, the participant has "total freedom" to construct her own investment policy and bears the total risk associated with this decision. The participants have total or partial freedom to select assets (i.e., stocks versus bonds, domestic versus international) they want to invest in and the amounts to be invested in these assets. Total freedom is rarely the case in practice, as pointed out in Chapter 3, and participants in Australia and Sweden do not use it.

In the CFDB plan, the participant does not have the ability to decide on the manner in which assets are allocated because this is delegated to the blue-ribbon board; however, the CFDB plan will guarantee the participants a certain ex ante accrual factor, ω, with which their contributions and accumulations will grow from year to year. Hence, the risk-taking posture of any one participant in a DC plan is likely to be different from that of the CFDB plan in its entirety.

We assume, under both schemes, that the participants will withdraw the amounts they have accumulated throughout their career immediately on retirement and will provide for their own annuity after retirement. Therefore, we ignore the costs and benefits of pooling on annuity payments. (This is discussed in Diamond 1994).

---

[11] See Asad-Syed et al. (1998) for details.

THE CONTRIBUTORY, FUNDED, DEFINED BENEFIT (CFDB) PLAN

It was argued earlier that a basic responsibility of the management of a pension plan is to match the amount of assets to the total size of the liabilities at each point in time. The two main tools in achieving this objective in the CFDB plan (or in any pension plan) are the investment policy and the contribution policy.[12]

The investment policy in the CFDB plan can be determined in the same way as in a traditional DB plan. The contribution policy, however, is somewhat different in the CFDB case. In a traditional DB plan, the oversight committee has the ability to increase or decrease the contributions of the plan sponsor from year to year. In the pure CFDB plan, the management or government has limited influence on the contributions of the participants because a deficit in the plan cannot simply be solved by increasing the amount the participants contribute. This follows, because the participants' contributions are directly linked to benefits. Hence, increasing the participants' contributions will automatically increase the obligation of the pension plan or imply a reduction in the guaranteed rate.[13] We return to this point in Chapter 8, as there is a risk that the long-term average return achieved will be below the guaranteed rate, and we rely on variable contributions to manage this risk. As a result, the nature of the guarantee changes; hence, there is more emphasis, in the variable contribution case, on guaranteeing the benefit rather than a fixed return.

It is possible in the CFDB scheme that the plan, at any time, will have a negative balance or that the total assets in the plan will not be sufficient to cover all liabilities. This is because this plan provides a guaranteed benefit through a guaranteed return to the participants, whereas the performance of the whole CFDB plan is impacted by market volatility and other unanticipated changes. If the total return of the CFDB plan is lower than the guaranteed rate of return, the plan could end up with a deficit.

The exact contribution policy in the CFDB system requires the timing of government financing, the amount paid into the system (whether the whole amount is paid immediately or amortized), and the opportunity cost of financing for the government to be articulated. In Muralidhar and van der Wouden (1998a), it is suggested, once liabilities exceed assets, the government will finance the whole deficit amount immediately with repayment to the government if the opposite should occur. The swap contract ensures such cash flows. The goal of pension reform must be to prevent the government from having to increase debt dramatically.

---

[12] See Muralidhar (2001), Chapter 3.
[13] This reduces political risk of the government increasing participant contribution if investment performance is weak.

COMPARISON BETWEEN CFDB AND DC PLANS

The previous section introduced the possibility that the CFDB pension plan could end up with a negative balance (i.e., if the government does not top up a deficit immediately or before a topping up). On the other hand, these situations cannot occur in the DC plan. Participants have individual accounts, and the amount each one accumulates depends on the contributions and the realized returns. However, in the DC plan it is possible that the participant will, owing to disappointing returns, retire with an annuity that is well below the level required for a minimum standard of living (Feldstein and Ranguelova 2001). In both pension schemes, it is possible that the participants will not meet their ex ante target wealth at retirement for reasons other than asset performance. A salary increase that is lower than expected, given a certain contribution rate, will affect retirement wealth in both pension plans.[14]

This chapter shows that the extent to which participants do not meet their targets is far greater in the DC plan than in the CFDB plan. The reason is that, in the DC plan, greater uncertainty in realized returns is passed on to the participants, who have fewer tools to mitigate this risk than an administrator of a CFDB plan.

The second conclusion arising from this chapter is that the expected debt for the country with a DC plan is much higher than the debt in the CFDB plan even with the most conservative assumptions.[15] To show this result, it is essential to clearly define the debt of the pension plan. We calculated the debt of the CFDB plan based on the "termination hypothesis," which assumes that the system will be terminated at a given date and that all participants must be compensated for their accrued rights.[16] The accrued rights in the CFDB pension plan are the promised pensions the participants have accumulated in their personal accounts at the guaranteed rate of return. Consequently, the debt in the CFDB plan is the difference between the realized asset balance of the CFDB plan and the promised wealth that participants would have accumulated with the guaranteed rate of return.[17]

[14] In Muralidhar and van der Wouden (1998a) the authors argue that the participant is always able, in the CFDB plan, to put aside additional savings in the third pillar to hedge against salary growth risk. Alternatively, the CFDB plan could include minimum pensions. In addition, in this pension plan, it is possible to index the participant's wealth conditionally to salary growth, depending on the financial status of the CFDB plan. In Boender, Heemskerk, and van Hoogdalem (1996) the authors describe the impact of conditional indexation of retirement benefits to the asset-liability strategy of a pension plan. The same methodology or ideas can be used in the CFDB plan for conditional indexing of wealth to salary inflation.

[15] We indicated earlier that the expected debt in the CFDB plan is explicit, whereas debt in the DC plan is implicit.

[16] See also East Asia: Philippines report (1997), Appendix I.

[17] The CFDB pension plan runs a deficit only if the aggregate of the promised wealth of participants exceeds total assets (i.e., the balance) of the CFDB plan.

In every period, debt in the DC plan, based on the "termination hypothesis," is equal to zero. However, the retirement wealth that the participant accumulates under this system could be well below the amount required to achieve a minimum standard of living. Heller (1998) and Muralidhar and van der Wouden (1998a) argue that the presence of poor retirees can be seen as an implicit debt for the country.[18] Feldstein and Ranguelova (2001) assume that the benchmark against which individuals can measure their performance is a 5.5 percent return (a portfolio of 60 percent in equities and 40 percent in bonds) and, hence, make a similar calculation. To make a direct comparison between both pension schemes, we define the debt of the DC plan as the difference between the amount a participant has accumulated under the DC scheme and the minimum wealth amount to achieve a target replacement rate (i.e., the accrued benefits in the CFDB plan) on the assumption of identical contribution and investment policies. This, in many ways, is the explicit debt obligation that a country like Mexico faces for having assured participants a pension outcome no worse than they would have earned under the former PAYGO DB scheme. In the case of Feldstein and Ranguelova (2001), there is an additional cost: the higher contribution rate that participants are charged to minimize the probability of low retirement wealth.

In addition, we make the following assumptions for both pension plans:

- Both plans provide participants a lump sum amount at retirement that is equal to the amount accumulated throughout their career.

- Both pension plans will be monitored from the moment the first participant joins the pension plan until the moment the last person retires. We assume that on day one participants of different age groups enroll in the plan. During the aging of the plan, there will be no new entrants and, in addition, we assume that all participants who started in the plan will participate until their retirement (i.e., there is no evasion and no mortality during working life). Modifying these assumptions will, in large part, change the absolute value of the difference between the CFDB and the DC plan and not the sign of the difference. Because these are fully funded schemes, we ignore population growth issues.

- We make a comparison of the two plans when the last participant retires, that is, on the closing date of the plans.[19] The expected debt of the DC and CFDB plans will be the accumulated debt at that particular moment. Participants retire

---

[18] Heller (1998) makes this point more forcefully.
[19] It is obvious that we can also make this comparison at intermediate points in time. However, because we want to capture the impact when all participants have retired, it is more obvious to compare the two plans as soon as the last participant retires.

during the aging of the plans. Consequently, the plans could run debts before the last participant retires. In the CFDB plan, these intermediate debts occur when the government has to finance a deficit in the plan (i.e., a situation in which the promised wealth of all participants exceeds the total assets of the plan or, correspondingly, when returns are less than the guaranteed return in the swap). The amount that the government contributed to the plan can be seen as an explicit debt for the CFDB plan. A debt in the DC plan occurs when participants retire with retirement wealth that is lower than the wealth they could have accumulated at the guaranteed rate of return in the CFDB plan. Because we compare the debt of the plans only when the last participant leaves the plan, we incorporate opportunity costs for rolling the intermediate debts up to this final moment. The opportunity costs can be seen as the cost of borrowing money to finance pension deficits. In the CFDB plan, at the final date, there will be the end balance of the CFDB plan and an account of all government contributions. Hence, the debt of the CFDB plan will be the closing balance of the pension plan less the government contributions. The difference between these accumulated debts of the DC and the CFDB schemes will be referred to as the welfare gains of moving away from a DC structure to a CFDB pension scheme.

ASSUMPTIONS FOR THE SIMULATIONS

ECONOMIC ENVIRONMENT

The consequences of the investment policies for both plans and the participants will be evaluated on the basis of 1,000 scenarios of the economic environment over each period in the life of the pension plan. The scenarios are generated by a model that describes each economic factor as a random walk and in which the relationships between the economic factors are maintained.[20] The most important characteristics of the generated scenarios are presented in Table 4.1.

Table 4.1 is based on assumptions of an expected real, risk-free rate of 2.5 percent, an expected real equity risk premium of 4 percent, and an expected inflation of 4 percent for these asset classes. The real returns are close to those assumed by the Bush Commission (3 percent real return for government bonds and 6.5 percent for equity). The correlations between these variables are provided in Appendix 4.1. For simplicity, we assume that real salary growth is 0 percent. Changing this variable does not change the results of this analysis.

---

[20] See Dert (1995) for a technical discussion of performing such analyses. These are standard techniques applied in the investment management business.

TABLE 4.1 Characteristics of the main economic variables

	Annual expected nominal value (%)	Standard deviation/ annual volatility (%)
Price and wage inflation	4.0	3.0
Domestic equity	10.5	15.0
Domestic fixed income	6.5	5.2

These assumptions are based on an analysis of U.S. markets and on comparisons of these assumptions with those made by leading asset management companies in their forward-looking asset-liability studies in early 2000. These real return assumptions are very reasonable for any market. In the case of developing markets, one would clearly expect these to be different, but it is not likely to change the results, as demonstrated in the section on sensitivity analyses.

Different economic scenarios will be used as input for the simulation model. More details on the simulation technique are provided in Appendix 4.2. The welfare of each participant in the DC and CFDB pension plans will be evaluated in each of these 1,000 economic situations. To provide readers with an idea of the nature of the simulation, Figure 4.1 shows the wealth development, under 15 different economic situations, of a 55-year-old participant who retires at age 65. Some paths have wealth above the target, whereas others fall short (i.e., the government incurs a debt).

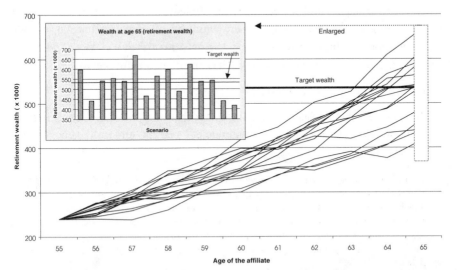

Figure 4.1. Wealth development of a 55-year-old participant until retirement under 15 different scenarios.

ADDITIONAL INVESTMENT ASSUMPTIONS

In addition to the assumptions for generating the economic environment, we make the following assumptions that will be applied to both participants in the DC plan and to the CFDB plan as a whole. These assumptions can be divided into two groups: (i) the assumptions on investment returns, and (ii) the assumptions on different inflation parameters.

The rates of return to monitor are as follows:

1. Target rate (i.e., the return for calculating the ex ante wealth target): The return used for the calculation of the ex ante target is the expected return on the investment policy.[21] This rate is the same for each participant.
2. CFDB guaranteed rate of return: The CFDB plan guarantees, in each year, a real rate of return that can be modeled as an investment in a synthetic government index bond with a certain premium (i.e., a return that guarantees a certain premium over price inflation). This is a fixed real rate, but the bond instrument through which it is paid will have the volatility of inflation.
3. Opportunity cost of debt: The financing of the pension plan debts by the government has an opportunity cost (i.e., cost of borrowing additional funds). The return on domestic fixed income is used to carry over debt to the future in the DC and the CFDB plans.[22]
4. Investment return: The investment return depends on the composition of the investment portfolio. We assume that the investment strategy is the same for each participant and is identical to the strategy in the CFDB plan. To simplify the problem, we use, as a base case, a static investment policy that allocates 100 percent to domestic fixed income. The sensitivity analyses give an indication of the impact of introducing more diversified investment portfolios.

The rates of inflation to monitor are as follows:

1. Wage inflation: We assume, for simplicity, that wage inflation is equal to price inflation[23] (i.e., a real-wage growth rate of 0 percent) and is the same for each participant.

---

[21] For instance, if a participant were to invest 100 percent in domestic fixed income, the expected rate of return would be 6.5 percent. A strategy that allocates 50 percent in domestic fixed income and 50 percent in domestic equity would generate an expected return of 8.5 percent.

[22] In the DC plan, this rate is used to carry forward the implicit debt for participants who have retired before the termination date of the plan. In the CFDB plan, this rate establishes the amount the government has put into the pension plan in intermediate periods for financing intermediate deficits.

[23] For simplicity, we assume a real salary growth rate of 0 percent; however, this assumption is not needed to emphasize the conclusions arising from this chapter. We show the impact of relaxing this assumption in Appendix 4.3, where a 1 percent real salary growth only confirms the basic conclusion.

TABLE 4.2 **Basic return and inflation parameter assumptions**

	Annual expected nominal rate (%)	Annual volatility (%)
Return assumptions		
Target rate	6.5	N/A
CFDB guaranteed rate of return[24]	6.5	3.0
Opportunity cost of debt[25]	6.5	5.2
Investment return[26]	6.5	5.2
Postretirement return	6.5	N/A
Inflation assumptions		
Wage inflation	4.0	3.0
Price inflation	4.0	3.0
Postretirement inflation	4.0	N/A

2. Price inflation: We assume that the annual price inflation is 4 percent with some volatility.
3. Postretirement inflation: This assumption is required to calculate the present value of the annuity at retirement (or the wealth required at retirement). We link this to price inflation.

The results in the next section are generated with specific assumptions for these returns and inflation parameters. Table 4.2 summarizes the values of these parameters, which will be referred to as the basic setting. Later, we introduce more diversified investment strategies, which result in some changes in the basic return assumptions.

RESULTS OF THE ANALYSIS

The results are divided into two sections. The first demonstrates the impact of the demographic changes in the plans, and the second shows the impact of investment regime changes. The first section contains analyses that will lay the foundation for the main conclusions, and the second is particularly important for developing countries that have high asset return volatility and more opportunities to diversify their asset allocations.

The impact of different population characteristics is shown in three subsections that focus on the composition of the pension plan. These include the following:

---

[24] This rate is like an investment in a synthetic government index bond with a premium of 2.5 percent over price inflation. Hence, it will carry the volatility of inflation.
[25] We assume this opportunity cost is the same as an investment in investment grade, domestic fixed income.
[26] As a basic case we assume a static investment strategy that allocates 100 percent to domestic fixed income. This investment strategy is the same for each participant and for the CFDB plan.

1. One participant in the plan,
2. Two participants in the plan, and
3. Forty participants in the plan.

The investment analysis evaluates the following two investment assumptions:

1. Increase in volatility of the investment portfolio, and
2. Diversification in the investment strategy.

Each subsection provides the retirement wealth of the participants under the DC and the CFDB plan and the welfare gain of choosing the CFDB pension plan over the DC plan.

DEMOGRAPHIC CHANGES IN THE PLAN

One Participant in the Plan

We start with a hypothetical worker who joins the plan without any initial wealth at age 25 with a starting salary of US$10,000 and retires at age 65. We use the return and inflation assumptions given in Table 4.2. In addition, we assume that the worker's target annuity at retirement is an annual payment of 70 percent of final salary. Further, we assume a life expectancy of 20 years postretirement and that the worker buys an inflation-adjusted annuity at retirement. Hence, retirement wealth of approximately US$541,406 is needed to provide this retirement income (on the assumption that postretirement rate of return is 6.5 percent and inflation is the same as preretirement inflation). This retirement wealth will be the ex ante target wealth of the participant.

To explore the impact of investment strategies over time, we assume that the nominal wage increases at the rate of price inflation and, at the beginning of each year, the participant invests his or her total annual contribution in investment-grade domestic fixed income. To simulate the participant's welfare, we need to determine an appropriate contribution rate. Given the basic assumptions on expected wage growth and the expected return on domestic fixed income, the participant needs to

TABLE 4.3 A hypothetical participant in the DC and the CFDB plans

Current age	Retirement age	Life expectancy at retirement	Initial balance ($)	Target wealth ($)	Current annual wage ($)	Annual contribution rate (%)
25	65	20	0	541,406	10,000	16.69

TABLE 4.4 **Results with one participant in the pension plan**

	Investment policy: expected return 6.5 percent, volatility 5.2 percent			
	Probability that participant will not meet the target wealth (%) (1)	Expected amount by which participant is below the target wealth ($) (2)	Downside risk when wealth is below the target (%) (3)	Expected debt of plan ($) (4)
DC	55.4	46,847	10.8	51,145
CFDB	53.7	35,177	8.2	51,145
Welfare gains of CFDB (i.e., the difference between DC and CFDB)				
Absolute	1.7	$11,670	2.6	$0
Relative	3.2	33.2%	31.7	0%

invest 16.69 percent of his or her wage each year to achieve the target retirement wealth of US$541,406. Table 4.3 summarizes the characteristics of this participant.

In the simulations, we keep track of this participant in the DC and the CFDB plan (which is no different from the DC plan because there is only one participant). Table 4.4 gives three important asset-liability statistics from the participant's point of view and the expected debt of the DC and the CFDB pension plan. A brief description follows, and Appendix 4.2 provides a more elaborate explanation.

Column 1: The probability that the participant will not meet his or her target wealth. This statistic provides the likelihood that the participant will retire with a retirement wealth lower than the target wealth.

Column 2: The expected amount by which the participant will be below the target wealth.

Column 3: The downside risk when the participant is below this target wealth.[27] Whereas Column 2 gives the expected amount by which the participant is below the target, Column 3 represents the volatility of this expected amount. Thus, a high value implies a higher risk that a participant's wealth is below the target.

Column 4: The expected debt of both pension plans, which has been explained in detail earlier.

In addition, the bottom half of Table 4.4 also presents the difference (absolute and relative, where absolute is the difference and relative is the ratio) between the DC

---

[27] The downside deviation is analogous to the definition of downside deviation of portfolio return (Sortino and van der Meer 1991) and belongs to the group of "Lower Partial Moments (LPM)" risk measures. In Leibowitz, Kogelman, and Bader (1994) the authors use these LPM measures to analyze the risk of certain asset portfolios.

and the CFDB plans for these statistics, which represent the welfare gains of moving away from a DC type of structure to a CFDB pension scheme.

Table 4.4 demonstrates that, under both schemes, the participant has a chance of achieving retirement wealth that is below the target. This uncertainty emerges from two possibilities: (1) from the uncertainty of the investment return, and (2) from the uncertainty in the salary growth (in this case through wage inflation rather than real salary growth variability). Because the participant has to bear both uncertainties in the DC plan, the expected amount by which the participant underperforms the target is higher and more profound under the DC scheme (see columns 1 and 2). Although the CFDB plan guarantees a certain real rate of return, it does not bear the uncertainty in the salary growth of its participants (the participant bears this risk). This explains the nonzero probability that the participant does not meet the target wealth. Hence, the rate at which the wealth of the participant accumulates under the CFDB plan is more stable than the wealth accumulation of the participant in his or her personal DC account.

The second key result is that the expected debt is the same for both plans (i.e., the difference in expected debt is US$0). This is because there is only one participant. These results clearly demonstrate that shifting most of the investment risk from the participant to the pension plan (i.e., as demonstrated in the CFDB plan) will benefit the participant and that the expected debt of the plan will not be greater than that of the DC scheme.

Two Participants in the Plan

The previous exercise can be conducted with more participants in the plan. If we have multiple identical participants, the only statistic in Table 4.4 that will change is the expected debt of the pension plan. This expected debt will be exactly the same as that shown in Table 4.4 multiplied by the number of identical participants enrolled in the plan. In Appendix 4.3, the results are given for a pension plan with two identical participants.

The more interesting extension is when there are participants of different ages in the plan. We added a second participant who has the same expected final salary

TABLE 4.5 Characteristics of the two participants in the systems

Current age	Retirement age	Life expectancy at retirement	Initial balance ($)	Target wealth ($)	Current annual wage ($)	Annual contribution rate (%)
25	65	20	0	541,406	10,000	16.69
45	65	20	94,738	541,406	21,911	16.69

TABLE 4.6 Results with two different participants in the plans

	Investment policy: expected return 6.5 percent, volatility 5.2 percent			
	Probability that participant will not meet the target wealth (%) (1)	Expected amount by which participant is below the target wealth ($) (2)	Downside risk when wealth is below the target (%) (3)	Expected debt of plan ($) (4)
DC	54.7	43,362	10.2	214,065
CFDB	53.8	29,930	7.2	188,104[28]
Welfare gains of CFDB (i.e., the difference between DC and CFDB)				
Absolute	0.9%	$13,432	3.0%	$25,961
Relative	1.67 %	44.9%	41.7%	13.8%

and the same target retirement wealth, but a different entry age. So as not to bias the simulations, because the two participants are at different stages of their lives, we give the older (i.e., second) participant the appropriate initial wealth in order to keep all other parameters identical. If it is assumed that the second participant will have the same contribution rate as the first (i.e., 16.69 percent of wages) and under the basic assumptions, the initial wealth of the second participant will be set at a level where the expected retirement wealth corresponds to the ex ante target.[29] The characteristics of the two participants are provided in Table 4.5.

The results of the simulation with these two participants are presented in Table 4.6.

Two interesting results follow from this extension. First, expected debt is about 13.8 percent higher in the DC plan than in the CFDB plan. Second, from the participants' perspective, the extent by which the participants' wealth is below the target wealth is significantly higher in the DC plan.

These two exercises allow us to conclude that the CFDB plan is more efficient from the perspective of the country and the participants when the pension plan covers

---

[28] The difference between this debt amount and the debt amount of two identical participants in Appendix 4.3 comes about because of our assumptions about the termination hypothesis and, retirement shortfalls and how they are financed. Because we assume that the first retiree's debts will be maintained until the plan terminates, debt is carried forward at the rate of interest equal to the expected return on government debt, which affects the analysis.

[29] This initial wealth is exactly the amount a 25-year-old individual would have accumulated at the age of 45 on the assumption of a yearly contribution of 16.69 percent and an expected rate of return of 6.5 percent. We can state that participants who have accumulated this amount are on target to meet their final retirement wealth and, in this case, the funded status of the participant is 100 percent.

TABLE 4.7 Characteristics of five participants in the system ranging from
25 to 29 years of age

Current age	Retirement age	Life expectancy at retirement (no. of years)	Initial balance ($)	Target wealth ($)	Current annual wage ($)	Annual contribution rate (%)
25	65	20	0	541,406	10,000	16.69
26	65	20	1,777	541,406	10,400	16.69
27	65	20	3,741	541,406	10,816	16.69
28	65	20	5,907	541,406	11,249	16.69
29	65	20	8,290	541,406	11,699	16.69
..	..	..	..	..	..	..

participants with different participation periods in the retirement plan. Diversification of liability risk is "exploited" by the CFDB plan.

Forty Participants in the Plan

In this section we extend the analysis to 40 participants, where each participant is of a different age at the time of enrollment in the pension plan. The ages of the 40 participants range from 25 to 64 years, and each individual has the same expected final salary and an ex ante target retirement income of 70 percent of final salary (that is, each individual targets the same retirement wealth). The annual contribution rate will be the same for all participants, and the initial wealth of each participant is set at a level such that, under the present assumptions, the expected retirement wealth will be the same as the target wealth.[30] Table 4.7 provides the characteristics of the individuals ranging from 25 to 29 years, and Appendix 4.4 provides the characteristics of all participants.

Table 4.8 summarizes the results of the two pension schemes with 40 participants.

The results with 40 participants in the plan are similar to the results with two participants. The welfare loss for participants is still higher under the DC scheme. However, it is clear that the expected debt of the DC plan is significantly higher (33.5 percent) than the debt in the CFDB plan.

This result highlights that the efficiency gains in the CFDB plan increase when the number of participants, with different participation periods, increases and that

---

[30] This means that the 45-year-old individual will be in an identical position under the current assumptions to that of the person in the previous result.

TABLE 4.8 Results with 40 participants in the plan

	Investment policy: expected return 6.5 percent, volatility 5.2 percent			
	Probability that participant will not meet the target wealth (%) (1)	Expected amount by which participant is below the target wealth ($) (2)	Downside risk when wealth is below the target (%) (3)	Expected debt of plan ($) (4)
DC	53.6	36,562	8.8	6,236,624
CFDB	53.3	23,590	5.7	4,670,100
Welfare gains of CFDB (i.e., the difference between DC and CFDB)				
Absolute	0.3%	$12,972	3.1%	$1,566,525
Relative	0.6%	55.0%	54.4%	33.5%

these efficiency gains are considerable. This is the risk-sharing property of the DB plan at work that many proponents of privatized schemes ignore.

INVESTMENT REGIME CHANGES IN THE PLAN

In this section we conduct two additional analyses on the plan with 40 different participants, focusing on only the investment policy of the retirement accounts. We conduct these exercises to demonstrate the impact of investment choice on welfare – especially in developing countries where the volatility of asset returns is higher and where the need for diversification is greater than in developed countries.

First, we increase the volatility in the asset portfolio substantially, and then we introduce the possibility of investing in two asset classes that are less than perfectly correlated.

Increase in Volatility

In the previous analysis we assumed that the retirement wealth of each individual in the DC plan and in the CFDB plan is invested in domestic fixed income. Table 4.9 shows the impact when we increase the volatility of this asset class substantially. We somewhat arbitrarily increased the annual volatility by 3.5 percent, which implies an annual volatility to domestic fixed income of 8.7 percent.

To see the impact of this increase in volatility, we compare the results in Table 4.9 to the results in Table 4.8. A few interesting conclusions are derived from the comparison. First, the relative difference between the expected debt in the DC plan and the CFDB plan is about the same (33.3 percent). However, what is more striking

TABLE 4.9 Results with 40 participants in the plan

	Investment policy: expected return 6.5 percent, volatility 8.7 percent			
	Probability that participant will not meet the target wealth (%) (1)	Expected amount by which participant is below the target wealth ($) (2)	Downside risk when wealth is below the target (%) (3)	Expected debt of plan ($) (4)
DC	55.8	60,556	13.7	9,656,368
CFDB	53.3	23,590	5.7	7,243,973
Welfare gains of CFDB (i.e., the difference between DC and CFDB)				
Absolute	2.5%	$36,966	8.0%	$2,412,395
Relative	4.7%	156.7%	140.4%	33.3%

is that the absolute expected debt increased substantially in both plans, resulting in a much higher absolute difference (US$2.4 million in the high volatility case versus US$1.6 million in the low volatility case). In other words, from a country perspective, the welfare gain of the CFDB plan increases substantially as the volatility of asset returns increases.

Other striking results are the participants' statistics. These statistics demonstrate major differences between the two plans. Because the investment risk in the DC plan is borne completely by the participants, the expected difference between the pension and target wealth at retirement for these participants is more than two-and-a-half times higher than the expected amount in the CFDB plan (US$60,556 for DC versus US$23,590 for CFDB). In addition, the volatility of this expected amount is also substantially higher in the DC plan (13.7 percent versus 5.7 percent). In other words, under the high volatility scenario, if participants do not meet their target wealth, they will end up with substantially lower retirement income in the DC plan.

In Appendix 4.3, which summarizes all these results and provides a few additional ones, the same analysis has been conducted with a volatility increase of 5 percent, which resulted in even higher expected debts in the DC plan and higher welfare gains in favor of the CFDB pension plan. Hence, in countries with very high volatility of investment portfolios, the welfare gains of moving away from the individual account DC structure are enormous.

Diversification in the Investment Portfolio

When the investment portfolio is diversified by introducing a second investment class, namely, domestic equity, it generates an equity risk premium of 4 percent

TABLE 4.10 Adjusted return and inflation assumptions

	Annual expected nominal rate (%)	Annual volatility (%)
Return assumptions		
Target rate	8.5	N/A
CFDB-guaranteed rate of return[31]	8.5	3
Opportunity cost of debt[32]	6.5	5.2
Postretirement return	6.5	N/A
Investment return	8.5	8.9
Inflation assumptions		
Wage inflation[33]	4	3
Price inflation	4	3
Postretirement price inflation	4	N/A

over domestic fixed income and has an annual volatility of 15 percent. We now assume that each individual in the DC plan and the entire CFDB plan will have an investment portfolio of 50 percent domestic fixed income and 50 percent domestic equity. This is less aggressive than the 60:40 equity:bond assumption of Feldstein and Ranguelova (2001). The 50:50 asset allocation generates an expected annual return of 8.5 percent and a volatility of 8.9 percent. Consequently, the CFDB plan offers a guaranteed real rate of return of 4.5 percent instead of the 2.5 percent used in all the previous simulations. The basic return assumptions shown in Table 4.2 will change as a result of the adjustment in the asset allocation (Table 4.10).

As a result of the higher expected returns during the career of the participants, they are able to lower their yearly contribution rate to reach the same target retirement wealth.[34]

Given these assumptions, the annual contribution rate for the 25-year-old participant, as described in Table 4.3, will be lowered to 10.53 percent. The contribution rate of the remaining 39 participants will also be lowered to 10.53 percent. Appendix 4.5 provides a detailed summary of the characteristics of the participants. This appendix

---

[31] This rate is like an investment in a synthetic government index bond with a real premium of 4.5 percent over price inflation.

[32] We assumed this opportunity cost to be unchanged. This creates some distortions in the incentives for governments, but these are unimportant for this analysis.

[33] We also assumed a salary growth equal to the price inflation (i.e., 0-percent real salary growth).

[34] Only the expected return during the participant's career changes, and thus the expected return after retirement (for buying the annuity) does not change. Consequently, given the same expected final salary, the participant targets the same absolute retirement wealth (U.S.$541,406) in this analysis as in the former ones.

TABLE 4.11 Results with 40 participants in the plan and a diversified portfolio

	Investment policy: expected return 8.5 percent, volatility 8.9 percent			
	Probability that participant will not meet the target wealth (%) (1)	Expected amount by which participant is below the target wealth ($) (2)	Downside risk when wealth is below the target (%) (3)	Expected debt of plan ($) (4)
DC	56.5	62,875	14.0	10,387,681
CFDB	53.3	23,305	5.7	5,860,749
Welfare gains of CFDB (i.e., the difference between DC and CFDB)				
Absolute	3.2%	$39,570	8.3%	$4,526,932
Relative	6.0%	169.8%	145.6%	77.2%

also shows that, besides the contribution rate, the initial wealth of the participants will change. Table 4.11 details the results of this analysis.

A comparison of the results of the diversified investment strategy with the results in the previous section (i.e., Table 4.9) gives some interesting results. The annual volatility of the diversified portfolio is about the same as in the earlier analysis (Table 4.9). Consequently, it results in higher expected debts than incurred with the low-volatility portfolio shown in Table 4.8.

The financial condition of the participants has not changed much by moving to the diversified portfolio; the expected amount by which the participants are below their target wealth is still significantly higher in the DC plan. On the other hand, there are some interesting changes in the expected debts of the pension plans. The expected debt in the DC plan increased, whereas the debt in the CFDB plan decreased. Consequently, owing to diversification, the absolute welfare gain of the CFDB plan nearly doubled.

Because the pension plan has access to greater diversification opportunities, the CFDB plan, which offers risk sharing, is able to leverage such efficiency gains from the asset portfolio. This result is particularly important for countries such as the United States with well-developed financial markets. It is especially important for developing countries that, although at present may not benefit from diversifying locally, are likely to benefit from international diversification.

SUMMARY

Previous research has focused on how a DC plan can be offered as a substitute for PAYGO DB schemes and how the risk that individuals retire poor can be mitigated through higher contributions. In the Feldstein and Ranguelova (2001) simulations, a doubling of contributions lowers the risk dramatically. In this chapter, we compare a DC plan with a CFDB plan. The analysis is general enough that the DC plan referred to in this chapter could be any of the following: a DC plan with a minimum guarantee, a Provident Fund plan, and a Provident Fund with dividend smoothing. The main conclusions that arise from this chapter are simple and straightforward.

It appears, by pooling participants who have different participation periods in the retirement plan, DB plans in general and the CFDB scheme in particular will have substantially lower welfare costs when viewed from the perspective of participants and a country. This result is very interesting not only for individual countries but also for regions consisting of multiple countries that are in the process of reforming their pension systems. Regions that are able to pool different participants with different demographic profiles will benefit the most from implementing a CFDB pension scheme. A good example is Euroland.

For countries with very high volatility of investment portfolios, the welfare gains of moving away from the individual account DC structure are enormous. In addition, for countries with access to greater diversification opportunities, the CFDB plan leads to substantial reduction in the welfare cost.

In this chapter, the investment strategy is identical for each individual and the CFDB plan as a whole throughout the time horizon of the evolution of the plan. Preliminary results suggest, under different investment environments,[35] the CFDB plan will outperform the DC plan even further. A simple extension is the determination of an optimal policy for the CFDB plan in every period. In addition, some have argued that the benefit from the lack of correlation between wage growth and asset returns can be captured by combining a PAYGO scheme with a funded DB or DC scheme (Feldstein and Ranguelova 2001). These papers fail to realize that the same result can be achieved in a funded DB plan with only a minor change – variable, rather than fixed, contributions. There is no need to create two plans, and we address this aspect in Chapter 8.

Further, the flexibility of the CFDB pension plan allows for adjustments in the financing strategy of the government. Currently, we assume that the government immediately tops up the total deficit when liabilities exceed total assets of the plan. However, preliminary analysis suggests that adjustments in this financing strategy or contribution policy could increase the efficiency of the CFDB plan even further.[36] This feature is also explored in Chapter 8.

---

[35] See Muralidhar and van der Wouden (1998a) for description.

[36] In Krishnamurthi et al. (1998a), Krishnamurthi et al. (1998b), and Dert (1995), the authors emphasize the importance of the contribution policy in an asset-liability context.

There are additional extensions to the analysis from this chapter that make it possible to predict even further efficiency gains in the CFDB plan. When the CFDB pension plan provides the retirement annuity, the plan can benefit even more. Further, different retirement ages of participants also benefit the performance of the whole pension plan. These statements arise from the fact that the adjustments described increase the diversity of the participants in the plan and, consequently, the diversity in the duration of their participation, which benefits the CFDB pension plan.

In short, the attractive risk-sharing properties of DB plans have been grossly ignored or underestimated by reformers in their rush to abandon PAYGO plans and give individuals greater choice. Unless the value of choice exceeds these welfare costs, countries and individuals will be worse off with currently implemented and contemplated DC pension reforms.

APPENDIX 4.1. Correlations of Economic Variables

	Price and wage inflation	Domestic equity	Domestic fixed income
Price and wage inflation	1	−0.3	−0.1
Domestic equity	−0.3	1	0.4
Domestic fixed income	−0.1	0.4	1

APPENDIX 4.2. Capturing Economic Uncertainty with Scenario Analysis

The statistical terms used throughout this chapter are explained in more detail in this appendix. These terms are commonly used in asset-liability studies for pension plans. In this chapter, two groups of statistics can be distinguished: the first group summarizes the position of the participants in the system, and the second provides a comparison between the DC and the CFDB plans. We first focus on the former group, and the same methodology is applied for calculating the statistics in the second group.

The analysis was conducted with 40 participants in the age group 25–64 years enrolled in the pension plan. We now focus on the 55-year-old participant in this system. Table A4.2.1 gives the characteristics of this participant.

We will now monitor the amount the participant accumulates in his or her personal account during the last 10 years of participation in the system and we conduct

TABLE A4.2.1 The profile of the 55-years-old participant in the system

Current age	Retirement age	Life expectancy at retirement	Initial balance ($)	Target wealth ($)	Current annual wage ($)	Annual contribution rate (%)
55	65	20	239,665	541,406	32,434	16.69

this analysis in 15 different economic scenarios. Figure 4.1 gives the development of retirement wealth of the participant under these different scenarios. A problem in simulation analysis with multiple variables is that higher moments (skew and kurtosis) are difficult to preserve to ensure consistency. As a result, certain variables (e.g., retirement wealth) created from the simulated variables (salaries and returns) may not have the same distribution properties of normality as the other variables.

Figure 4.1 immediately demonstrates that the wealth of this participant develops in a different way under different economic simulations. Consequently, total wealth at retirement (i.e., at age 65) will also be different. The bar graph in the figure gives the final wealth at retirement under the 15 different situations versus the target. This means the following for the asset-liability statistics from the perspective of the participant:

1. The probability that the participant will not meet the target wealth: Because there are 5 scenarios in which the wealth at retirement is lower than the target wealth, this probability is 33.3 percent (5 out of 15 scenarios).
2. The expected amount by which the participant is below the target wealth: This is the amount by which the participant could expect to be lower than the target wealth. The probability that one scenario occurs is 6.67 percent (1 out of 15 scenarios); thus, the expected amount in one scenario that the retirement wealth is lower than the target will be the probability that this scenario occurs (i.e., 6.67 percent) multiplied by the amount by which the retirement wealth is below the target wealth. Consequently, the total expected amount is the aggregation of these amounts over all the scenarios.
3. Downside risk: This statistic is related to the previous one which gives the expected value of the underperformance. On the other hand, the downside risk gives the volatility of this expectation. A high volatility means that retirement wealth could be much lower than the target wealth.

APPENDIX 4.3. Overview of All the Results

Description of the cases		Probability that participants will not meet their target wealth (%) (1)	Expected amount by which participants are below their target wealth ($) (2)	Downside risk when wealth is below the target (%) (3)	Expected debt of the system ($) (4)
1 participant: 25 years	DC	55.4	46,847	10.8	51,145
Basic assumptions	CFDB	53.7	35,177	8.2	51,145
Return: 6.5%; Volatility: 5.2%	Absolute welfare gain	1.7	11,670	2.6	0
2 participants: 25 and 25	DC	55.4	46,847	10.8	102,290
Basic assumptions	CFDB	53.7	35,177	8.2	102,290
Return: 6.5%; Volatility: 5.2%	Absolute welfare gain	1.7	11,670	2.6	0
2 participants: 25 and 45	DC	54.7	43,362	10.2	214,065
Basic assumptions	CFDB	53.8	29,930	7.2	188,104
Return: 6.5%; Volatility: 5.2%	Absolute welfare gain	0.9	13,432	3.0	25,961
40 participants: 25 to 64 years	DC	53.6	36,562	8.8	6,236,624
Basic assumptions	CFDB	53.3	23,590	5.7	4,670,100
Return: 6.5%; Volatility: 5.2%	Absolute welfare gain	0.3	12,972	3.1	1,566,525
40 participants: 25 to 64 years	DC	55.8	60,556	13.7	9,656,368
3.5% volatility increase	CFDB	53.3	23,590	5.7	7,243,973
Return: 6.5%; Volatility: 8.7%	Absolute welfare gain	2.5	36,966	8.0	2,412,395
40 participants: 25 to 64 years	DC	56.5	62,875	14.0	10,387,681
Diversification: debt + equity	CFDB	53.3	23,305	5.7	5,860,749
Return: 8.5%; Volatility: 8.9%	Absolute welfare gain	3.2	39,570	8.3	4,526,932
40 participants: 25 to 64 years	DC	56.6	70,855	15.6	11,177,035
5.0% volatility increase	CFDB	53.3	23,590	5.7	8,402,621
Return: 6.5%; Volatility: 10.2%	Absolute welfare gain	2.5	47,265	9.9	2,774,415
40 participants: 25 to 64 years	DC	53.7	52,264	8.6	8,949,348
1% real wage growth	CFDB	53.3	34,573	5.7	6,631,054
Return: 6.5%; Volatility: 5.2%	Absolute welfare gain	0.4	17,691	2.9	2,318,294

APPENDIX 4.4. Characteristics of the 40 Participants in the Pension Plan

Current age	Retirement age	Life expectancy at retirement (no. of years)	Initial balance ($)	Target wealth ($)	Current annual wage ($)	Annual contribution rate (%)
25	65	20	0	541,406	10,000	16.69
26	65	20	1,777	541,406	10,400	16.69
27	65	20	3,741	541,406	10,816	16.69
28	65	20	5,907	541,406	11,249	16.69
29	65	20	8,290	541,406	11,699	16.69
30	65	20	10,909	541,406	12,167	16.69
31	65	20	13,780	541,406	12,653	16.69
32	65	20	16,925	541,406	13,159	16.69
33	65	20	20,364	541,406	13,686	16.69
34	65	20	24,120	541,406	14,233	16.69
35	65	20	28,218	541,406	14,802	16.69
36	65	20	32,683	541,406	15,395	16.69
37	65	20	37,544	541,406	16,010	16.69
38	65	20	42,830	541,406	16,651	16.69
39	65	20	48,573	541,406	17,317	16.69
40	65	20	54,808	541,406	18,009	16.69
41	65	20	61,572	541,406	18,730	16.69
42	65	20	68,903	541,406	19,479	16.69

(continued)

APPENDIX 4.4. (*continued*)

Current age	Retirement age	Life expectancy at retirement (no. of years)	Initial balance ($)	Target wealth ($)	Current annual wage ($)	Annual contribution rate (%)
43	65	20	76,844	541,406	20,258	16.69
44	65	20	85,440	541,406	21,068	16.69
45	65	20	94,738	541,406	21,911	16.69
46	65	20	104,791	541,406	22,788	16.69
47	65	20	115,652	541,406	23,699	16.69
48	65	20	127,382	541,406	24,647	16.69
49	65	20	140,043	541,406	25,633	16.69
50	65	20	153,702	541,406	26,658	16.69
51	65	20	168,431	541,406	27,725	16.69
52	65	20	184,306	541,406	28,834	16.69
53	65	20	201,411	541,406	29,987	16.69
54	65	20	219,833	541,406	31,187	16.69
55	65	20	239,665	541,406	32,434	16.69
56	65	20	261,008	541,406	33,731	16.69
57	65	20	283,969	541,406	35,081	16.69
58	65	20	308,663	541,406	36,484	16.69
59	65	20	335,211	541,406	37,943	16.69
60	65	20	363,743	541,406	39,461	16.69
61	65	20	394,401	541,406	41,039	16.69
62	65	20	427,331	541,406	42,681	16.69
63	65	20	462,694	541,406	44,388	16.69
64	65	20	500,658	541,406	46,164	16.69

APPENDIX 4.5. Characteristics of the 40 Participants in the Pension Plan with Revised Assumptions Owing to Diversification in the Asset Portfolio

Current age	Retirement age	Life expectancy at retirement	Initial balance ($)	Target wealth ($)	Current annual wage ($)	Annual contribution rate (%)
25	65	20	0	541,406	10,000	10.53
26	65	20	1,142	541,406	10,400	10.53
27	65	20	2,427	541,406	10,816	10.53
28	65	20	3,869	541,406	11,249	10.53
29	65	20	5,482	541,406	11,699	10.53
30	65	20	7,284	541,406	12,167	10.53
31	65	20	9,293	541,406	12,653	10.53
32	65	20	11,528	541,406	13,159	10.53
33	65	20	14,011	541,406	13,686	10.53
34	65	20	16,765	541,406	14,233	10.53
35	65	20	19,815	541,406	14,802	10.53
36	65	20	23,190	541,406	15,395	10.53
37	65	20	26,919	541,406	16,010	10.53
38	65	20	31,036	541,406	16,651	10.53
39	65	20	35,576	541,406	17,317	10.53
40	65	20	40,578	541,406	18,009	10.53
41	65	20	46,084	541,406	18,730	10.53
42	65	20	52,140	541,406	19,479	10.53
43	65	20	58,796	541,406	20,258	10.53
44	65	20	66,108	541,406	21,068	10.53

(*continued*)

APPENDIX 4.5. (*continued*)

Current age	Retirement age	Life expectancy at retirement	Initial balance ($)	Target wealth ($)	Current annual wage ($)	Annual contribution rate (%)
45	65	20	74,133	541,406	21,911	10.53
46	65	20	82,937	541,406	22,788	10.53
47	65	20	92,589	541,406	23,699	10.53
48	65	20	103,166	541,406	24,647	10.53
49	65	20	114,750	541,406	25,633	10.53
50	65	20	127,431	541,406	26,658	10.53
51	65	20	141,308	541,406	27,725	10.53
52	65	20	156,485	541,406	28,834	10.53
53	65	20	173,079	541,406	29,987	10.53
54	65	20	191,216	541,406	31,187	10.53
55	65	20	211,031	541,406	32,434	10.53
56	65	20	232,673	541,406	33,731	10.53
57	65	20	256,303	541,406	35,081	10.53
58	65	20	282,095	541,406	36,484	10.53
59	65	20	310,240	541,406	37,943	10.53
60	65	20	340,944	541,406	39,461	10.53
61	65	20	374,431	541,406	41,039	10.53
62	65	20	410,945	541,406	42,681	10.53
63	65	20	450,750	541,406	44,388	10.53
64	65	20	494,133	541,406	46,164	10.53

5

The Transition from PAYGO to Funding with a Common Portfolio: Application to the United States[1]

THE PROBLEM OF TRANSITION FROM PAYGO TO PARTIAL OR FULL FUNDING: IS IT WORTH DOING, AND IF SO, HOW?

There is broad agreement, as shown in Chapter 3, that the funded system tends to outperform pay-as-you-go (PAYGO) in many respects.[2] One need not assume, therefore, that there should be an immediate switch to funding (Samuelson 1975). Participants perceive funding as superior to PAYGO because they pay a lower contribution (with lower volatility) for the same cost ratio. This is only because the rest of the (cost of) benefits are provided from the return on accumulated capital (i.e., they are made richer). Therefore, to move to funding means the capital must be accumulated first to fund the unfunded liabilities of the existing PAYGO system. This is known as the "transition problem," and the key concerns are (i) how to do it and (ii) who should bear the cost. We will deal with these issues in general and, in this chapter, eventually apply the analysis to the United States.

How do we move from PAYGO to a (fully or partially) funded system? This is regarded as the major obstacle to moving to a capitalized system. It is widely believed that this funding would impose an intolerably heavy burden on the transition generation, which would be required to pay a double contribution: one to build the new capitalized system and the other to social security (SS) to pay the current promised pensions. Drawing on the basics of pension finance and with the help of simulation analysis, we demonstrate that this view generally exaggerates the transition cost.[3] We also provide a more generalized analytical approach to the transition in Appendix 5.5.

---

[1] The assistance of Maria Luisa Ceprini for early work on the American reform is gratefully acknowledged. This chapter leverages many ideas developed in Modigliani et al. (2001).

[2] Feldstein (1997) has addressed similar issues.

[3] Valdes-Prieto (1997) has argued that this double contribution may be overstated, but arrives at the conclusion for a different set of reasons and by imposing different burdens on transition generations.

A GENERALIZED TRANSITION MECHANISM

In this section, we outline the basic mechanism to accomplish the transition from a PAYGO to a funded system and illustrate it by means of a simple simulation.

DESCRIPTION OF THE BASIC TRANSITION MECHANISM

For the sake of exposition, we initially focus on the special case of an economy that is stationary with respect to population and productivity and whose PAYGO system is balanced. The centerpiece of our transition plan is the creation of a new public fund (NF), which, like SS, is financed by mandated contributions and offers defined benefits but is fully funded. The required contribution rate will be established so that, when the NF reaches maturity, it is able to pay all the benefits at the established rate (e.g., to provide a 50-percent replacement rate on average salary at age 65). In other words, the contribution rate is fixed from the beginning at the equilibrium level required when the NF reaches maturity (steady state). The fund reaches maturity when all the participants have paid the same required contribution over their entire working life. Clearly, the required contribution will depend on the rate of return on assets and other relevant parameters, as shown in Chapter 3, Table 3.1.

The NF will pay pensions from the very beginning following the rules appropriate to a funded system (i.e., will pay pensions to those who reach the retirement age on the basis of what they have actually contributed to the NF). The amount of these pensions will be established at the date of retirement by applying the appropriate rules to the participant's credit balance accumulated at the fixed rate of return. Note the difference with the rules of a PAYGO system, where pensions are paid to retired people on the basis of length of service whether or not they ever contributed to the fund. In the NF, only those who have had the opportunity to make the full, required years of contribution will, on retirement, be entitled to the full pension from the NF.

However, the NF pensions will not actually be paid to the pensioners. Instead, the aggregate flow of pensions due in a given period will be transferred in bulk to SS. Social security in turn will use that flow, together with the amount raised from contributions (and possibly government subsidies), to pay for the pensions according to the existing rules and also to pay a fixed contribution to the NF. Note that the NF account does not have to balance in each period: it will actually show a surplus, increasing its assets until maturity. Because the amounts to be paid out are fixed by established rules, the flow from the NF reduces the contributions to be raised by SS, dollar for dollar. For example, if the flow from the NF is equal to 10 percent of wages, contributions can be 10 percent lower. However, the SS obligation, to transfer the fixed contribution to the NF, will initially result in a current account deficit in SS that has to be made up somehow. By whom and how this supplement will be paid is also examined.

The flow of transfers from the NF to SS will initially be small because only few participants will have reached the retirement age, and they will have very small balances, having contributed to the fund for only a short time. However, the flow will grow rapidly because the number of people retiring will grow for several years related to life expectancy and those retiring will have progressively larger balances, for they will have contributed longer to the fund.

The key idea of our solution is that the NF flow of pensions will keep growing as it approaches "maturity." Provided the permanent contribution rate to the NF (and by construct to SS) has been set at the appropriate steady-state level consistent with the rate of return, demographics, and the intended replacement rate, the flow of pensions generated by the NF will eventually equal the flow of benefits to be paid by the old PAYGO system, which is the cost ratio. In Appendix 5.5 we provide the analytical solution for how the contribution rate (and degree of fundedness) can be uniquely determined. From that point on, SS will not need to levy contributions to pay for the pensions but only to cover the fixed contribution. Thus, at maturity (steady state), the only contribution to be paid will be the fixed contribution under a funded scheme. This, as one can infer from Table 3.1 (Chapter 3), will generally be much lower than the PAYGO contribution, which is the cost ratio.

Note that the time it takes for the NF to reach maturity, permitting full abatement of the contribution by as much as 75 percent, is substantial. It is at least as long as the length of the standard contributive life plus the length of retirement and is something in the order of 60 years. But, as shown here, a cut in contributions can begin much earlier.

A HYPOTHETICAL STATIONARY ECONOMY

We illustrate our basic approach by applying it to a purely hypothetical stationary economy, which satisfies the assumptions underlying Table 3.1 in Chapter 3. Effectively, we assume $\rho = 0$. Life expectancy on reaching retirement is assumed to be 18 years, and the rate of return on pension system assets is taken as 5 percent. Under these assumptions, the cost ratio (CR) or PAYGO contribution is 22.5 percent. But the contribution required by a funded system is only 4.8 percent! Figure 5.1 and Table A5.1.1 in the appendix illustrate the details of the transition path.

In the figure, the top horizontal line at 22.5 percent represents the cost ratio, which is a constant because the economy is stationary (and the replacement rate is

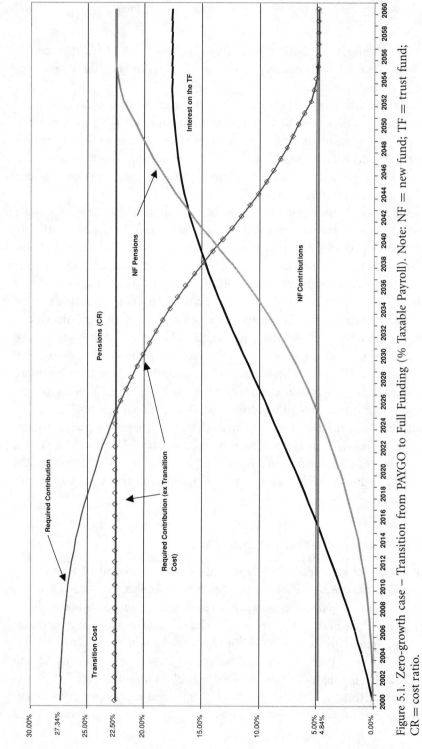

Figure 5.1. Zero-growth case – Transition from PAYGO to Full Funding (% Taxable Payroll). Note: NF = new fund; TF = trust fund; CR = cost ratio.

assumed constant). The bottom (heavy) horizontal line at 4.84 percent shows the contribution rate to the NF. The heavy curve, rising from left (0 percent) to right (22.5 percent), is the critical component of the plan, for it represents the flow of pensions paid by the new plan to SS (NF pensions). It starts at zero, grows at an accelerating rate until the 2030s, and then decelerates, growing slowly until it reaches a ceiling equal to the cost ratio of 22.5 percent (or p) just before 2060. The rise in the NF pensions, in turn, "crowds out" the required contributions to SS, as shown by the falling curve starting at 27.3 percent (22.5 percent plus the 4.8 percent contribution to the NF) and ends with a floor equal to the NF contribution. The miraculous reduction in the contribution, from the 22.5 percent of the PAYGO to the 4.8 percent of the funded system, is made possible by the large accumulation of capital resulting from the 4.8-percent contribution and interest thereof, which exceeds pension payments as long as the number of participants increases, that is, until maturity (at which point the number stabilizes). At maturity, the accumulation reaches a level of some 3.53 times payroll, which at a 5-percent rate of return represents interest equal to 17.65 percent of payrolls (interest on TF). This, together with the fixed contribution of just over 4.84 percent, covers p (22.5 percent).

As pointed out in the introduction, the transition to the (low-contribution) funded system involves a cost – of initially raising contributions above the PAYGO level – which essentially represents the unfunded liabilities of PAYGO. We can measure the transition cost by the amount of such added contributions: they are represented in the graph by the difference between the required contributions and the PAYGO cost ratio (where positive). It can be seen that the cost starts at 4.8 percent and gradually declines to zero by the twenty-fifth year because the NF pensions reduce the required contribution. This cost of transition from a permanent contribution rate of 22.5 percent to 4.8 percent, or some 75 percent lower, appears surprisingly small with our approach: it averages less than 3.3 percent of payrolls for 25 years or about 15 percent of the PAYGO payroll tax.[4] This is in sharp contrast to the common perception that the transition cohorts have to pay, throughout their lives, a double contribution: one to the old SS and one to the new funded system. This seemingly counterintuitive result basically reflects the power of compound interest at a realistic level.

The next question is: How can the transition cost be allocated? There are many ways to spread the cost among different groups. For instance, one could place the burden on current workers by increasing their contribution rate to the level indicated by the "required contribution" curve or on current retirees by lowering pensions temporarily. Either action or any combination of the two would reduce consumption

---

[4] It would average only 1.4 percent of payrolls over the 60-year period.

and increase saving. Alternatively, the government could absorb the transition cost, and employees' contributions would remain constant until the transition cost ceases and would decline thereafter, as shown in Figure 5.1. The government contribution, in turn, could be financed by increased public saving through higher taxes or lower government consumption or finally by borrowing and increasing government debt with the burden falling on future generations. It must be understood, however, that the last method would be counterproductive (as shown in Chapter 3), for the increase in debt would offset the new saving of the system. This would negate one of the important benefits of funding, namely, that of increasing national saving and capital.

We now examine alternative paths and some intergenerational equity issues.

GENERALIZATIONS: ALTERNATIVE PATHS TO FULLY FUNDED EQUILIBRIUM

We have seen that, at maturity, the NF is able to pay pensions equal to p and these outlays are fully financed by the fixed contribution, say c^*, plus the income it obtains from its (equilibrium) assets rA^*, where c^* and A^* are measured as ratios to aggregate wages and r is the gross rate of return (i.e., not adjusted for population growth and productivity growth). Thus, in the steady state the following relation holds (as $\rho = 0$):

$$c^* + r A^* = p \tag{5.1}$$

This implies that assets must reach a unique equilibrium value given by

$$A^* = (p - c^*)/r. \tag{5.2}$$

Thus, for the simulation, the equilibrium asset-to-wage ratio is

$$(22.5 - 4.84)/5 = 3.53^5. \tag{5.3}$$

If at any point the cost ratio changes because of changes in life expectancy or any other variable, the Social Security Administration will need to establish the new c^* for given r to determine the new equilibrium. These simulations are relatively easy to conduct and should be relatively easy to phase in given the long life of a defined benefit SS scheme.

An important implication is, whenever the system has accumulated an amount of net assets to wages ratio equal to the equilibrium ratio, it has reached a position

---

[5] With growth, one would need to adjust the denominator, thereby leading to a higher ratio.

of long-run equilibrium (equivalent to maturity) in the sense that it can pay the benefit embodied in the cost ratio with a permanent required contribution equal to the equilibrium contribution rate. In the preceding example, if the system manages somehow to accumulate an asset–wage ratio of 3.53, then it can pay the 22.5 percent cost ratio with a contribution rate of 4.84 percent because the difference is covered by the return on the assets accumulated. This conclusion is important because it is intuitively clear there must be many possible ways of accumulating the equilibrium asset–wage ratio. In other words, although our simulation shows one possible path resulting in the accumulation of the equilibrium wealth, many other paths must arrive at that result. This observation has the important implication of greatly broadening the paths to final equilibrium accessible by our approach.

This conclusion can be illustrated by a simple example. In the simulation, those in the labor force up to the year 2025 would be hurt by the reform, for they will have to increase their contribution above the PAYGO rate. However, those present thereafter will be better off because the contribution falls and the decline is fairly rapid for a while. This clearly raises the question of intergenerational equity. Could one "smooth" the gains from the reform by assuring some gains or smaller losses for earlier generations while reducing those of some later generations?

For instance, we may want to begin cutting the contribution, perhaps 5 years earlier. In Figure 5.1 this would mean that the contribution curve would be 1 percentage point below the original one and must presumably remain below it at least until the year 2030. This assumption can be seen to be perfectly possible but, on condition that, at some later point, the alternate path will cross the old path and remain, at least for a while, above it. The reason can be explained (roughly) by the consideration that the height of the contribution line, at any point, is a major determinant of the slope of the path of wealth accumulation. Hence, in the period when the contribution is lower, wealth accumulates more slowly, falling below the standard path. Therefore, for the net asset to wage ratio to reach the equilibrium level, it must at some later date catch up by growing faster, which means a contribution rate above the standard. It is, in principle, even possible to maintain the alternate path below (or at least never above) the equilibrium path until the terminal year of the standard version (2060). However, in this case the asset–wage ratio will be too low, and therefore the contribution rate will have to remain for a while above the long-run equilibrium value of 4.8 percent – possibly requiring a longer time before the steady state is reached (especially if we impose the requirement that the contribution path be monotonically declining). Many such paths are demonstrated in Chapter 6 in our discussion on the Spanish system. The principle should be clear: One can, within some limits, improve the lot of the older generations but only at the expense of the younger ones (who, however, are privileged by the first transition solution).

MERGING TWO FUNDS INTO ONE

Up to this point, we have relied on the two-fund approach: the old SS and the NF, because we believe that this formulation is helpful to bring out the fundamental logic of our approach. But having done so, we may now ask whether the two-fund structure is, in fact, essential to the proposed reform. It is easily shown (with the help of the results of the last section) that the result can be achieved just as well, and in fact more conveniently, by relying on a single fund – the New SS. Therefore, implementation of our reform approach does not require the creation of an NF.

This proposition can be readily verified from Table A5.1.1 by "consolidating" the sources of funds, which include government contributions, household contributions, interest on assets and NF pensions (columns [8] and [9] for SS with [2] and [3] for the New Fund, respectively), and the uses, which include the contributions to the NF, the NF surplus, and the SS cost ratio (columns [1] and [4] for the New Fund with [6] for SS, respectively) for any year. Carrying out this consolidation, one finds the following simple result. For any year,

System surplus = NF surplus + SS surplus = Total contributions to the pension system (from the participants and the government, if any) + return on assets − cost ratio, (5.4)

where assets mean the accumulated surplus, capitalized at the fixed rate.

Because at any point of time the assets are given and p is similarly a constant or an exogenously given target, the system surplus is an increasing function of the total contribution.

Now we know from the last section, to complete the transition, it is sufficient that the assets reach the critical level determined by the cost ratio, the rate of return, and the long-run equilibrium contribution that characterizes the steady state and that can readily be calculated independent of whether there are two funds or one.

We can conclude that, at least as long as the cost ratio is constant, our approach will lead to a termination of the transition on condition that: (i) at the beginning of the reform, the total contribution exceeds the cost ratio so as to generate an initial surplus; and (ii) thereafter, the contribution rate is kept high enough to result in a (sufficiently) positive surplus that increases the assets towards an equilibrium, which will exist provided p eventually stabilizes.

Clearly, there will be many possible eligible paths for the contribution rate, all eventually monotonically declining (because a positive surplus implies increasing assets, but of different shapes and duration). In general, the lower the contribution path, the longer it takes to complete the transition. The initial gap between contributions and the cost ratio can be created by increasing participants' contributions or through a government subsidy, as explained earlier and in the following paragraph.

This conclusion, unfortunately, does not mean that our approach guarantees a smooth transition just by the choice of an appropriate monotonically declining contribution. It does so, provided p is constant (or declining) but not necessarily if the cost ratio is expected to rise significantly above the current level, threatening the solvency of the PAYGO system. But this is precisely what is happening in the United States and, to some extent, in many other countries with PAYGO. The simulation presented in the next section (and Appendixes 5.2 and 5.3) is therefore of special interest.

NEED FOR REFORM AND PROPOSED SOLUTIONS FOR THE UNITED STATES

Many analysts such as Diamond (1997); Schieber and Weaver in ACSS (1997), Geanakoplos et al. (1999); Kotlikoff (1996); Kotlikoff, Smetters, and Walliser (1998); Feldstein and Samwick (1997); and Seidman (1999) developed simulations to demonstrate the transition to a funded scheme and examine who would benefit and lose from such a transition. With the exception of Diamond (1997) and Seidman (1999), most other researchers would favor the switch to funding private accounts. The following simulations attempt to do the same for our proposal, but this is done in the context of creating a (partially) funded DB plan.

THE SOCIAL SECURITY SYSTEM IN THE UNITED STATES: THE NEED FOR REFORM

We provide only summary information on the U.S. system to demonstrate the need for reform. Schieber and Shoven (1999) provide a more complete history and description of the U.S. Social Security system. Current total contributions to Social Security are 12.4 percent of taxable wages. Under the existing defined benefits structure, the benefits are predictably based on a participant's life contributions. That structure entitles the participant to retire at some stated age (65 at present and gradually increasing over time) with a quasi-real pension which, on average, represents a replacement rate of roughly 50 percent of the "average life income" (the average wage of the participant's best 35 years). But the average replacement rate hides the very "progressive" nature of the U.S. Social Security program. In fact, the marginal replacement rate declines notably as the life income of the recipient rises.

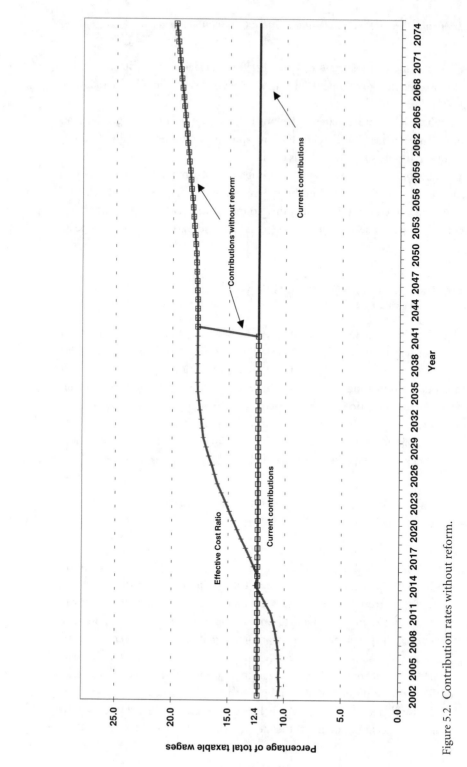

Figure 5.2. Contribution rates without reform.

In Figure 5.2 (underlying data are provided in Appendix Table A5.2.1), we show the cost ratio forecast by the SSA for the "intermediate cost case" (SSA 2002). It can be seen that this line rises above the current contribution line by the middle of the next decade, meaning that SS starts running a current deficit. The cost ratio keeps rising because of the increasingly unfavorable behavior of population and productivity; hence, the deficit continues to increase. For a while this deficit can be covered by the assets accumulated through the surplus of past years. But by the early 2040s, the buffer will be exhausted and the cost ratio will be some 50 percent above current PAYGO contributions. Thus, to keep the system solvent without changing benefits, the contribution would have to jump dramatically from 12.4 percent to 17.8 percent in 2042 and then gradually to 19.5 percent. This is shown in Figure 5.2 under "Contributions without reform." Alternatively, one would have to enforce a one-third decline in benefits (reneging on past promises) or some combination of these two unsavory measures. Furthermore, there is no assurance that even so drastic a remedy could avert more problems later.

These problems and possible solutions have been discussed ad nauseam.[6] But many of the solutions offered so far require a combination of the following: (i) a prospective rise in contributions, (ii) a cut in benefits, and (iii) an increase in investment risk to be borne by the participants (Feldstein 1995, Greenstein 1999, Kotlikoff and Sachs 1998, ACSS 1997, Ferrara 1997, Schieber and Shoven 1999, and the Bush Commission Report). We have argued in previous chapters, as have Seidman (1999) and Aaron and Reischauer (1998), that the major problem with existing Social Security arrangements is the method of financing pensions, not in the defined benefit structure. We hold that the present structure of defined benefits in the United States provides a sound basis with strong public support; the problem is how to finance it. In what follows we present a feasible long-run solution to this financial problem, including the transition path. But before doing so we examine some significant alternative proposals.

A REVIEW OF MAJOR PROPOSALS

Clinton's Promise – A Missed Opportunity

A painless transition could have been made to a fully funded system without changing benefits, by using (i) the (transitory) current and prospective Social Security surplus, (ii) the budget surpluses under the Clinton Administration that were pledged

---

[6] See Munnell (1977), Blahous (2000), NCRP (1998), NASI (1999), Baker (1999), Schieber and Shoven (1999), and Aaron and Reischauer (1998).

to Social Security, and (iii) an imaginative investment policy for the Trust Fund (TF) aiming for the highest return consistent with long-run stability and with proper concern for minimizing the role of government in financial markets (Seidman 1999). Appendix 5.3 shows that our approach could have worked very effectively for the United States, where budget surplus utilization could have generated a gradual but full transition together with participants' contributions initially constant and then monotonically declining, though this outcome partly reflects a set of favorable circumstances unique to the United States.

Given the Bush Administration's decision to utilize the budget surplus for tax rebates and the economic slowdown between 2000 and 2002, the United States can adopt a second-best partially funded solution, which would ensure the maintenance of current benefits but for which the contribution rates will be stabilized at a level 1.12 percent higher than current taxes. The additional contribution is the cost that participants must bear for the tax cut policy enacted by the Bush Administration.

As shown earlier, the transition to full or partial funding requires additional resources, and at one point in the late 1990s, it appeared that the United States would be able to use budget surpluses to achieve full or partial funding. By committing a portion of the budget surplus to Social Security, as recommended by President Clinton, the United States could have achieved full funding and *reduced contributions to 6.2 percent by the late 2050s*. Because this is no longer feasible, we leave the description of this specific case and the comparison with the proposal of the Clinton Administration to Appendix 5.2.

The Bush Administration Proposal

The Bush Administration has not stated its position clearly enough and has leaned toward the proposals of Professor Martin Feldstein and the "privatization" of Social Security. Moreover, the Bush Commission on Social Security presented three proposals for consideration rather than one, making it difficult to pinpoint which proposal is most favored by President Bush. Diamond and Orszag (2002) demonstrate the flaws in the three proposals: one would not lead to long-term solvency (Model 1); the other two (Models 2 and 3) would lead to a reduction in replacement rates, result in more risk for participants (as shown in Chapter 4), and would require an injection of 1.5 to 1.7 percent of payroll for 75 years from the general budget. Because any proposal that requires a reduction of benefits is probably politically unfeasible, and any solution that does not restore fiscal balance and solvency is irrelevant, we consider the generic proposal that requires the creation of private accounts.

To create such accounts, it has been proposed that participants fund these accounts (either by mandate or voluntarily) with a 2-percent diversion of Social Security contributions to private accounts. The accounts would be managed by the private sector, and participants would have some choice. Early versions of these proposals (Feldstein and Samwick 1997) planned to use the projected budget surplus to cover the 2-percent diversion (either through rebates to participants or by filling the hole in PAYGO pension payments as a result of this 2-percent diversion). The Bush Commission is less direct about where these funds will come from because Social Security will need the funds to pay current and future retirees (and the outlook projects growing budget deficits).

The participant's final pension would be a combination of the funded DC and PAYGO DB pensions. The idea was to use the accumulation in the DC accounts to offset obligations under PAYGO (either dollar for dollar or by using proportions of the DC and DB pensions to determine the final pension), thereby attempting to achieve the minimum DB payout with DC schemes. Because the volatility of DC pensions is not trivial, these proposals have considered either guaranteeing the PAYGO pension or potentially requiring participants to increase contributions by as much as (an additional) 2 percent (Feldstein and Ranguelova 2001) in an attempt to minimize the probability that participants would retire with lower than the currently promised pensions. We have demonstrated the cost of guarantees in DC schemes in Chapter 4, and it is not trivial. Furthermore, where participants have choice in asset allocation and fund manager selection, the dispersion in performance, and hence the cost of the guarantee, is likely to be higher than where there is limited or no choice. The alternative – to raise contributions – imposes a direct cost on participants, who are now burdened with a contribution rate anywhere between 14.4 to 16.4 percent (the basic 12.4 percent + 2 percent for private accounts + 2 percent to ensure a high probability of achieving the retirement target); thus, although participants may have choice, there is no assurance that the government will not incur additional costs should they still retire poor.

Our Proposal

As demonstrated in the zero growth case, additional resources are needed to make the transition, and, as shown in Appendix 5.2, a transition could have been made to a fully funded system. With a change in political leadership and economic conditions, the budget surplus, and all the projections for it to continue well into the future, disappeared under the impact of tax cuts and a slowing economy. As a result, a key resource for our transition was taken away. The question then is: Is the transition still feasible? And, if so, toward what alternative system are we moving?

In the absence of government surpluses, any additional contributions must come from participants, for debt-financed government contributions are not appropriate given their perverse implications. The best alternative is to tax participants but, in so doing, there are two critical considerations: (i) that the size of the tax be minimized, and (ii) that the pain be borne equally by all participants and cohorts (to ensure intergenerational equity). In many ways, what this requires is the sort of increase in contributions proposed by the Greenspan Commission but with the higher objective of creating a partially funded structure that would, ideally, insulate the system against future crises.

To demonstrate our transition, we rely on the more convenient one-fund approach with the values of the relevant parameters estimated by the SSA for the "intermediate case," and we assume a reasonable estimate of a (gross) real return of 5.2 percent. We address the appropriateness of this return in the next section. An essential feature of our plan is to guarantee at all times the (defined) benefits currently offered by SS. We ensure this result by using as our cost ratio the very same one used by the SSA in its (intermediate) cost projection (SSA 2002).

Figure 5.3 and Table A5.3.1 in Appendix 5.3 provide the details of this simulation. We have established, with a 5.2 percent rate of return (adjusted for approximately 1 percent of growth), a 1.1 percent *permanent* increase in contributions will provide enough resources to ensure the maintenance of all current benefits. Appendix 5.5 demonstrates the analytical technique by which the 1.1-percent permanent increase is determined. Under this plan, the asset-to-wage ratio is expected to reach a ceiling of 1.6 times wages, which seems quite acceptable. This would generate returns from investments of about 6.4 percent (shown in Figure 5.3 as the gradually increasing line labeled "Interest from Trust Fund") with the balance of the cost ratio covered by the higher fixed contribution rate (Household contribution with proposed plan). Although full funding might be preferred by some because the lower contribution rate implies lower labor market distortions, in light of the current economic situation the solution we propose is the most feasible and equitable. In addition, we demonstrate some interesting possible benefits from partial funding in Chapter 8.

Comparing Our Proposal with the Adjustment of the PAYGO System

One argument in favor of PAYGO is the consideration that the deficit of the current system is not really that serious (Munnell 1999).[7] The SSA has calculated that, up to 2075, the receipts will be short of promised benefits by only about 2 percent of payrolls (only 0.8 percent higher than the required contribution under our solution); thus, we could solve the problem for at least the next 75 years while maintaining PAYGO by opting for an immediate increase in the Old Age Survivor (OAS) contribution

---

[7]   This criticism has also been elaborated in personal correspondence.

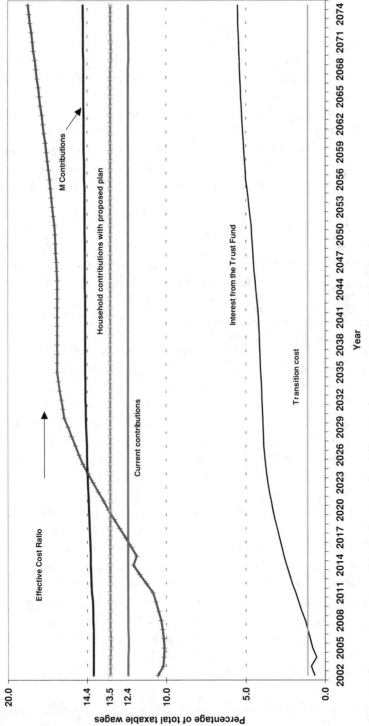

Figure 5.3. Comparison of contribution rates under different reform scenarios (Partial Funding).

from the current 11 percent to perhaps 13 percent (which would make the combined Old Age Survivor and Disability Insurance – (OASDI) – contribution approximately 14.5 percent). But this approach – call it the M solution – produces a path of contributions that is dramatically worse than our full-funding approach, as can be seen from Figure A5.2.1, and slightly more expensive than our proposal in Figure 5.3. In Figure 5.3, a horizontal line at a height of approximately 14.5 percent represents the M-contribution path. More important, though, as shown in Chapter 3, under the basic economic forecasts for economic and population growth, the PAYGO contribution is more susceptible to change and does not contribute to national savings.

FINANCIAL ISSUES

This section deals with some major financial issues, and the more technical issues on the choice of the rate of return are explained in Appendix 5.4.

MANAGING THE TRUST FUND PORTFOLIO

An essential feature of our reform is that all the assets accumulated in the process of funding must be invested through the TF in a common portfolio. This will be benchmarked to a portfolio consisting, in principle, of an equal share of all traded securities. This requires very limited management to track changes in the composition of the benchmark. This very limited management should be overseen by a highly prestigious, independent, blue-ribbon board, much like the Federal Reserve Board. Such boards have been created in Canada and Ireland, where initial reports suggest a positive experience with strong principles of governance. Assets could be managed in-house at a very small cost or entrusted to several private managers for a fee established through competitive bidding. Seidman (1999) has examined the feasibility of such an approach and quotes Cavanaugh (1996) to demonstrate that the portfolio can be managed at extremely low cost (through a competitive bidding process) and insulated from political decisions. Further, Angeles (1996) examines the questions that should be asked prior to investing public money in private markets.

The management of the portfolio leaves no room for discretion, with the obvious advantages of eliminating the danger of political manipulation. But it also has a drawback – namely, that the managers follow the market passively – and therefore their decisions do not reflect their views about the true value of companies in their portfolio. It follows that, as the TF grows to be a larger share of the market, the valuation function is left to the owners of a declining fraction of capital. This is frequently and understandably regarded as an undesirable development. The problem is even more troublesome if one considers the issue of whether the TF or its managers should be entitled to vote their shares.

We would like, therefore, to submit an alternative approach for consideration inspired by the very recent launching of a new type of instrument – the so-called Exchange Traded Funds or ETFs (e.g., S and P 500 Depository Receipts [SPDRs] or "I-shares"). Suppose n managers have been chosen, each of whom manages $1/n$ of the portfolio. Imagine next, instead of instructing them to hold the benchmark portfolio, they are contracted to guarantee the approximate return that the TF would obtain from holding the benchmark.[8] The fund managers should find this contract advantageous because they have the option of total hedging by actually choosing to hold the benchmark. At the same time, they are free to choose some other portfolio that they regard as promising a higher return for a performance fee, though, of course, that involves taking some risk. With this type of contract, each manager will have an incentive to use his or her information to hold the most promising portfolio, which is precisely what happens today with private managers of institutional or private money, except that private managers are not held to a guaranteed return. Any such value added above the benchmark return can be shared with the managers. In short, this type of contract can ensure the benchmark return for the TF while keeping open the possibility that the market may reflect the information and expectations of all investors without excluding those whose portfolio is strictly benchmarked.

Some labor groups have protested the investment of Social Security funds in stock markets, for they feel this unduly favors the owners of capital. However, increasingly, pension funds (including union pension funds) are the major shareholders in companies, which suggests that this fear is unfounded because labor is gradually becoming the owner of capital.[9]

DESCRIPTION AND OPERATION OF THE SWAP CONTRACT

We demonstrated in the appendix to Chapter 1 and Chapter 3 that, with a fixed contribution, to offer defined (real) benefits, either individually or in aggregate, a funded pension system must be able to count on a fixed (real) rate of return that is the same for all participants (excluding adjustments for redistribution). We achieve this through two devices: (i) investment of participants' contributions in one *common* diversified portfolio and (ii) a swap between Social Security and the Treasury.

---

[8] Firms will need to make an accommodation for transactions costs, degree of tracking, and so on, to bid on the same.

[9] Diamond (1999) discusses investment in equities.

Our proposed portfolio, even though maximally diversified, cannot ensure a guaranteed return. For this reason, we propose that the SSA and the Treasury enter into a contract to swap the return of the market portfolio against a fixed real rate. Under this contract, the SSA would exchange the (uncertain) return derived from its market portfolio for payment by the Treasury of a fixed real return in the order of 5.2 percent. Political risk is managed because any interference with the investments will lead to higher payments by the Treasury in the swap.

The obvious question is: What is the appropriate real rate? Because this is a difficult technical question and we do not pretend to have unique expertise in this issue, our analysis and a tentative answer are relegated to Appendix 5.4. We also deal with managing the risk of getting the rate incorrect (in the short term) in Chapter 8. However, a review of market capitalization of equities and bonds suggests that the allocation across those two major assets should be in a 70:30 proportion. Suffice it to say here that our tentative answer would be a real return of 5 to 5.5 percent. This conclusion is based on the record of more than a century of stock market returns as well as corporate profits since the end of the 1950s. It suggests that the unlevered, pretax rate of return on corporate capital averages 8 to 8.5 percent. (Pretax profit is the relevant measure since the tax would accrue to the Treasury together with the net of tax portion.) Our assumption of a 5 to 5.5 percent return is achievable even with the return assumptions of the Bush Commission. Our recommended rate would offer the Treasury an expected risk premium of around 3 percent on the swap. Without pretending to settle the current debate on the appropriate risk premium, we submit that 3 percent is a reasonable premium for the Treasury given its long life and the externality in the form of improvement in the welfare of participants by making it possible to offer defined benefits.

If the swap is such a "reasonable" deal, could it not be offered by private investors or speculators? The answer, of course, is that the risk premium earned by the Treasury is much larger than that accruing to private investors because it alone benefits from the externality resulting from the rise in tax revenue. In Chapter 7, we discuss private offerings of guaranteed returns.

From an operational perspective, one could imagine that at the time the swap is arranged, the Treasury would set up a sinking fund that would be credited (or debited) with the difference between the return of the market (grossed up by an estimate of the tax levied on the profit of the equities held by the TF) and the fixed rate (say, our 5.2 or 5.5 percent). A lower and upper limit would be established for the sinking fund. If the accumulation went above the upper limit, the surplus could be transferred to the budget, and, at the same time, consideration would be given to raising the fixed swap rate and reducing contributions accordingly. Corresponding actions would be taken if the sinking fund went below the lower limit.[10] Any such "contributions" by the government could be financed through higher taxes on participants and, in Chapter 8, we examine how this process can be managed through variable contributions as well.

This approach clearly shifts to the government the risk that the market return deviates from the return guaranteed to Social Security. We contend that the government is in a position to absorb this risk because of its size and indefinite life. Furthermore, the government can spread the risk of a single portfolio over a whole cohort and that of a single cohort of workers over a large number of cohorts. More important, the government should be prepared to undertake the role of the insurer of last resort in consideration of the externality that would come from guaranteeing peace of mind to older citizens. We return to this in Chapter 8, where we demonstrate how the risks of short-term variability of asset returns and wage growth can be managed effectively through variable contributions.

A SIMULATION OF THE WORKING OF THE SINKING FUND

We conducted an historical simulation of the performance of a few portfolios over two historical periods: (i) a 75-year period from 1926 to 2001 and (ii) a shorter 40-year period from 1961 to 2001.[11] We assumed, for simplicity, that returns from stocks are broadly represented by the Standard & Poors 500 stock index and that the bond portfolio is represented by returns from an investment in the 20-year Treasury bond.[12] We assumed U.S.$100 to have been invested in a series of portfolios on Day 1 with growth at the respective rates. This approach ignores periodic contributions, but we are more interested in capital market performance and risks. We then created four different static portfolio allocations (ALCO 1 has 30 percent in equities, ALCO 2 has 40 percent in equities, ALCO 3 has 50 percent in equities, and ALCO 4 has 60 percent in equities). The results of this analysis are provided in Table 5.1, and ALCO 5 represents the guaranteed real return performance (5.2 percent). The performance of the "sinking fund" is demonstrated in Table 5.2.

---

[10] One alternative would be to average the performance of the portfolio over a longer period to ensure less volatile periodic payments in the swap. We thank Professor David Blake for this comment.

[11] We acknowledge the problems of historical simulation as it represents only one path over many possible future paths. Ideally, techniques such as bootstrapping or the Monte Carlo simulation should be adopted, but these simulations are meant to be indicative and not necessarily conclusive; hence, the easier alternative is adopted here.

[12] Data are taken from Ibbotson Associates (various years).

TABLE 5.1 Historical simulation of the risks of the swap contract under different asset allocations

Guaranteed real return | 5.2%

I. 1926–2000 (75 Years)

	ALCO 1	ALCO 2	ALCO 3	ALCO 4	Benchmark ALCO 5
S&P 500 returns (%)	30	40	50	60	0
20-yr Treasury Bond returns (%)	70	60	50	40	0
Benchmark (inflation + guaranteed rate %)	0	0	0	0	100
	100	100	100	100	0
Starting balance (begin 1926)	$100	$100	$100	$100	$100
End balance (end 2000)	$22,277.98	$34,637.60	$52,216.85	$76,362.98	$39,027.82
Percentage of time below benchmark (ann %)	52.00	48.00	49.33	44.00	N/A
Percentage of time below benchmark (cum %)	73.33	62.67	38.67	21.33	N/A
Geometric mean (return ann %)	7.47	8.11	8.70	9.25	8.28
Average return (%)	7.89	8.62	9.35	10.07	8.37
Worst underperformance vs BM (ann %)	(22.30)	(25.38)	(28.46)	(31.54)	N/A
Worst underperformance vs BM (cum $)	($16,749.84)	($10,531.04)	($4,791.68)	($3,264.31)	N/A

II. 1961–2000 (40 Years)

	ALCO 1	ALCO 2	ALCO 3	ALCO 4	ALCO 5
S&P 500 returns (%)	30	40	50	60	0
20-yr Treasury Bond returns (%)	70	60	50	40	0
Benchmark (inflation + guaranteed rate %)	0	0	0	0	100
	100	100	100	100	0
Starting balance (begin 1961)	$100	$100	$100	$100	$100
End balance (end 2000)	$3,008.15	$3,630.06	$4,336.14	$5,127.86	$4,073.37
Percentage of time below benchmark (ann %)	52.50	47.50	50.00	40.00	N/A
Percentage of time below benchmark (cum %)	95.00	90.00	80.00	75.00	N/A
Geometric mean (return ann %)	8.88	9.40	9.88	10.34	9.71
Average return (%)	9.37	9.90	10.43	10.97	9.75
Worst underperformance vs BM (ann %)	(22.30)	(25.38)	(28.46)	(31.54)	N/A
Worst underperformance vs BM (cum $)	($1,279.73)	($1,092.93)	($892.98)	($681.17)	N/A

Notes: ann = annualized; cum = cumulative; BM = benchmark.

TABLE 5.2 **Historical simulation of the sinking fund under different asset allocations**

1926–2000 (75 Years)
Performance of the sinking fund (in U.S. dollars)

	ALCO 1	ALCO 2	ALCO 3	ALCO 4
1926	5.22	5.60	5.99	6.37
1927	21.04	24.61	28.21	31.83
1928	33.35	43.12	53.22	63.67
1929	27.14	35.06	43.09	51.20
1930	22.03	25.11	27.81	30.12
1931	3.90	1.08	(2.26)	(6.09)
1932	20.35	14.45	8.15	1.51
1933	34.68	34.33	32.83	30.20
1934	36.25	34.20	30.95	26.59
1935	54.20	58.37	60.85	61.59
1936	74.29	84.06	92.02	97.97
1937	40.86	41.78	40.53	37.12
1938	62.38	68.33	71.74	72.48
1939	63.85	68.63	70.73	70.05
1940	56.95	58.16	56.59	52.27
1941	25.13	23.44	19.09	12.22
1942	15.23	17.15	16.04	11.92
1943	18.57	26.42	30.90	31.81
1944	21.45	34.48	44.02	49.69
1945	54.04	77.05	96.43	111.41
1946	(19.66)	(0.06)	15.68	26.93
1947	(69.11)	(46.66)	(27.80)	(13.28)
1948	(87.19)	(63.11)	(42.69)	(26.71)
1949	(67.32)	(36.32)	(8.84)	14.07
1950	(80.06)	(33.33)	11.29	52.21
1951	(115.93)	(54.40)	7.42	67.55
1952	(121.94)	(48.12)	28.13	104.63
1953	(145.22)	(72.18)	2.64	77.01
1954	(77.32)	35.31	156.88	284.65
1955	(64.85)	79.53	241.60	419.00
1956	(130.91)	19.79	191.80	383.32
1957	(178.84)	(38.75)	116.77	284.86
1958	(180.43)	8.90	230.40	482.82
1959	(223.56)	(18.33)	226.01	509.50
1960	(217.53)	(3.93)	246.10	531.06
1961	(209.00)	48.01	357.61	720.86
1962	(256.37)	(10.29)	279.87	612.67
1963	(267.05)	21.04	369.11	778.40
1964	(275.15)	49.49	447.59	922.84
1965	(322.23)	31.13	470.41	1.002.18

(*continued*)

TABLE 5.2 (*continued*)

		ALCO 1	ALCO 2	ALCO 3	ALCO 4
	1966	(439.22)	(105.94)	300.81	783.77
	1967	(549.21)	(169.57)	311.09	903.09
	1968	(671.21)	(264.10)	258.08	909.76
	1969	(925.82)	(548.46)	(66.63)	531.89
	1970	(1.034.53)	(631.50)	(121.70)	505.45
	1971	(1.070.29)	(611.05)	(29.48)	686.83
	1972	(1.149.63)	(623.90)	51.47	895.44
	1973	(1.563.04)	(1.089.48)	(492.33)	239.54
	1974	(2.113.37)	(1.716.08)	(1.238.04)	(681.15)
	1975	(2.307.42)	(1.795.82)	(1.162.51)	(403.07)
	1976	(2.414.58)	(1.792.88)	(1.017.51)	(80.54)
	1977	(2.946.07)	(2.355.58)	(1.625.53)	(751.34)
	1978	(3.576.82)	(2.962.50)	(2.195.73)	(1.268.54)
	1979	(4.465.10)	(3.777.85)	(2.900.87)	(1.816.33)
	1980	(5.432.99)	(4.610.68)	(3.521.63)	(2.124.15)
	1981	(6.463.12)	(5.660.17)	(4.605.69)	(3.264.31)
	1982	(6.581.53)	(5.550.00)	(4.219.68)	(2.559.25)
	1983	(7.217.96)	(6.035.74)	(4.475.03)	(2.480.61)
	1984	(7.784.31)	(6.486.93)	(4.791.68)	(2.648.29)
	1985	(7.817.84)	(6.108.95)	(3.873.51)	(1.043.91)
	1986	(7.673.05)	(5.610.05)	(2.928.01)	445.24
	1987	(8.886.61)	(6.775.95)	(4.005.69)	(487.44)
	1988	(9.636.82)	(7.227.68)	(4.041.46)	36.67
	1989	(9.930.63)	(6.884.81)	(2.804.73)	2.485.66
	1990	(11.571.24)	(8.512.08)	(4.460.05)	732.90
	1991	(11.555.26)	(7.692.18)	(2.519.92)	4.181.63
	1992	(12.504.80)	(8.339.75)	(2.765.57)	4.453.60
	1993	(12.801.34)	(8.087.68)	(1.834.71)	6.189.90
	1994	(15.143.48)	(10.531.04)	(4.343.41)	3.688.27
	1995	(13.798.01)	(7.562.02)	846.52	11.818.14
	1996	(15.268.10)	(8.177.32)	1.625.85	14.740.96
	1997	(14.346.00)	(5.391.12)	7.191.84	24.302.93
	1998	(13.485.83)	(2.544.09)	13.059.06	34.593.95
	1999	(16.103.14)	(4.233.89)	13.234.83	38.107.70
	2000	(16.749.84)	(4.390.22)	13.189.04	37.335.16
Worst-case scenario		(16.749.84)	(10.531.04)	(4.791.68)	(3.264.31)

The first conclusion, given the two periods and a target guaranteed real return of 5.2 percent (adjusted by adding the consumer price inflation), is that allocations to equities of 50 percent and above (ALCO 3 and ALCO 4) achieve the funding target over both historical periods; allocations with less than 50 percent in equities are less likely to succeed and do not achieve the annualized nominal target return of 8.28

percent and 9.71 percent for the two periods, respectively. However, just because the target is achieved at the end of 2000 does not mean that these portfolios do not imply risk for the Treasury.

We define four typical asset management risk measures and make some estimate of them. The risk measures are (i) percentage of time (using monthly data) that these allocations provide an annual return below the guaranteed rate, (ii) percentage of time that these allocations have cumulative allocations below the guaranteed return fund (i.e., the percentage of time that the sinking fund has a negative position), (iii) the degree to which the portfolio could underperform the guaranteed rate on an annual basis (worst underpeformance on an annual basis expressed in percent returns), and (iv) the degree to which the portfolio could underperform the guaranteed rate on a cumulative basis (worst underpeformance on a cumulative basis or worst drawdown expressed in dollar terms).

The results across these parameters, for all portfolios and both periods, are relatively mundane in that higher allocations to equity result in (i) a higher percentage of time that the performance is above the guaranteed rate of return on both an annual and cumulative basis, (ii) higher annual "downside" risk (the worst underperformance), and (iii) lower cumulative decreases in the sinking fund (these are a lower percentage of final wealth). The higher annual "downside" risk is more an embarrassment measure than a true risk to the system because a social security arrangement is a multiyear arrangement and annual drawdowns are less relevant than cumulative drawdowns. In summary, this section has shown how the swap contract might work and has evaluated some statistics on the risks to such a swap had it been applied to the United States. The simulations suggest, with allocations as low as 50 percent to equities, a 5.2-percent guaranteed real rate can be financed without excessive risk over different horizons.

These simulations have not allowed for international diversification and investment in other nonpublic assets (the Canadian Pension Plan Board permits private equity investments), and we know that the greater the ability to diversify risk, the higher the likelihood that a target return can be achieved with lower volatility of returns.

HOW THE RATE OF RETURN AFFECTS THE MERITS OF ALTERNATIVE SCHEMES

There is one more question concerning the rate of return that requires brief discussion. Does the advantage of the funded system over PAYGO depend on a high rate of return? Here one must distinguish between the merits of the systems in the long-run equilibrium and the problems of transition from one system to the other.

With respect to the first question, the answer is straightforward – the funded system dominates PAYGO on the basis of the level and potential volatility of the long-term contribution rate, provided the rate of return on capital exceeds the rate of growth of real income. Indeed, it is clearly a necessary (and also sufficient) condition for the equilibrium long-term contribution rate under funding to be lower than that of PAYGO. (It will be recognized that such a conclusion is in line with a well-known proposition about dynamic optimization of per capita consumption.) It is hardly conceivable that this condition could fail to hold – at least as far ahead as one can see.

The situation is somewhat different with regard to the transition problem. As we have demonstrated, if p does not increase over the relevant horizon (or if the PAYGO system could take care of its pension obligations without raising the contribution rate), then, for any reasonable positive rate of return, our system will ensure a transition to full funding in finite time to a permanently lower contribution with a monotonically decreasing rate of contribution (except for and provided that an initial additional contribution can be made by the participants, the government, or through Social Security surplus to start the TF accumulation). The rate of return would, of course, affect the equilibrium contribution and the length of the transition.

But the preceding conclusion does not necessarily hold when the PAYGO system is not self-sustaining and is heading for insolvency, as is the case in the United States. In particular for the United States, in the absence of a government subsidy, the system would run into deficit by the end of the first quarter of this century and run down the TF by 2042. Even with the proposed program of generous government subsidies that President Clinton had mooted, it would not be able to deliver the promised benefits without a hefty increase in PAYGO contributions. In this situation, one part of the TF interest must be used to plug the growing hole due to the rising cost ratio. There is, then, no guarantee that our system, even if we assumed government contributions from the imaginary surplus, could deliver the "miracle" of transforming a PAYGO system into a fully funded one, in finite time and without ever raising contributions, unless the rate of return is high enough. That is why we have demonstrated an alternative that requires a slightly higher contribution rate to be levied on participants (Appendix 5.3 has a lower return than in Appendix 5.2).

We have not established the precise minimum feasible rate, but we have run a few more simulations, not reported here, from which we have established that the "miracle" in the full-funding scenario is still possible with a rate of 5 percent, though at the cost of raising the equilibrium contribution to 7.4 percent and with less aggressive cuts and with contributions potentially being raised by a small amount in the early years.[13] In the partially funded alternative, a lower rate of return of

---

[13] These increases are caused by disability insurance deficits in those years.

5 percent is compensated for by permanently raising contributions by 1.4 percent. However, we recall that these standard paths can be modified, utilizing a trade-off between the time of the first cut and the duration of the transition period in the fully funded case and between the rate of return and the permanent increase in contributions in the partial funding case.

On the other hand, with a 4-percent gross return the "miracle" is no longer possible under the full-funding scenario because the system is never able to accumulate enough assets so that the return on these assets, together with the equilibrium contributions, is sufficient to cover the terminal cost ratio. Even in this case, the full transition is possible, but requires additional contributions by the government, the participants, or both. In the partially funded alternative, a 4-percent real return requires a 2.5-percent permanent increase in contributions – in which case the M-solution may be preferred. The solution proposed by Seidman (1999) utilizes the 4-percent return assumption and requires an initial increase in contributions and a slight reduction in benefits to conduct the transition.

IMPACT OF THE INCREASE IN THE STOCK OF CAPITAL ON THE RATE OF RETURN

The last issue, which must be recognized, is that of the possible feedback of the introduction of a fully funded or partially funded system on the rate of return. There is no question that, by the time the funded system reaches equilibrium, it will result in a substantial increase in the amount of national capital. To illustrate, we have shown, with a 5.2-percent rate of return and a 20-percent cost ratio, the TF net assets under full (partial) funding should amount in steady state to roughly 3.1 (1.6) times the wage bill, or nearly 2.3 (1.1) times national income because the wage bill is around 75 percent of national income. Now, the ratio of private wealth to national income can be placed at around 4.5; thus, the new system would imply a rise in the wealth–income ratio by an impressive additional 50 (25) percent. However, this is not the full story, for the effect on interest rates should depend on the growth of productive tangible capital, which is less than wealth because the latter includes holding government debt. If we eliminate this component, the ratio of capital to income has recently tended to be just below 4. Therefore, the rise in the capital–income ratio could be close to 57 (30) percent. Such a development could have a significant effect in reducing the rate of return on corporate capital. One must be cautious in accepting such an estimate. On the one hand, the rise in TF wealth could induce some offsetting reduction in personal wealth. But, on the other hand, it must be remembered that, in an open economic system, one should focus on the growth of "world" capital not just American capital. Under the partially funded solution, this problem is diluted because the asset-to-income ratio is substantially lower.

SUMMARY

In this chapter, we endeavored to show how the current Social Security structure of defined benefits in the United States, whose future is seriously threatened, can be permanently preserved by gradually replacing the current PAYGO financing with a new funded, defined benefits system. We use the United States as an example to demonstrate not only how benefits can be preserved but also how different transition scenarios can be developed to satisfy the objectives of such reform (i.e., speed of transition, intergenerational equity, partial versus full funding). The new scheme directly supports the welfare objectives of the present Social Security schemes, as it maintains current benefits.

This conclusion is supported by many considerations, among which the following are crucial:

First, under PAYGO, the contributions, which are in effect compulsory saving, are used to finance pensions and hence consumption. In the new funded system, these savings are invested in financial assets that grow large by the time of retirement and produce a return that makes it possible to maintain the required cash contribution below the PAYGO contribution by a large factor (in 2075 by approximately 6 percentage points or some 30 percent of the required rate under PAYGO).

Second, the United States missed a unique chance to permanently lower Social Security contributions by squandering the budget surplus. This surplus, if applied to Social Security, could have led to significant gains for workers and lower labor market distortions. The lesson from this experience is that future surpluses should be utilized to achieve more comprehensive reform and that delays can be costly.

We recommend a transition to partial funding and investing these assets in a common fund holding a strictly indexed portfolio of all marketable securities (equity and debt) managed by the government and private managers on the basis of the lowest bidder. Such a portfolio has desirable efficiency properties and leaves no discretion to those in charge of the TF. If feasible, we further advocate allocating the assets of the TF to individual accounts from an accounting point of view (i) to make participants more aware of the relation between their contributions and the growth of their balance, (ii) to eliminate the temptation of Congress to divert the TF assets to other purposes, and (iii) to make it possible for participants to borrow from their accounts. In addition, the SSA must enter into a swap with the Treasury to ensure DB.

Unfortunately, there are costs in the transition from PAYGO to the funded system, as savings need to be boosted, at least temporarily, to fund the unfunded pension liability. We lay out an operational program for the transition and with moderate additional burden – that is, an additional payroll levy averaging 1.12 percent. The advantage of this solution is that it ensures intergenerational equity, though some current participants close to retirement may feel disadvantaged by such changes.

Clearly, solutions such as doing nothing or trying to fix the existing PAYGO system are not reasonable alternatives. Hence, the unavoidable transition cost is worth bearing. We suggest that our permanent solution is preferable to the set of proposals that goes under the misnomer of "privatization" of Social Security (including those of the Bush Administration). These proposals generally involve only great risk; hence, they entail a substantially higher long-run contribution rate to guarantee benefits. What is worse is that their basic feature is the principle of mandated contributions to individually managed accounts. These are not only much more expensive to manage but also imply giving up the social-welfare-promoting principle of defined benefits in favor of a defined contributions approach with its serious risks – especially for poorer, less sophisticated participants – and high cost to government if a minimum outcome is guaranteed. Last, but not least, these proposals would greatly contribute to unnecessarily and arbitrarily increasing the inequalities in the distribution of pension income.

APPENDIX 5.1. Details on the Transition Dynamics under Zero Growth

See Table A5.1.1.

APPENDIX 5.2. The Ideal Simulation Compared with the Clinton Administration Proposal

In the 1990s the Clinton Administration proposed a Social Security plan that sought to take advantage of the then-prevailing budget surplus. It proposed to reform the system by applying some of the surplus toward funding. This would have meant setting aside allocations from the surplus as early as 2000. In addition, the Clinton plan foresaw the possibility of investing some of the TF reserves in the capital markets. The plan basically consisted of maintaining the current PAYGO system and the current contribution rate as long as possible (see the horizontal line with height of 12.4 percent [until 2056] in Figure A5.2.1). The figure also shows the cost ratio forecast by the SSA for the "intermediate cost case." It can be seen that this line rises above the contribution line by the middle of the next decade, meaning that Social Security starts running a current deficit. The cost ratio keeps rising because of the increasingly unfavorable behavior of population and productivity; hence, the deficit continues to increase. For a while this deficit can be covered by the assets accumulated through the surplus of past years (up to the second decade) and the transfer of the

TABLE A5.1.1 Transition dynamics in the zero-growth case (percentage of taxable wages)

Assumptions:
Life expectancy = 18
Interest rate = 5%
Lag interest on previous year's TF

	New Fund					Uses	Old SS	Sources
	Sources		Uses					
Year	Contributions to New Fund	New Fund accrued interest = $[(5_{t-1}]*5\%$	New Fund pensions	New Fund surplus = (1) + (2) − (3)	New Fund assets = $[(5_{t-1}] + (4)$	Pensions or cost ratio	Required financing = (6) − (3) + (1)	Transition cost or government contributions = max[(7) − (6), 0]	Household contributions if government bears cost
	(1)	(2)	(3)	(4)	(5)	(6)	(7)	(8)	(9)
2000	4.84	0.00	0.02	4.82	4.84	22.50	27.32	4.82	22.50
2001	4.84	0.24	0.02	5.06	9.90	22.50	27.32	4.82	22.50
2002	4.84	0.50	0.03	5.31	15.21	22.50	27.31	4.81	22.50
2003	4.84	0.76	0.06	5.54	20.75	22.50	27.28	4.78	22.50
2004	4.84	1.04	0.11	5.77	26.51	22.50	27.23	4.73	22.50
2005	4.84	1.33	0.17	6.00	32.51	22.50	27.17	4.67	22.50
2006	4.84	1.63	0.24	6.23	38.74	22.50	27.10	4.60	22.50
2007	4.84	1.94	0.32	6.46	45.19	22.50	27.02	4.52	22.50
2008	4.84	2.26	0.42	6.68	51.87	22.50	26.92	4.42	22.50
2009	4.84	2.59	0.53	6.90	58.78	22.50	26.81	4.31	22.50
2010	4.84	2.94	0.66	7.12	65.89	22.50	26.68	4.18	22.50
2011	4.84	3.29	0.81	7.32	73.22	22.50	26.53	4.03	22.50
2012	4.84	3.66	0.98	7.52	80.74	22.50	26.36	3.86	22.50
2013	4.84	4.04	1.16	7.72	88.46	22.50	26.18	3.68	22.50
2014	4.84	4.42	1.36	7.90	96.36	22.50	25.98	3.48	22.50
2015	4.84	4.82	1.59	8.07	104.43	22.50	25.75	3.25	22.50

130

Year								
2016	4.84	5.22	1.83	8.23	112.66	22.50	25.51	3.01	22.50
2017	4.84	5.63	2.10	8.37	121.03	22.50	25.24	2.74	22.50
2018	4.84	6.05	2.39	8.50	129.53	22.50	24.95	2.45	22.50
2019	4.84	6.48	2.69	8.63	138.16	22.50	24.65	2.15	22.50
2020	4.84	6.91	3.02	8.73	146.89	22.50	24.32	1.82	22.50
2021	4.84	7.34	3.35	8.83	155.72	22.50	23.99	1.49	22.50
2022	4.84	7.79	3.71	8.92	164.64	22.50	23.63	1.13	22.50
2023	4.84	8.23	4.08	8.99	173.63	22.50	23.26	0.76	22.50
2024	4.84	8.68	4.47	9.05	182.68	22.50	22.87	0.37	22.50
2025	4.84	9.13	4.88	9.09	191.78	22.50	22.46	0.00	22.46
2026	4.84	9.59	5.31	9.12	200.90	22.50	22.03	0.00	22.03
2027	4.84	10.04	5.76	9.12	210.02	22.50	21.58	0.00	21.58
2028	4.84	10.50	6.23	9.11	219.13	22.50	21.11	0.00	21.11
2029	4.84	10.96	6.73	9.07	228.20	22.50	20.61	0.00	20.61
2030	4.84	11.41	7.26	8.99	237.19	22.50	20.08	0.00	20.08
2031	4.84	11.86	7.80	8.90	246.09	22.50	19.54	0.00	19.54
2032	4.84	12.30	8.38	8.76	254.85	22.50	18.96	0.00	18.96
2033	4.84	12.74	8.99	8.59	263.45	22.50	18.35	0.00	18.35
2034	4.84	13.17	9.62	8.39	271.84	22.50	17.72	0.00	17.72
2035	4.84	13.59	10.29	8.14	279.98	22.50	17.05	0.00	17.05
2036	4.84	14.00	10.99	7.85	287.83	22.50	16.35	0.00	16.35
2037	4.84	14.39	11.73	7.50	295.33	22.50	15.61	0.00	15.61
2038	4.84	14.77	12.50	7.11	302.44	22.50	14.84	0.00	14.84
2039	4.84	15.12	13.31	6.65	309.09	22.50	14.03	0.00	14.03
2040	4.84	15.45	14.16	6.13	315.22	22.50	13.18	0.00	13.18
2041	4.84	15.76	14.98	5.62	320.84	22.50	12.36	0.00	12.36
2042	4.84	16.04	15.77	5.11	325.96	22.50	11.57	0.00	11.57
2043	4.84	16.30	16.53	4.61	330.57	22.50	10.81	0.00	10.81
2044	4.84	16.53	17.25	4.12	334.68	22.50	10.09	0.00	10.09
2045	4.84	16.73	17.94	3.63	338.32	22.50	9.40	0.00	9.40

(continued)

TABLE A5.1.1 (*continued*)

Assumptions:
Life expectancy = 18
Interest rate = 5%
Lag interest on previous year's TF

	Sources								
		New Fund						Old SS	
	Sources		Uses			Uses		Sources	
Year	Contributions to New Fund	New Fund accrued interest = $[(5_{t-1}]*5\%$	New Fund pensions	New Fund surplus = $(1)+(2)-(3)$	New Fund assets = $[(5_{t-1}]+(4)$	Pensions or cost ratio	Required financing = $(6)-(3)+(1)$	Transition cost or government contributions = $\max[(7)-(6),0]$	Household contributions if government bears cost
	(1)	(2)	(3)	(4)	(5)	(6)	(7)	(8)	(9)
2046	4.84	16.92	18.58	3.18	341.49	22.50	8.76	0.00	8.76
2047	4.84	17.07	19.19	2.72	344.22	22.50	8.15	0.00	8.15
2048	4.84	17.21	19.75	2.30	346.52	22.50	7.59	0.00	7.59
2049	4.84	17.33	20.27	1.90	348.41	22.50	7.07	0.00	7.07
2050	4.84	17.42	20.74	1.52	349.94	22.50	6.60	0.00	6.60
2051	4.84	17.50	21.26	1.08	351.01	22.50	6.08	0.00	6.08
2052	4.84	17.55	21.85	0.54	351.55	22.50	5.49	0.00	5.49
2053	4.84	17.58	22.10	0.32	351.87	22.50	5.24	0.00	5.24
2054	4.84	17.59	22.30	0.13	352.00	22.50	5.04	0.00	5.04
2055	4.84	17.60	22.44	0.00	352.00	22.50	4.90	0.00	4.90
2056	4.84	17.60	22.51	(0.07)	351.93	22.50	4.83	0.00	4.83
2057	4.84	17.60	22.51	(0.07)	351.86	22.50	4.83	0.00	4.83
2058	4.84	17.59	22.51	(0.08)	351.78	22.50	4.83	0.00	4.83
2059	4.84	17.59	22.51	(0.08)	351.70	22.50	4.83	0.00	4.83
2060	4.84	17.59	22.51	(0.08)	351.62	22.50	4.83	0.00	4.83

TABLE A5.2.1 Details on simulation with the transition cost financed through "Surpluses" (comparison with Clinton Administration Proposal) (percentage of taxable wages)

Assumptions:
Life expectancy = 18 years
Interest rate = 5.5%
Lag interest on previous year's TF

	Pensions or cost ratio	Household contribution to pensions	Tax rebate	Government subsidy	Total contributions = (2) + (3) + (4)	Trust Fund accrued interest = (9)t−1*(Int Rate-p)	Inflows to SS = (6) + (5)	Social security surplus = (7) − (1)	Trust Fund = (9)t − 1 + (8)	Total assets/ benefits = (9)/(1)	Clinton Administration contributions
	(1)	(2)	(3)	(4)	(5)	(6)	(7)	(8)	(9)	(10)	(11)
2002	10.53	12.38	0.33	2.20	14.91	0.83	15.74	5.21	33.91	322	12.38
2003	10.44	12.37	0.32	2.00	14.69	1.12	15.81	5.37	39.28	376	12.37
2004	10.49	12.38	0.32	2.40	15.10	0.75	15.85	5.36	44.63	425	12.38
2005	10.46	12.39	0.33	2.50	15.22	1.07	16.29	5.83	50.47	482	12.39
2006	10.49	12.39	0.33	3.00	15.72	1.31	17.03	6.54	57.01	543	12.39
2007	10.57	12.41	0.33	3.40	16.14	1.54	17.68	7.11	64.12	607	12.41
2008	10.67	12.40	0.35	3.80	16.55	1.80	18.35	7.68	71.79	673	12.40
2009	10.84	12.40	0.36	4.10	16.86	2.15	19.01	8.17	79.97	738	12.40
2010	11.03	12.40	0.38	4.30	17.08	2.48	19.56	8.53	88.50	802	12.40
2011	11.25	12.40	0.43	4.50	17.33	2.83	20.16	8.91	97.41	866	12.40
2012	11.69	12.40	0.45	4.60	17.46	3.21	20.67	8.98	106.38	910	12.40
2013	12.14	12.41	0.48	4.60	17.48	3.58	21.06	8.93	115.31	950	12.41
2014	12.58	12.41	0.50	4.50	17.41	3.96	21.37	8.79	124.10	987	12.41
2015	12.36	12.40	0.50	0.00	12.90	4.34	17.24	4.88	128.99	104.4	12.40
2016	12.74	12.40	0.52	0.00	12.92	4.51	17.44	4.70	133.69	1050	12.40
2017	13.11	12.40	0.54	0.00	12.94	4.71	17.65	4.54	138.22	1054	12.40
2018	13.49	12.40	0.57	0.00	12.97	4.89	17.86	4.37	142.60	1057	12.40
2019	13.86	12.40	0.59	0.00	12.99	5.08	18.06	4.20	146.80	1059	12.40
2020	14.24	12.40	0.61	0.00	13.01	5.26	18.27	4.03	150.82	1059	12.40
2021	14.59	12.40	0.63	0.00	13.03	5.43	18.46	3.87	154.69	1060	12.40

(continued)

133

TABLE A5.2.1 (*continued*)

Assumptions:

Life expectancy = 18 years
Interest rate = 5.5%
Lag interest on previous year's TF

	Pensions or cost ratio	Household contribution to pensions	Tax rebate	Government subsidy	Total contributions = (2) + (3) + (4)	Trust Fund accrued interest = $(9)t-1*$(Int Rate-ρ)	Inflows to SS = (6) + (5)	Social security surplus = (7) − (1)	Trust Fund = $(9)t-1$ + (8)	Total assets/ benefits = (9)/(1)	Clinton Administration contributions
	(1)	(2)	(3)	(4)	(5)	(6)	(7)	(8)	(9)	(10)	(11)
2022	14.95	12.40	0.65	0.00	13.05	5.57	18.62	3.67	158.36	1059	12.40
2023	15.30	12.40	0.68	0.00	13.08	5.70	18.78	3.48	161.84	1058	12.40
2024	15.66	12.40	0.70	0.00	13.10	5.83	18.92	3.27	165.11	1055	12.40
2025	16.01	12.40	0.72	0.00	13.12	5.94	19.06	3.05	168.16	1050	12.40
2026	16.26	12.40	0.74	0.00	13.14	6.05	19.19	2.94	171.10	1053	12.40
2027	16.50	12.40	0.75	0.00	13.16	6.13	19.28	2.78	173.88	1054	12.40
2028	16.75	12.41	0.77	0.00	13.17	6.19	19.36	2.62	176.49	1054	12.41
2029	16.99	12.41	0.78	0.00	13.19	6.25	19.44	2.45	178.94	1053	12.41
2030	17.24	12.41	0.80	0.00	13.21	6.30	19.51	2.27	181.21	1051	12.41
2031	17.34	12.41	0.81	0.00	13.22	6.34	19.56	2.22	183.42	1058	12.41
2032	17.45	12.41	0.82	0.00	13.23	6.42	19.65	2.20	185.62	1064	12.41
2033	17.55	12.40	0.83	0.00	13.23	6.50	19.73	2.18	187.80	1070	12.40
2034	17.66	12.40	0.84	0.00	13.24	6.57	19.81	2.16	189.96	1076	12.40
2035	17.76	12.40	0.85	0.00	13.25	6.65	19.90	2.14	192.10	1082	12.40
2036	17.76	12.40	0.85	0.00	13.25	6.72	19.98	2.21	194.31	1094	12.40
2037	17.76	12.40	0.85	0.00	13.25	6.80	20.05	2.29	196.60	1107	12.40
2038	17.77	12.40	0.86	0.00	13.26	6.88	20.14	2.37	198.97	1120	12.40
2039	17.77	12.40	0.86	0.00	13.26	6.96	20.22	2.45	201.42	1134	12.40
2040	17.77	12.40	0.86	0.00	13.26	7.05	20.31	2.54	203.96	1148	12.40
2041	17.77	12.40	0.86	0.00	13.26	7.14	20.40	2.63	206.59	1162	12.40
2042	17.77	12.40	0.86	0.00	13.26	7.27	20.54	2.76	209.36	1178	12.40
2043	17.78	12.40	0.87	0.00	13.27	7.41	20.68	2.90	212.26	1194	12.40
2044	17.78	12.40	0.87	0.00	13.27	7.56	20.82	3.05	215.30	1211	12.40

2045	17.78	12.40	0.87	0.00	13.27	7.71	20.98	3.20	218.50	1229	12.40
2046	17.81	12.40	0.87	0.00	13.27	7.87	21.14	3.33	221.83	1246	12.40
2047	17.84	12.40	0.88	0.00	13.28	7.99	21.26	3.43	225.26	1263	12.40
2048	17.86	12.40	0.88	0.00	13.28	8.11	21.39	3.53	228.79	1281	12.40
2049	17.89	12.40	0.89	0.00	13.29	8.24	21.52	3.63	232.42	1299	12.40
2050	17.92	12.40	0.89	0.00	13.29	8.37	21.66	3.74	236.16	1318	12.40
2051	17.98	12.40	0.89	0.00	13.29	8.50	21.80	3.81	239.97	1334	12.40
2052	18.05	12.40	0.90	0.00	13.30	8.69	21.98	3.94	243.90	1351	12.40
2053	18.11	12.40	0.90	0.00	13.30	8.88	22.18	4.07	247.97	1369	12.40
2054	18.18	12.40	0.91	0.00	13.31	9.08	22.38	4.21	252.18	1387	12.40
2055	18.24	12.40	0.91	0.00	13.31	9.28	22.59	4.35	256.53	1406	12.40
2056	18.31	12.40	0.92	0.00	13.32	9.49	22.81	4.50	261.02	1425	18.31
2057	18.38	12.40	0.92	0.00	13.32	9.66	22.98	4.60	265.62	1445	18.38
2058	18.46	12.40	0.93	0.00	13.33	9.83	23.16	4.70	270.32	1465	18.46
2059	18.53	12.40	0.93	0.00	13.33	10.00	23.34	4.81	275.13	1485	18.53
2060	18.60	12.40	0.94	0.00	13.34	10.18	23.52	4.92	280.05	1506	18.60
2061	18.68	12.40	0.94	0.00	13.34	10.36	23.71	5.03	285.08	1526	18.68
2062	18.75	12.40	0.95	0.00	13.35	10.55	23.90	5.14	290.22	1548	18.75
2063	18.83	12.40	0.95	0.00	13.35	10.74	24.09	5.26	295.48	1569	18.83
2064	18.90	12.40	0.96	0.00	13.36	10.93	24.29	5.38	300.87	1592	18.90
2065	18.98	12.40	0.96	0.00	13.36	11.13	24.49	5.51	306.38	1614	18.98
2066	19.06	12.40	0.97	0.00	13.36	11.34	24.70	5.64	312.02	1637	19.06
2067	19.14	12.40	0.97	0.00	13.37	11.54	24.91	5.77	317.79	1660	19.14
2068	19.22	12.39	0.98	0.00	13.37	11.76	25.13	5.91	323.70	1684	19.22
2069	19.30	12.39	0.98	0.00	13.38	11.98	25.35	6.05	329.76	1709	19.30
2070	19.38	12.39	0.99	0.00	13.38	12.20	25.58	6.20	335.96	1734	19.38
2071	19.46	12.39	0.99	0.00	13.39	12.43	25.82	6.36	342.32	1759	19.46
2072	19.53	6.19	1.00	0.00	7.19	12.67	19.86	0.33	342.64	1754	19.53
2073	19.61	6.20	1.00	0.00	7.20	12.68	19.88	0.27	342.91	1749	19.61
2074	19.68	6.20	1.01	0.00	7.20	12.69	19.89	0.21	343.12	1743	19.68
2075	19.76	6.20	1.01	0.00	7.21	12.70	19.91	0.15	343.26	1737	19.76
2076	19.83	6.20	1.01	0.00	7.21	12.70	19.91	0.08	343.35	1731	19.76
2077	19.90	6.20	1.02	0.00	7.22	12.70	19.92	0.02	343.37	1725	19.76
2078	19.97	6.20	1.02	0.00	7.22	12.70	19.93	(0.04)	343.33	1719	19.76
2079	20.04	6.20	1.03	0.00	7.23	12.70	19.93	(0.11)	343.22	1713	19.76
2080	20.11	6.20	1.03	0.00	7.23	12.70	19.93	(0.18)	343.03	1706	19.76

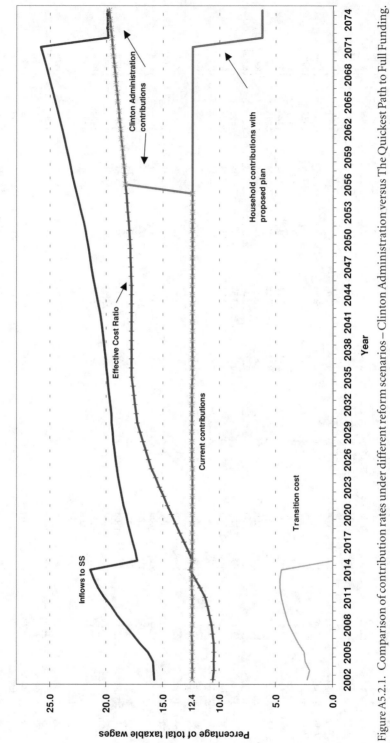

Figure A5.2.1. Comparison of contribution rates under different reform scenarios – Clinton Administration versus The Quickest Path to Full Funding.

Administration's proposed share of on-budget surpluses to Social Security. But by the late 2050s the buffer is exhausted whereas the cost ratio is some 50 percent above PAYGO contributions. Thus, to keep the system solvent with unchanged benefits, the contribution would have to jump dramatically from 12.4 percent to 18.5 percent and then gradually to 19.5 percent. This is shown in Figure A5.2.1 by the line marked "Clinton Administration." Alternatively, one would have to enforce a one-third decline in benefits (reneging on past promises) or some combination of these two unsavory measures. Furthermore, there is no assurance that even that drastic remedy could avoid more problems later. In short, the Administration's plan did not provide a long-term solution to the Social Security crisis. However, by committing the budget surplus to Social Security, some attempt was being made to foster additional savings.

Figure A5.2.1 demonstrates the contribution path that would have ensured the quickest arrival to the equilibrium, steady-state level of contributions and assets with the addition of the surplus subject to the constraint that the contribution should never exceed the current level of 12.4 percent. Not surprisingly, we find the fastest admissible path to full funding is one that maintains the highest possible contribution (which ensures the quickest accumulation of capital), but that highest contribution is obviously the current one. This contribution is to be maintained up to the date at which the equilibrium amount of assets is accumulated. At that point, the contribution itself is suddenly cut down to the equilibrium level, and steady state is reached (provided the cost ratio remains stable after that time). It turns out that, with the cost ratio forecast for the United States and an assumed guaranteed return of 5.5 percent, the equilibrium value of the asset–payroll ratio is just over 3 and the corresponding equilibrium contribution rate is some 6.2 percent. Had we implemented our reform a few years earlier in 2000, this could have also been achieved with a lower rate of return of 5.2 percent – that is, steady state could have been achieved more rapidly. In short, delays are already affecting the cost of a transition to a more stable system. The (shortest) time required to reach the steady state depends on the initial path and other factors affecting Social Security receipts.

In the case of the United States, given the initial TF, the initial contribution rate of 12.4 percent, and the assumed contribution from the government surplus, we find the minimum time is 60 years. This "shortest path" is shown in Figure A5.2.1 by the combination of two horizontal lines, one starting at the current contribution rate of 12.4 percent and terminating in 2072 and the other beginning in the same year at 6.2 percent and corresponding to the steady state.

But the "fastest track" reported above does not seem like a desirable solution because it creates "unbearable" intergenerational equity problems. Relying on a streamlined version of labor force participation, we can see that those entering the labor force between now and 2020, and thus retiring by 2072, will have continued

TABLE A5.3.1 Details on simulation with participants bearing the cost of transition (Partial Funding) (percentage of taxable wages)

Assumptions:
Life expectancy = 18 years
Interest rate = 5.2%
Lag interest on previous year's TF

	Pensions or cost ratio	Household contributions	Tax rebate	Additional contribution	Total contributions = (2) + (3) + (4)	Trust Fund accrued interest = $(9)_{t-1}*$(Int Rate-ρ)	Inflows to SS = (6) + (5)	Social security surplus = (7) − (1)	Trust Fund = $(9)_{t-1}$ + (8)	Total assets/ benefits = (9)/(1)	Clinton Administration contributions
	(1)	(2)	(3)	(4)	(5)	(6)	(7)	(8)	(9)	(10)	(11)
2002	10.85	12.40	0.33	1.12	13.85	0.68	14.53	3.68	30.03	277	12.40
2003	10.51	12.40	0.32	1.12	13.84	0.90	14.74	4.23	34.26	326	12.40
2004	10.47	12.40	0.32	1.12	13.84	0.55	14.39	3.92	38.18	365	12.40
2005	10.46	12.39	0.33	1.12	13.84	0.80	14.64	4.18	42.36	405	12.49
2006	10.49	12.39	0.33	1.12	13.84	0.97	14.81	4.32	46.68	445	12.39
2007	10.57	12.41	0.33	1.12	13.86	1.12	14.98	4.41	51.09	483	12.41
2008	10.67	12.40	0.35	1.12	13.87	1.28	15.15	4.48	55.57	521	12.40
2009	10.84	12.40	0.36	1.12	13.88	1.50	15.38	4.54	60.11	555	12.40
2010	11.03	12.40	0.38	1.12	13.90	1.68	15.58	4.55	64.67	586	12.40
2011	11.25	12.40	0.43	1.12	13.95	1.88	15.83	4.58	69.24	615	12.40
2012	11.69	12.40	0.45	1.12	13.98	2.08	16.05	4.36	73.60	629	12.40
2013	12.14	12.41	0.48	1.12	14.00	2.26	16.26	4.12	77.73	640	12.41
2014	12.58	12.41	0.50	1.12	14.03	2.44	16.47	3.89	81.61	649	12.41
2015	12.36	12.40	0.50	1.12	14.02	2.61	16.63	4.27	85.88	695	12.40
2016	12.74	12.40	0.52	1.12	14.04	2.75	16.79	4.05	89.94	706	12.40
2017	13.11	12.40	0.54	1.12	14.06	2.90	16.96	3.85	93.78	715	12.40
2018	13.49	12.40	0.57	1.12	14.09	3.04	17.12	3.64	97.42	722	12.40
2019	13.86	12.40	0.59	1.12	14.11	3.18	17.28	3.42	100.84	727	12.40
2020	14.24	12.40	0.61	1.12	14.13	3.31	17.44	3.20	104.04	731	12.40
2021	14.59	12.40	0.63	1.12	14.15	3.43	17.59	2.99	107.03	733	12.40
2022	14.95	12.40	0.65	1.12	14.17	3.53	17.71	2.76	109.79	734	12.40
2023	15.30	12.40	0.68	1.12	14.20	3.62	17.82	2.52	112.30	734	12.40

Year											
2024	15.66	12.40	0.70	1.12	14.22	3.71	17.92	2.27	114.57	732	12.40
2025	16.01	12.40	0.72	1.12	14.24	3.78	18.02	2.01	116.58	728	12.40
2026	16.26	12.40	0.74	1.12	14.26	3.85	18.11	1.85	118.43	729	12.40
2027	16.50	12.40	0.75	1.12	14.28	3.88	18.16	1.66	120.09	728	12.40
2028	16.75	12.41	0.77	1.12	14.29	3.91	18.21	1.46	121.55	726	12.41
2029	16.99	12.41	0.78	1.12	14.31	3.94	18.25	1.26	122.81	723	12.41
2030	17.24	12.41	0.80	1.12	14.33	3.95	18.28	1.04	123.85	718	12.41
2031	17.34	12.41	0.81	1.12	14.34	3.96	18.30	0.96	124.81	720	12.41
2032	17.45	12.40	0.82	1.12	14.35	3.99	18.34	0.89	125.70	720	12.40
2033	17.55	12.40	0.83	1.12	14.35	4.02	18.38	0.82	126.53	721	12.40
2034	17.66	12.40	0.84	1.12	14.36	4.05	18.41	0.75	127.28	721	12.40
2035	17.76	12.40	0.85	1.12	14.37	4.07	18.44	0.68	127.96	721	12.40
2036	17.76	12.40	0.85	1.12	14.37	4.09	18.47	0.70	128.67	724	12.40
2037	17.76	12.40	0.86	1.12	14.37	4.12	18.49	0.73	129.40	728	12.40
2038	17.77	12.40	0.86	1.12	14.38	4.14	18.52	0.75	130.15	733	12.40
2039	17.77	12.40	0.86	1.12	14.38	4.16	18.54	0.77	130.92	737	12.40
2040	17.77	12.40	0.86	1.12	14.38	4.19	18.57	0.80	131.72	741	12.40
2041	17.77	12.40	0.87	1.12	14.38	4.22	18.60	0.83	132.55	746	12.40
2042	17.77	12.40	0.87	1.12	14.38	4.27	18.65	0.88	133.43	751	12.40
2043	17.78	12.40	0.87	1.12	14.39	4.32	18.71	0.93	134.36	756	12.40
2044	17.78	12.40	0.87	1.12	14.39	4.38	18.77	0.99	135.35	761	12.40
2045	17.78	12.40	0.88	1.12	14.39	4.44	18.83	1.05	136.40	767	12.40
2046	17.81	12.40	0.88	1.12	14.39	4.50	18.90	1.09	137.48	772	12.40
2047	17.84	12.40	0.89	1.12	14.40	4.54	18.93	1.10	138.58	777	12.40
2048	17.86	12.40	0.89	1.12	14.40	4.57	18.98	1.11	139.69	782	12.40
2049	17.89	12.40	0.89	1.12	14.41	4.61	19.02	1.12	140.82	787	12.40
2050	17.92	12.40	0.90	1.12	14.41	4.65	19.06	1.14	141.96	792	12.40
2051	17.98	12.40	0.90	1.12	14.41	4.68	19.10	1.11	143.07	796	12.40
2052	18.05	12.40	0.91	1.12	14.42	4.75	19.17	1.12	144.19	799	12.40
2053	18.11	12.40	0.91	1.12	14.42	4.82	19.24	1.13	145.32	802	12.40
2054	18.18	12.40	0.92	1.12	14.43	4.88	19.31	1.13	146.45	806	12.40
2055	18.24	12.40	0.92	1.12	14.43	4.95	19.38	1.14	147.59	809	12.40
2056	18.31	12.40	0.93	1.12	14.44	5.02	19.45	1.14	148.73	812	17.40
2057	18.38	12.40		1.12	14.44	5.06	19.50	1.11	149.85	815	17.46
2058	18.46	12.40		1.12	14.45	5.09	19.54	1.09	150.93	818	17.53

(continued)

TABLE A5.3.1 (*continued*)

Assumptions:
Life expectancy = 18 years
Interest rate = 5.2%
Lag interest on previous year's TF

	Pensions or cost ratio	Household contributions	Tax rebate	Additional contribution	Total contributions = (2) + (3) + (4)	Trust Fund accrued interest = $(9)_{t-1}*$(Int Rate-ρ)	Inflows to SS = (6) + (5)	Social security surplus = (7) − (1)	Trust Fund = $(9)_{t-1}$ + (8)	Total assets/ benefits = (9)/(1)	Clinton Administration contributions
	(1)	(2)	(3)	(4)	(5)	(6)	(7)	(8)	(9)	(10)	(11)
2059	18.53	12.40	0.93	1.12	14.45	5.13	19.59	1.06	151.99	820	17.59
2060	18.60	12.40	0.94	1.12	14.46	5.17	19.63	1.03	153.02	823	17.66
2061	18.68	12.40	0.94	1.12	14.46	5.20	19.67	0.99	154.01	825	17.73
2062	18.75	12.40	0.95	1.12	14.47	5.24	19.70	0.95	154.96	826	17.80
2063	18.83	12.40	0.95	1.12	14.47	5.27	19.74	0.91	155.87	828	17.88
2064	18.90	12.40	0.96	1.12	14.48	5.30	19.78	0.87	156.75	829	17.95
2065	18.98	12.40	0.96	1.12	14.48	5.33	19.81	0.83	157.57	830	18.02
2066	19.06	12.40	0.97	1.12	14.48	5.36	19.84	0.78	158.36	831	18.09
2067	19.14	12.40	0.97	1.12	14.49	5.38	19.87	0.73	159.09	831	18.17
2068	19.22	12.39	0.98	1.12	14.49	5.41	19.90	0.68	159.77	831	18.24
2069	19.30	12.39	0.98	1.12	14.50	5.43	19.93	0.63	160.40	831	18.32
2070	19.38	12.39	0.99	1.12	14.50	5.45	19.95	0.57	160.97	831	18.39
2071	19.46	12.39	0.99	1.12	14.51	5.47	19.98	0.52	161.49	830	18.46
2072	19.53	12.39	1.00	1.12	14.51	5.49	20.00	0.47	161.96	829	18.53
2073	19.61	12.40	1.00	1.12	14.52	5.51	20.02	0.42	162.38	828	18.61
2074	19.68	12.40	1.01	1.12	14.52	5.52	20.04	0.36	162.74	827	18.68
2075	19.76	12.40	1.01	1.12	14.53	5.53	20.06	0.30	163.05	825	18.75
2076	19.83	12.40	1.01	1.12	14.53	5.54	20.08	0.25	163.29	823	18.75
2077	19.90	12.40	1.02	1.12	14.54	5.55	20.09	0.19	163.48	822	18.74
2078	19.97	12.40	1.02	1.12	14.54	5.56	20.10	0.13	163.61	819	18.74
2079	20.04	12.40	1.03	1.12	14.55	5.56	20.11	0.07	163.68	817	18.73
2080	20.11	12.40	1.03	1.12	14.55	5.57	20.12	0.01	163.69	814	18.73

their contribution at the current rate and thus contributed to the buildup of capital. However, they will draw no advantages from the sudden reduction of contribution by 50 percent, which will benefit only those entering the labor force after 2072! But we have shown our approach to be consistent with a host of alternative contribution paths. It is easy to see that intergenerational equity problems will be relieved by any paths that reduce the contribution rate before the end of the fastest path at the cost of slowing down the accumulation and, hence, postponing the arrival of the steady state. Such a lengthening allows older generations to share in the forthcoming improvement at the cost of reducing the advantages to later generations hence our proposed solution in the main text.

APPENDIX 5.3. Details on Transition for Our Proposal

See Table A5.3.1.

APPENDIX 5.4. Choice of the Rate of Return

One of the basic tenets of our proposals is that the rate of return promised to the assets accumulated through mandated contributions to Social Security should approximate, as closely as possible, the (marginal) risk-adjusted return on capital – that is, the number of real dollars per year that a $100 investment adds to real GNP before taxes on average over a suitable period of time and appropriately adjusted for risk. The relevant return is *before tax* because the corporate profit tax is a return to the Treasury, which must be added to the after-tax return.

One can obtain an estimate of this amount with the help of historical data on the average return on equities by using the hypothesis that in the long run Tobin's Q should be 1. We can begin with estimates of the return on stocks available for the United States for roughly two centuries (Siegel 1994 and 1999). These suggest that, over several decades, the average return on equity has been remarkably stable – around 7 percent. However, one must take into account two important adjustments. First, the return on equity corresponds to profit, and profit is not a satisfactory measure of the return on capital when the firm is financed partly by debt (i.e., when it has a "levered" capital structure). Rather, the return on capital is the return on a portfolio consisting of the same fraction of all outstanding marketable liabilities – shares and bonds (or, equivalently, a weighted average of the return on equity and debt) – weighted by the share of each instrument in the "market capitalization" of firms. This is precisely the procedure we advocate: investing in an indexed portfolio consisting of an appropriate share of the market portfolio of stock and bonds. Now, a quick examination of available data (e.g., Federal Reserve Flow of Funds Accounts of the United States) suggests the share of equity in total capitalization is, on average, 70 percent. Combined with an estimate of the real interest rate of approximately 3 percent, this results in an estimate of return on capital of about 6 percent. Bosworth (1996) arrived at an estimate of 6.2 percent for the real return on the capital employed in the American economy.

However, this is an estimate of return on total corporate capital *after* corporate income tax. Corporate income tax of about 30 percent on the levered profit, plus a 30-percent debt at a real interest rate of around 3.3 percent, results in an estimated 8 percent of the pretax return on total capital divided as follows: 1 percent for interest and 7 percent for equity before tax, of which 2 percent is attributable to tax. This estimate of a pretax return on the unlevered market portfolio is close to a well-known estimate of Poterba (1998), which concludes that "the pre-tax return on capital in the corporate non-financial sector has averaged 8.5 percent over the 1959–1996 period (p. 1)."[14] On the basis of these considerations, we have arrived at an estimate of 8 to 8.5 percent in pretax, unlevered returns.

It must be recognized, however, that the estimate of an extra 2 percent return to the Treasury from incremental tax revenue could be biased. It rests on the assumption that all the TF investment in the unlevered equity of corporations is accompanied by an equal expansion in the stock of equities demanded, or, equivalently, all other holders of market securities do not reduce their desired holdings. This, of course, need not be true: for instance, it is conceivable that the rise in savings due to the TF would reduce foreign lending and investment in domestic stocks. If this should happen, our estimate of the tax gain is overestimated. On the other hand, the increased capital stock increases profits as well as other income, such as labor, and to this extent our estimate is downward biased. For example, Feldstein and Samwick (1999) follow this route, and end up with a very similar estimate of the tax effect. Presumably, only experience can establish the true effect. That experience dictates if and when it may become appropriate to retouch the contribution rate – up or down.

APPENDIX 5.5. The General Analytical Solution to the Transition – Determining the Optimal Contribution and Asset–Wage Ratio

For the United States we advocate a solution consisting of a (modest) one-step, permanent increase in the contribution rate, which results in a partially funded, partially

---

[14] See Poterba (1998).

PAYGO structure capable of ensuring a "permanent" financing of current benefits. We show here that such a solution can be adopted anywhere under suitable conditions and also show how it can be estimated operationally. The suitable condition is essentially that the cost ratio p_t should gradually converge to a long-term steady state value p^*. This condition is clearly satisfied by the long-term projections for the United States by the SSA.

We have defined the following in Chapter 3:

- a_t to be assets in a funded system at time t,

- w_t to be the wage bill at time t,

- r to be the (long-run) return on capital and ρ to be growth in real wages (which, to simplify the exposition, is assumed here to be fixed), and

- A_t to be the asset-to-wage ratio at time t.

We assume c to be the stepped-up, new, fixed-contribution rate (contributions divided by wages). Then the surplus of a funded system, s_t, is given by

$$s_t = A_{t-1}(r - \rho) + c - p_t = A_t - A_{t-1}. \tag{A5.5.1}$$

Let T denote the time when steady state is reached. Then, from A5.5.1,

$$s_T = A_{T-1}(r - \rho) + c - p^* = 0. \tag{A5.5.2}$$

We also know, from the way assets are accumulated in the system, that A_{T-1} will be determined by the growth in initial assets, plus contributions, minus pensions (both accumulated at compound interest to the terminal date). If we define Σ_t as the summation operator from time 0 to t and Π_t as the product operator from time 0 to t and set ρ equal to zero, then we can restate A_{T-1} as follows:

$$A_{T-1} = A_0 \Pi_{T-1}(1 + r)^t + c \left\{ (\Pi_{T-1}(1 + r)^t - 1)/r \right\} - \Sigma_{T-1} \left\{ p_t \Pi_{T-1-t}(1 + r)^t \right\} \tag{A5.5.3}$$

With equations A5.5.2 and A5.5.3, we have two equations in two unknowns (c and A_{T-1}) that can be solved simultaneously to obtain the value of the new steady contribution c. In particular, the choice of c and A_{T-1} that we used in our proposed reform, and in the simulations thereof, is the (unique) solution of (A5.5.2) and (A5.5.3) for the values of the parameters relevant to the United States as shown in Table A5.3.1:

$$(T = 80, \ p^* = 20.1\%, \ r - \rho = 4\%, \ A(0) = 0.3).$$

If we look at our final parameters of A_{T-1} of 1.6369 and c of 14.55% (12.40% basic contribution, plus a tax rebate of 1.03%, plus an additional contribution of

1.13%), then equation A5.5.2 balances with A5.5.3 very close to balance (differences arise probably because ρ is nonstationary, which thus affects the compounding). Finally, we note that governments may want to impose restrictions on the value of A, and this is an additional constraint to our more general solution. This is discussed further in Chapter 8.

6

Social Security Reform in Spain

With Pedro Sainz de Baranda

The public pension system in Spain administered by the social security administration (Instituto Nacional de la Seguridad Social or INSS) is one of the pillars of the social protection system. The system is currently a PAYGO scheme that has come under increased financial pressure as a result of three trends that have affected several countries – especially in Europe:

1. Increased generosity – Politicians have increased pensions in real terms for those segments of society in greater need. Furthermore, the pension system has sometimes been used as an electoral weapon.
2. Deterioration in the labor markets – The increase in unemployment during the 1980s and 1990s has eroded the payroll tax base below its theoretical potential.
3. Demographic changes – An increase in life expectancy, combined with a dramatic decline in fertility rates since 1975, has raised the old age dependency ratios. Projections suggest further increases in this ratio. To maintain pension commitments, all else being equal, there will be greater fiscal pressure on the existing wage base.

The future of the Spanish public pension system has spurred many debates and prompted many proposals for reform in recent years. The agreements of the Pacto de Toledo (1995) that led to several positive reforms in the system have been particularly important. The economic expansion in the second half of the 1990s, and from 2000 to 2003, created small surpluses for the Spanish public pension system and, in some circles, a potentially false sense of security of its financial viability. However, the government has postponed reforms until after the 2004 general elections given the tensions and strikes witnessed in neighboring France over proposed reforms. This postponement comes despite suggestions from several agencies, including the

Organization for Economic Cooperation and Development, that reforms are critical for the sustenance of the pension system (Garrido 2003).

This chapter recommends lasting reform for the Spanish system utilizing elements such as partial or total funding described in previous chapters. We first provide a brief description of the Spanish public pension system (sistema contributivo de la Seguridad Social), including its financial performance in the last two decades. We then evaluate the future of the system by examining its susceptibility to key demographic and macroeconomic factors that can, and will, affect the future financial outlook of the public pension system. Following that, we evaluate the impact of potential reforms on the system, including two specific ones already discussed by employers, policy makers, and unions: (i) the implementation of flexible retirement after age 64 and (ii) the extension of the number of years used to calculate the retirement pension from the last 15 years before retirement to the last 35 years. Thereafter, we examine in detail the applicability of our reform proposal and the transition to funding (similar to Chapter 5) the Spanish social security system. The simulations show the impact of funding by itself and in combination with additional reforms to benefits. We demonstrate that successful implementation should allow the system to meet its obligations to current and future retirees without raising the payroll tax to current or future workers. Furthermore, simulations of the reformed system suggest that the payroll tax could be substantially decreased, particularly after 2045.

THE SOCIAL SECURITY SYSTEM IN SPAIN

The social security system in Spain has its roots in social protection policies started at the turn of the century.[1] The current system tasks the state with providing a public social security system for all citizens that will guarantee certain services and provide monetary contributions when necessary. The politics surrounding the system in the early 1990s led to the so-called Pacto de Toledo, which resulted in the introduction of a few reforms and has shaped some of the current characteristics of the system.

DESCRIPTION OF THE SOCIAL SECURITY SYSTEM

The social security system in Spain provides three major types of protection and services:

1. **Monetary payments**
   Contributive payments – Contributive pensions, temporary disability, and maternity benefits are earned as a result of contributions to the social security

---

[1]   Boletin Oficial de la Cortes Generales (1995).

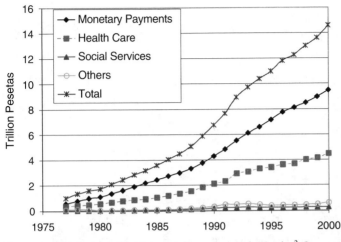

Figure 6.1. Evolution of social security expenses in Spain.[2] Source: Sainz de Baranda (2001).

system during the worker's active years and are dependent on the individual's contributive history.

Noncontributive payments – They include complements to pensions below certain levels and other monetary payments intended to maintain a minimum standard of living for all citizens in need.

2. **Universal health care protection**
3. **Social services** – Social assistance programs for disfavored groups such as the disabled or the elderly.

The system can be distilled into two main components: (a) a contributive component (represented by contributive pensions) and (b) a universal component to which every citizen is entitled regardless of contributive history. Figure 6.1 shows the evolution of expenses in nominal terms for the different types of protection, and that monetary payments dominate.

Similarly, there are two main sources of funds:

1. Contributions from workers in the program
2. Government transfers from the general budget (taxation).

Figure 6.2 shows the evolution of the sources of funds in nominal terms, and contributions clearly dominate.

---

[2] Ministerio de Trabajo y Asuntos Sociales (2000).

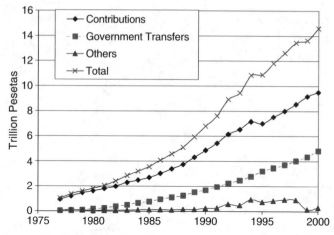

Figure 6.2. Evolution of social security revenues in Spain.[3] Source: Sainz de Baranda (2001).

Contributive and noncontributive pensions are managed by the INSS, health services by the Instituto Nacional de la Salud, and social services by the Instituto Nacional de Servicios Sociales. To introduce "solidarity," the finances are managed jointly for all services by the Tesorería General de la Seguridad Social. For many years, this solidarity resulted in using surpluses in the contributive pension system to finance noncontributive (universal) programs.

Since the reform of 1997, the government has been moving toward a clarification of the funding sources. Health care and noncontributive pensions tend to be supported by government transfers (general taxation), whereas contributive benefits, including pensions, are funded by the contributions. This change, however, was not fully implemented until 2000, and part of the surpluses of the pension system in the 1990s was used to fund health care costs. Only in 2000 were surpluses from the pension system allocated to a "pension fund." For ease of exposition, we focus on the contributive protection system only, and details on the more expansive system are provided in Sainz de Baranda (2001).

Contributions

Contributions to the social security system are calculated as a percentage of the contribution regulatory base (CRB). The CRB is the equivalent of the gross salary received by an employee, excluding the contribution to the social security system made by the employers. Table 6.1 shows the payments that have to be made to the social security system. The table demonstrates that employer contributions are

---

[3] Ibid.

TABLE 6.1 Payments made to the social security system (percent of CRB)

	(General scheme)		
	Employer	Employee	Purpose
General contingencies	23.6	4.7	Contributive pensions
Job-site accidents	Varies with job	0	Temporary disability
Unemployment	6.0	1.6	Fund subsidies for unemployed workers
FOGASA	0.4	0	Pay salary and severance in bankruptcies
Training	0.6	0.1	Fund training programs for workers in need

Source: Sainz de Baranda (2001).

approximately 30 percent, and total contributions exceed 36 percent! Contributions for general contingencies represent more than 90 percent of funding for contributive programs.

Of these, only the first two items in Table 6.1 are managed by social security contributive programs. The other three items in Table 6.1 are managed by independent entities focused on fighting unemployment and supporting unemployed workers. The Instituto Nacional de Empleo (INEM), an independent entity, pays the general contingencies contributions of unemployed workers who have the right to receive a contributive unemployment subsidy.

Retirement Pensions

PREREQUISITES. Participants must have paid the legal contributions to social security for at least 15 years, must be 65 years old, and must not be engaged in any professional activities.

AMOUNT PAID. There are fourteen annual payments, each calculated as a percentage of the pension regulatory base (PRB). The PRB is calculated (starting January 1, 2002) as

$$PRB = \frac{\sum_{i=1}^{24} CRB_i^n + \sum_{i=24}^{180} \check{CRB}_i^r}{210} \tag{6.1}$$

Where CRB_i^n is the contribution regulatory base for the ith month before retirement in nominal terms (not adjusted for inflation) and $\check{CRB}_i^r$ is an equivalent term but adjusted by the consumer price inflation (CPI) up to the twenty-fourth month prior to retirement. Since the CRB is roughly the monthly gross salary, on an annual basis,

TABLE 6.2 Analysis of the finances of the contributive programs in Spain (1980–2000)

	1980	1981	1982	1983	1984	1985	1986	1987	1988
Number of pensions[a] (×1000)	4,631	4,728	4,902	5,074	5,249	5,411	5,547	5,697	5,82
Pension payments (b Pts)	875	1,107	1,318	1,591	1,870	2,120	2,408	2,647	2,95
Payment for all programs[b] (b Pts)	1,031	1,280	1,522	1,812	2,094	2,354	2,658	2,917	3,25
Total contributive expenses[c] (b Pts)	1,069	1,327	1,578	1,879	2,171	2,441	2,756	3,025	3,37
Total contributive expenses (percent of GDP)	7.1	7.8	8.0	8.3	8.5	8.7	8.5	8.4	8.
Average pension (kPts/year)	189	234	269	314	356	392	434	465	5C
Contributors[a,d] (×1000)	10,543	10,485	10,384	10,472	10,657	10,979	11,307	11,286	11,38
Contribution payments (b Pts)	1,598	1,769	1,972	2,284	2,459	2,683	3,001	3,370	3,73
Contribution payments (percent of GDP)	10.5	10.4	10.0	10.1	9.6	9.5	9.3	9.3	9.
Average contribution (kPts/year)	152	169	190	218	231	244	265	299	32
Balance of the program (b Pts)	529	442	393	406	288	242	245	345	35
Balance of the program (percent of GDP)	3.5	2.6	2.0	1.8	1.1	0.9	0.8	1.0	0.
Balance w/o min. complements (b Pts)[e]									
Balance w/o min. complements percent GDP[e]									

[a] Average.
[b] Includes temporary disability and maternity leave.
[c] Adding an estimate of the management cost.

14× PRB would be 100 percent of the gross salary if this had been constant for the last 180 months and there was no inflation in the previous 2 years. Real salary increases (decreases) during the past 15 years, and inflation (deflation) in the last 2 years, would make the PRB-to-last-salary ratio lower (higher) than 100 percent. The pension becomes 100 percent of the PRB for people with 35 years of contributions or greater. It decreases at a rate of 2 percent per year of contribution down to 80 percent of PRB for people with 25 years of contribution and then at a rate of 3 percent per year of contribution down to 50 percent of the PRB for people with 15 years of contributions.[4]

OTHER FEATURES. Surviving spouses of pensioners, or active workers with certain contribution profiles, receive pensions. In addition, all existing pensions are indexed to the CPI.[5] The system also provides for maximum and minimum pensions, and

[4] Currently, workers who were contributive members to some specific programs before January 1, 1967, have an option to retire early, starting at age 60. The people who so choose will get an 8 percent reduction of their pension per year up to age 65.

[5] It is worth noting that the indexing to the CPI is done in relation to the CPI forecast and should be adjusted at year-end to reflect the actual CPI. However, only when the CPI is higher than

989	1990	1991	1992	1993	1994	1995	1996	1997	1998	1999	2000
5,956	6,110	6,268	6,429	6,640	6,836	6,971	7,131	7,294	7,420	7,516	7,560
3,329	3,781	4,223	4,721	5,249	5,688	6,190	6,717	7,078	7,453	7,796	8,357
3,688	4,213	4,746	5,310	5,832	6,274	6,822	7,397	7,738	8,092	8,467	9,116
3,824	4,369	4,922	5,507	6,048	6,506	7,074	7,671	8,024	8,392	8,780	9,453
8.5	8.7	9.0	9.3	9.9	10.0	9.7	9.9	9.8	9.6	9.4	9.4
559	619	674	734	791	832	888	942	970	1,004	1,037	1,105
1,904	12,428	12,802	12,953	12,934	12,784	12,934	13,098	13,463	14,053	14,786	15,508
4,297	4,861	5,422	6,142	6,524	7,147	6,980	7,513	7,993	8,540	9,156	9,900
9.5	9.7	9.9	10.4	10.7	11.0	9.6	9.7	9.7	9.8	9.8	9.8
361	391	423	474	504	559	540	574	594	608	619	638
473	493	500	636	476	641	−94	−158	−31	148	375	453
1.1	1.0	0.9	1.1	0.8	1.0	−0.1	−0.2	0.0	0.2	0.4	0.4
827	905	964	1,155	1,017	1,200	474	447	578	761	991	1,068
1.8	1.8	1.8	2.0	1.7	1.9	0.7	0.6	0.7	0.9	1.1	1.1

Includes unemployed workers with contributive coverage from INEM.
On the assumption that the noncontributive benefit of complements to minimum pension had not been funded out of the contributions.
ource: Sainz de Baranda (2001).

the replacement rate drops to 87 percent for people who contribute at the maximum level.

When a pensioner earns a pension below the minimum established by law, the social security system pays a complement through the contributive system to increase the income up to a decent subsistence level. This is clearly a noncontributive benefit and was recognized as such at the agreements of the Pacto de Toledo. Nonetheless, this benefit is still being financed from the contributions rather than by government transfers from the general budget.

EVOLUTION OF THE ECONOMICS OF THE SYSTEM UP TO THE YEAR 2000

Table 6.2 shows the financial evolution of the contributive programs in Spain isolated (to the extent possible) from overall social security finances.[6] The income from

the forecast have the pensions been revised. The government has lacked the political courage to adjust to the low side when the CPI was below expectations.

[6] A portion of the management expenses of social security has been allocated to the contributive programs. Management expenses for the contributive system were a total of about 3.7 percent

TABLE 6.3 Population in Spain: Some key recent historical data

	1971	1981	1991	May 1996	Jan 1998
Total population	**34,216,274**	**37,741,460**	**38,919,910**	**39,669,385**	**39,85 2,652**
0–15 years	10,076,820	10,271,646	8,103,708	6,930,284	6,570,530
15–64 years	20,799,873	23,196,732	25,387,404	26,542,607	26,778,356
>64 years	3,339,581	4,273,082	5,428,798	6,196,494	6,503,766
Youth dependency ratio*	48.4	44.3	31.9	26.1	24.5
>64 dependency ratio**	16.1	18.4	21.4	23.3	24.3
Total dependency ratio	64.5	62.7	53.3	49.5	48.8

* Ratio of population under 16 to population between 16 and 64.
** Ratio of population over 64 to population between 16 and 64.
Source: Sainz de Baranda (2001).

workers' contributions has been steady at around 9.5 to 10 percent of the gross domestic product (GDP) over the last two decades, whereas the cost of the contributive programs increased steadily from about 7 percent to 9 to 10 percent of GDP as a result of improved coverage and deteriorating demographics.

Note that the contributive system of social security has always produced surpluses (except for a short period in 1995 and 1996 after the payroll tax was lowered by 1 percentage point). However, these surpluses have always been used to fund other noncontributive programs. The trend started to change in 2000 when part of the surplus was allocated to the pension reserve fund. The situation is even more favorable when the finances are analyzed on the assumption that the noncontributive complements for minimum pensions are funded out of the general budget and not out of contributions. In this case, the surplus would have been approximately 1 percent of GDP for the past few years.

SUMMARY OF RECENT DEMOGRAPHIC TRENDS IN SPAIN

The key source for demographic data in Spain is the Instituto Nacional de Estadística (INE). Table 6.3 summarizes some of the key figures for the population in Spain since the 1970s.

The trends are clear and consistent with observations in other European countries:

1. A reduction in the fertility rate has resulted in fewer births and a significant reduction in the youth dependency ratio in the 1980s and 1990s.

of the contributions, of which half involves management of the temporary disability benefits. The trend has been for a management cost of 2.1 percent of the paid amounts for pensions and 27 percent of the paid amounts for temporary disability.

2. An increase in the life expectancy has resulted in increases in the old age dependency ratio.

Both factors combined have resulted in a rapid aging of the population of Spain in the past few decades. Sainz de Baranda (2001) has made two fascinating observations:

1. Southern countries of the European Union (EU) have had a later but more dramatic decrease in fertility rates, having reached the lowest levels ever seen in the EU.
2. The average maternity age in Spain has increased significantly in recent years and has become one of the highest in the EU.

Detailed demographic simulations for Spain are provided in Sainz de Baranda (2001). They assume a number of different demographic scenarios – all of them suggest growing problems for the PAYGO system.

RECENT MACROECONOMIC AND LABOR TRENDS AND PROJECTIONS

The Spanish economy has improved significantly in recent years. Fiscal restraint has been exercised as part of Stage 3 of the European Monetary Union. This brought fiscal deficits to near balance from about 7 percent of GDP in the early 1990s. Qualifying for the Monetary Union, coupled with a better fiscal outlook, stimulated faster output and resulted in a sharp decline in interest rates and inflation, further strengthening the fiscal outlook (IMF 2000).[7] Figure 6.3 illustrates the trends in GDP growth and CPI variation for the past years together with the shortrun outlook.[8]

The central government outlook includes a small social security surplus in each of the 4 years included in the forecast (2001 to 2004). The recent expansive cycle in the economy was mainly driven by job creation. Productivity growth (measured as the difference between GDP growth and job creation) remained at modest levels around 0.5 to 1.2 percent since 1995. Government projections call for annual productivity growth of 1.1 percent until 2004.

The occupied labor force in Spain has been rather low in relation to its working age population for two reasons: (i) high unemployment and (ii) low labor force participation.

[7] Ministerio de Economía (2001) contains the short-run (2000–2004) projections for the Spanish economy published by the Ministry of Economy.
[8] GDP growth in 2001 and 2002 has been in excess of 6 percent (higher than projected in 2001), thereby creating a more favorable environment for reform. CPI has fluctuated between 3 and 4 percent from 2000 to 2003.

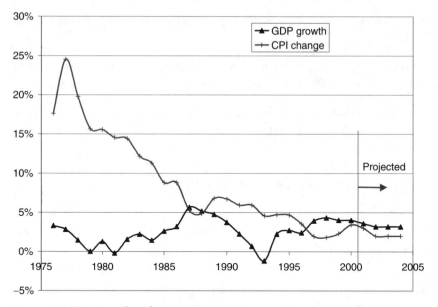

Figure 6.3. GDP Growth and CPI, 1977–2004. Source: Sainz de Baranda (2001).

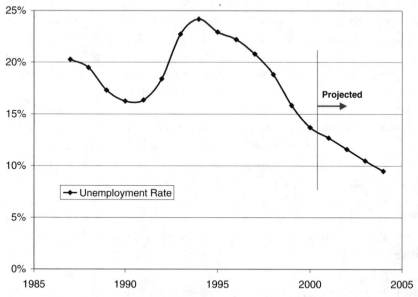

Figure 6.4. Unemployment rate in Spain: Recent trends and shortrun outlook. Source: Sainz de Baranda (2001).

Spain has been notorious for labor market degradation since the late 1970s and has had the highest unemployment rate of any EU country for most of the past two decades. The rate of unemployment, however, has been decreasing rapidly in the last few years.

Figure 6.4 illustrates recent data and the forecast for the near future. Unemployment has declined from 15.32 percent in 1999 to approximately 10.5 percent in 2001 and 11.5 percent in 2002. Nevertheless, there is room for further reduction to the 4 to 5 percent level, although this may require additional structural reforms. The reduction in unemployment can play a key role in allowing for successful transition to a more robust system with lower contributions.

It is impossible to provide accurate projections for the evolution of the economy over a 50-year period. To assess the major trends that can be expected in the evolution of the finances of the social security system, we will carry out a simulation for a potential central path (no business cycles) for the economy.

Beyond 2004, the central scenario is developed as follows:

- Assume a more modest rate of output growth of 2.5 percent starting in 2005.

- Inflation is kept at 2 percent.

- The government maintains fiscal balance outside of social security beyond 2003.

- The number of jobs grows at an annual 1.4 percent during the initial period until the unemployment rate reaches a minimum (we assume 5 percent is structural unemployment).

- Productivity growth is taken as 1.1 percent initially, which is the same figure used for the shortrun outlook. As the labor supply becomes tighter (decreasing unemployment), the rate of productivity growth increases up to a maximum of 1.5 percent annually. The GDP growth adapts to the new rate of growth of productivity and jobs.

- Finally, to calculate the active population (and, thus, the unemployment rates), labor force participation rates (LFPRs) are projected forward from their current levels.

Figure 6.5 shows some key parameters of the economy as projected for the baseline population scenario outlined above and the central macroeconomic scenario.

FINANCIAL PROJECTIONS FOR THE CONTRIBUTIVE SOCIAL SECURITY SYSTEM

Details of the projected income and expenses of the contributive programs of the social security system into 2050 are provided in Sainz de Baranda (2001).

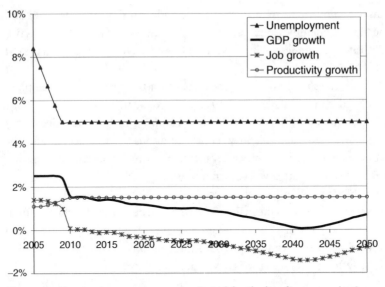

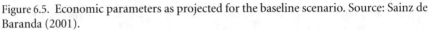

Figure 6.5. Economic parameters as projected for the baseline scenario. Source: Sainz de Baranda (2001).

There are two sources of income, as follows:

1. A payroll tax (contributions for general contingencies and jobsite accidents).
2. Returns on the pension fund. The returns will be a function of the total capital accumulation and the investment policy if funding is considered. They are a nonissue in the current PAYGO system.

Our assumption is that the ratio of contributions to GDP remains constant at 9.8 percent throughout the projection period. On the basis of the methodology in Sainz de Baranda (2001), the financial projections for the contributive portion of the Spanish social security system were calculated for the baseline case and several alternative scenarios.

BASELINE SCENARIO AND THE NEED FOR REFORM

Table 6.4 and Figure 6.6 show the projections for the baseline demographic and macroeconomic scenarios outlined in Sainz de Baranda (2001).

The system is expected to have a surplus up to the decade of 2020. The surplus peaks at 1.7 percent of GDP around 2009, mainly as a result of a decrease in the weight of the retirement pension program. The increase in the dependency ratio will drive the program into large deficits – over 7 percent of GDP – toward the end of

TABLE 6.4 Financial projections for the baseline
demographic scenario (percent of GDP)

Year	Contributions	Total expense	Balance
2000	9.8	8.8	1.1
2005	9.8	8.2	1.6
2010	9.8	8.1	1.7
2015	9.8	8.5	1.3
2020	9.8	9.2	0.6
2025	9.8	10.2	−0.4
2030	9.8	11.6	−1.7
2035	9.8	13.1	−3.3
2040	9.8	14.8	−5.0
2045	9.8	16.5	−6.6
2050	9.8	16.9	−7.1

Source: Sainz de Baranda (2001).

the projected period (2050). Clearly, something needs to be done to correct these
trends, otherwise, contributions will rise dramatically or benefits will have to be cut.

PROPOSALS FOR REFORM

The previous projections follow a somewhat similar pattern to those suggested by
recent studies (Herce and Alonso Meseguer 2000, IMF 2000). A minor difference is

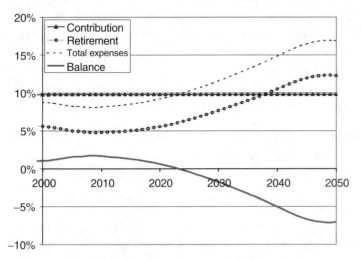

Figure 6.6. Financial projections for the baseline demographic scenario (percent of GDP).
Source: Sainz de Baranda (2001).

that the other studies suggest a slightly lower expected surplus for the first years of the twenty-first century, probably resulting from the good economic performance of Spain in 2000.[9] The alarming deterioration expected beyond 2020, driven by demographic factors, has been the subject of extensive debates. For countries in the European Monetary Union, the restriction on fiscal deficits would make financing an imbalance in the contributive system of social security (of 7 percent of GDP) a very difficult endeavor. The most likely options would be to reduce the imbalance through an increase in contributions or a cut in benefits.

Many proposals have been put forward to reform social security in Spain. They can be grouped into two broad categories: (i) those that maintain the current PAYGO and (ii) those that move towards a mixed funded-PAYGO system. We briefly examine these proposals.

MAINTAINING THE CURRENT PAYGO SYSTEM

The simplest way to ensure financial viability is to increase contributions or reduce expenditures. This is currently the chosen path of the Spanish authorities. Among the potential ways to increase the contribution revenue, the following are often cited:

- Reduce unemployment rates.
- Increase participation rates, particularly for women.
- Increase the payroll tax.

The first two fail to prevent the problem of future insolvency, although they certainly reduce it. Our forecasts would be even more negative if the unemployment rates and female participation rates were to remain at current levels. Raising contribution payroll tax to fund pensions will increase the fiscal burden on labor, making the country less attractive for investments.

The proposals cited to reduce expenditures typically entail a reduction in current benefits and are discussed in detail in Appendix 6.1. These include:

- Increasing the number of years of contribution used to calculate pensions.
- Increasing the penalty for early retirement or shorter contributive history.
- Postponing the retirement age.
- Fostering part-time retirement at ages over 65.

Increasing the number of years used to calculate the pension can reduce expenditure and eliminate some potential distortion that encourage early retirement.

---

[9] Also, our calculations exclude the complements to minimum pensions as a contributive expense.

Increasing the retirement age, or making it more flexible, appears to be a reasonable approach – particularly if one considers that people tend to join the labor force at a later age and retain good health for many years. Some of these measures can be used in conjunction with other reforms, such as our move to a funded DB, to ensure the viability of the pension system. In 2001, the Spanish government reached an initial agreement with unions and employers to allow workers to continue to be active at ages over 65. The government could exempt this employment from social security contributions and have workers receive a pension proportionate to their inactive time (if they remain as part-time workers). The government also proposed to increase the years of contribution used to calculate pension from 15 to 35. This measure was strongly opposed by the unions (Sainz de Baranda 2001). The potential impact of these reforms on the financial outlook of the contributive programs of social security is discussed as part of the evaluation of our reform proposal.

CONVERTING TO A MIXED PAYGO-FUNDED SYSTEM WITH PARTIAL PRIVATIZATION

This position has been defended convincingly by economists at Fundacion de Estudios de Economia Aplicada (FEDEA) – specifically in Jimeno (2000), Herce (2001), and Herce and Alonso Meseguer (2000). Advocates of a mixed system in Spain suggest that the PAYGO portion of the pension scheme can be taken as an investment in human capital to complement the investment in physical capital of the funded portion. We return to these types of proposals in Chapter 8 and demonstrate that the case for mixed systems is predicated on other issues as well.

APPLICABILITY OF OUR REFORM PROPOSAL FOR SPAIN

The confluence of several factors makes our proposed reform attractive for Spain:

- The need for significant reform of the social security system to prevent it from sliding into deep financial crisis in the middle decades of this century. Although this assertion is in itself not devoid of controversy (García 2000), as in the United States, our own projections strongly support it.

- The fact that the Spanish economy has a capital level below the "Golden Rule" and could, thus, improve economic welfare by implementing a funded pension system. The gross national savings rate is about 22 percent in Spain, and the marginal product of capital is higher than the average observed rate of growth.

- The high degree of satisfaction with the current "defined benefit" system. This makes "privatization" of the pension system a very difficult political endeavor.

- The (transitory) current and prospective social security surplus can be used as the "embryo" of the Spanish pension fund (SPF) to facilitate the transition. The government is aiming for fiscal balance in this decade. Therefore, there is limited scope to fund special contributions from the general budget. If needed, other sources, such as surpluses from INEM, can be tapped.

- The Spanish capital markets are relatively underdeveloped. There appears to be ample opportunity for growth in the equity markets and for corporate bonds to disintermediate the banks as sources of corporate financing. The pension fund can foster the development of the Spanish financial markets.

One of the key issues is whether the expected social security surpluses, if invested as proposed here, will be sufficient to finance the deficits projected for the middle years of this century. To explore this, several simulations were run using the baseline scenario described previously. In these simulations, the initial social security surplus was accumulated in an interest-bearing fund through an investment in the markets and a swap between INSS and the treasury. Interest generated by assets constitutes a second source of income for social security. When the system runs a deficit, the assets accumulated in the fund are used to balance the system until the fund is drained. It is assumed that payroll taxes remain at a constant level throughout the period, unless otherwise stated.

The performance of the proposal is reviewed in Sainz de Baranda (2001) under three real return scenarios (3 percent, 5 percent, and 7 percent). Figure 6.7 shows the results of simulations using a real rate of return on the fund's assets of 5 percent. The following three curves are shown in each figure:

- The total accumulated assets on the pension fund as a percent of GDP (right scale).

- The balance of the social security system when the interest on the fund's assets is added to the contributions as a second source of income.

- The financing needs to restore balance.

The need for external financing will be zero for as long as the system runs a surplus or there are sufficient assets in the fund to cover the deficit.

With a 5-percent real rate of return on the fund's assets, the financial health of the system improves. Surpluses continue until about 2035. The fund reaches a maximum of about 50 percent of GDP in the years immediately before 2035. Starting in 2036, assets from the fund are used to finance the current deficit of the social security system. By 2048, the fund is drained.

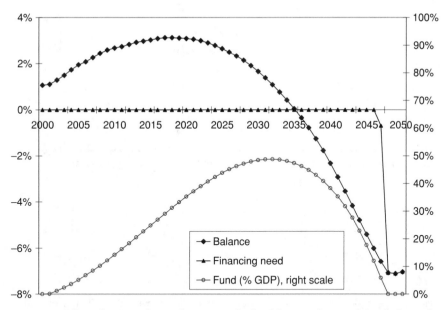

Figure 6.7. Effect of a 5% real rate of return on the funds' assets. Source: Sainz de Baranda (2001).

Appendix 6.4 includes some historical returns on equities and fixed income securities in Spain. As with the U.S. case, a real rate of return of 5 percent is not deemed unreasonable. With this rate, the financial health of the system improves, but its long-term viability is not guaranteed. Sainz de Baranda (2001) has demonstrated that a 7 percent real return completes the transition, but this return assumption may be too aggressive. Additional reforms are required in conjunction with the creation of the SPF and investment in the market.

The following sections consider three key options: (i) flexible retirement over age 64, (ii) extending the contribution years used to calculate the pension from 15 to 35, and (iii) contributing the expected surplus from the Employment Institute (INEM) financed through payroll taxes to the pension fund. We do not consider a one-time increase in contributions, as in Chapter 5, given the already high level of contributions.

Combining an Investment Fund with Additional Reforms

INTRODUCING A FLEXIBLE RETIREMENT AGE. One of the possible alternatives is to combine the creation of the SPF with the implementation of a flexible retirement age. The impact of the flexible retirement age on the finances of the system (without

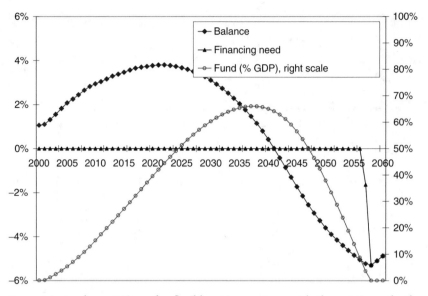

Figure 6.8. Implementation of a flexible retirement age with the creation of a fund. Assumes a 5% real rate of return. Source: Sainz de Baranda (2001).

the creation of the fund) is described in Appendix 6.1. Figure 6.8 shows the results of a simulation in which those projections are combined with the creation of a fund earning a real return of 5 percent.

A combination of these two reforms improves the financial outlook of the system. Surpluses would continue until 2042. The fund would accumulate assets up to a maximum of about 65 percent of GDP around 2040. Starting in 2042, assets from the fund will be used to finance the current deficit of the social security system, which reaches over 4 percent of GDP around 2050. The fund is drained by the year 2055. Therefore, although this solution is a step in the right direction toward solving the pension crisis, it is not sustainable in the long term.

CONTRIBUTING SURPLUSES FROM INEM TO THE PENSION FUND. General scheme wages are taxed, not only to finance the contributive programs of social security but also for programs to fight unemployment and support unemployed workers. These taxes are a total of 8.65 percent of the CRB (7 percent paid by the employer and 1.65 percent by the employee) and fund programs managed by independent entities – primarily by INEM, which receives a payroll tax of 8.25 percent, and by Fondo de Garantia Salarial or Wage Guarantee Fund (FOGASA) with the other 0.4 percent.

Table 6.5 summarizes the financing of INEM over the past few years. The main source of financing is the payroll tax, which represents approximately 2 percent of

TABLE 6.5 Summary of INEM finances as a percentage of GDP

	1997	1998	1999	2000e	2001e
Government transfers	0.33	0.25	0.16	0.05	0.00
External transfers	N/A	N/A	0.12	0.11	0.10
Payroll taxes	1.87	1.88	2.09	1.97	1.95
Total Income	2.32	2.25	2.37	2.13	2.05
Subsidies	1.83	1.71	1.44	1.33	1.28
Employment policies	0.49	0.54	0.82	0.80	0.77
Total Expenses	2.32	2.25	2.26	2.13	2.04

Source: Sainz de Baranda (2001).

GDP and, as part of social security contributions, should remain a stable fraction of GDP as long as the tax rules are not changed. In addition, transfers from the general budget had to be used while the unemployment rate was high to supplement the payroll tax. These transfers have declined progressively and were expected to be zero from 2001. There is also a small transfer from the EU captured as external transfers in Table 6.5.

The main expense is the subsidy paid to unemployed workers. However, this item has declined steadily as a fraction of GDP, for unemployment fell in the past years. The second item relates to programs that actively promote employment, such as training. This item has increased as the reduction in unemployment freed up resources to invest in this type of program.

Beyond 2002, it can safely be assumed that the source of financing will remain approximately 2 percent of GDP for as long as the payroll tax is not changed. However, as the unemployment rate falls from the current level of approximately 11 percent to the steady-state level of 5 percent, the expenses should decrease substantially. We estimate this decrease as follows:

- We fit a straight line to the past subsidy expense (percent of GDP) as a function of the unemployment rate. This line was used to estimate the subsidy as a function of future unemployment rates.

- The expense in programs to promote employment per unemployed worker is maintained constant at the 2001 level throughout the projection period (in real terms).

With these simple assumptions, we can estimate the surplus of INEM. Figure 6.9 shows the results. There is a rapid increase in the surplus up to 1 percent of GDP around 2009, when "full employment" is reached. The surplus increases slightly from there, up to almost 1.2 percent of GDP, by 2050.

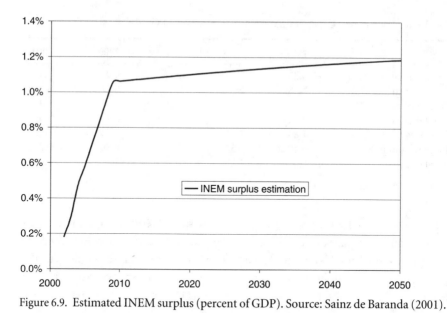

Figure 6.9. Estimated INEM surplus (percent of GDP). Source: Sainz de Baranda (2001).

As the economy approaches full employment, expenses in unemployment-related programs should decline sharply. One alternative would be to cut the payroll tax, which is clearly desirable. However, the next simulations assume that the payroll tax is not cut initially but rather that the INEM surplus is contributed to the pension fund.

Two simulations were conducted. In the first, the INEM surplus is added to the pension fund until 2015. Subsequent surpluses in INEM would be trimmed through payroll tax cuts. In the second, the surplus continues to be added to the fund until 2060, and after that year the payroll tax is cut. Figures 6.10 and 6.11 illustrate these simulations, respectively. When the contributions from the INEM surplus are stopped in 2015, the social security system runs current deficits starting around 2040, which reach 6 percent of GDP in 2055. At about the same time, the fund is drained. If the INEM surplus contributions are kept up to 2060 as in Figure 6.11, there is a current surplus for the period and the fund grows to about 120 percent of GDP. Under these circumstances, the system is financially viable.

It would appear that adding the INEM surplus to the pension fund for an extended period could prevent the anticipated financial crisis of the social security system. It also means postponing a reduction in the very high payroll tax for decades. The effectiveness of this reform is also strongly dependent on the rapid reduction of unemployment to generate a significant surplus in INEM. However, research shows

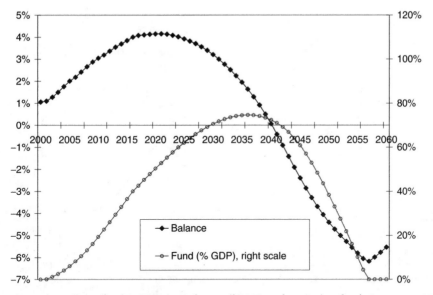

Figure 6.10. Contributing INEM surplus until 2015 to the pension fund. Assumes a 5% real rate of return. Source: Sainz de Baranda (2001).

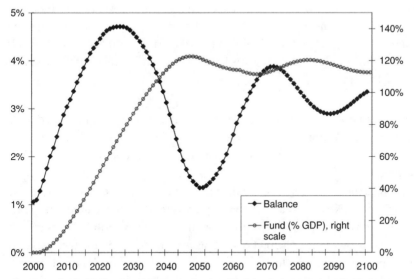

Figure 6.11. Contributing INEM surplus until 2060 to the pension fund. Assumes a 5% real rate of return. Source: Sainz de Baranda (2001).

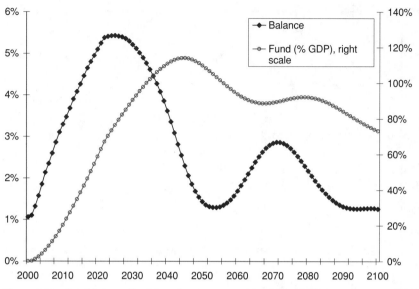

Figure 6.12. Combining a flexible retirement age with adding INEM surpluses until 2021. Assumes a 5% real rate of return. Source: Sainz de Baranda (2001).

that citizens are willing to use existing taxes to fund such programs rather than being refunded these monies only to be taxed later (Modigliani and Modigliani 1987).

It should also be noted that, in this simulation and all other simulations the maximum fund-to-GDP ratio does not occur in the year the surplus (flow) is zero. It occurs when the surplus-to-existing-stock ratio is equal to the growth of the economy in nominal terms.

FLEXIBLE RETIREMENT AGE AND CONTRIBUTING INEM SURPLUSES TO THE PENSION FUND. A more robust solution can be obtained by combining the introduction of flexible retirement policies with the contribution of INEM surpluses to the fund.

Figure 6.12 shows an additional simulation in which the introduction of a flexible retirement policy is assumed and INEM surpluses are added to the fund until 2021. The system runs current surpluses throughout the projection period. This approach permits a reduction in the payroll tax starting around 2020 (because the balance is positive and stays positive) while ensuring the financial viability of the system.

A possible second path would be to continue INEM surplus contributions to the fund. This would keep the current surpluses in the social security system and would build the fund to a critical level, which would allow larger payroll tax cuts at

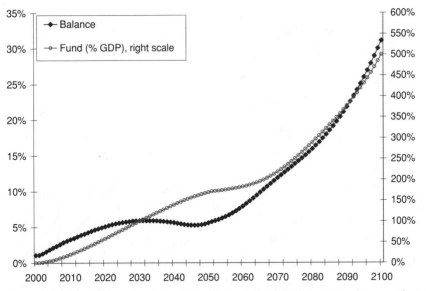

Figure 6.13. Combining a flexible retirement age with adding INEM surpluses until 2050. Assumes a 5% real rate of return. Source: Sainz de Baranda (2001).

a later date. Figure 6.13 illustrates this scenario with INEM surpluses added to the fund until 2050. The fund approaches 200 percent of GDP by 2050 and continues to grow beyond that point. The system shows increasing current surpluses beyond 2050. Under this scenario, a large payroll tax cut can be implemented without compromising the financial viability of the system. We return to this point in the section on potential payroll tax cuts.

EXTENDING CONTRIBUTION YEARS USED TO CALCULATE PENSION. Another reform package could be structured to combine the creation of the pension fund with an extension of the number of contribution years used to calculate the pension benefit from 15 to 35 years. This runs the risk of reducing the overall pension.

Figure 6.14 shows an additional simulation that combines these two reforms. The real return on the pension fund is assumed to be 5 percent. The system runs current surpluses until 2045. Beyond that year, current deficits drain the fund until its depletion around 2070. However, improving the finances of the system is better than combining the creation of the fund with a flexible retirement age policy (Figure 6.8). Given our previous simulations, it is obvious that adding INEM surpluses to the fund for a period of time can ensure the financial viability of the system. However, the pension reduction is meaningful (Figure A6.1.2).

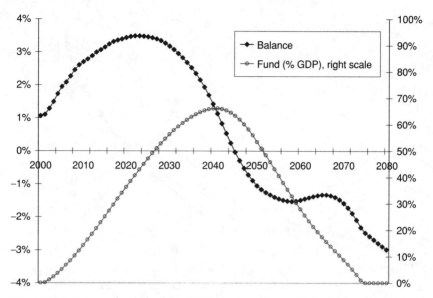

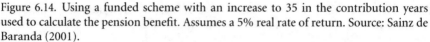

Figure 6.14. Using a funded scheme with an increase to 35 in the contribution years used to calculate the pension benefit. Assumes a 5% real rate of return. Source: Sainz de Baranda (2001).

One additional simulation, shown in Figure 6.15, includes the following combination of reforms:

- Creation of a pension fund earning a real return of 5 percent.
- Contributing social security surpluses and INEM surpluses until 2025 to the fund.
- Flexible retirement age.
- Extending the calculation period for the PRB to 35 years but changing the pension calculation method so the decline in the effective replacement rate is partially mitigated.

With this combination, not only are payroll taxes cut in 2025 to trim the surplus in INEM, but the pension fund also continues to grow and the system shows steady surpluses, which increase rapidly after 2050. Therefore, additional payroll tax cuts can be implemented. The following section explores possible paths for payroll tax cuts under some of the scenarios presented earlier.

Potential Paths for Payroll Tax Cuts

Of all the potential reforms explored in the previous sections, the most promising includes a combination of three key issues:

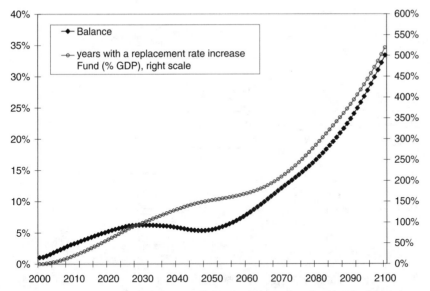

Figure 6.15. Using a funded scheme (including INEM surpluses) with a flexible retirement age and longer required participation. Assumes a 5% real rate of return. Source: Sainz de Baranda (2001).

1. Creation of an SPF with an investment policy similar to that recommended in Chapter 5, combined with the swap instrument with a 5 percent real guaranteed rate. Current and future social security surpluses will be transferred to the fund.
2. Contribution of prospective surpluses from INEM to the fund – at least for a transitory period.
3. Reforms in pension calculation, such as the implementation of a more flexible retirement age policy aimed at promoting later retirement and extending the years used to calculate the base pension from 15 to 35 years. The latter would result in a significant decrease in pensions, which could be partly compensated for by increasing the pension in relation to the PRB.

In Figure 6.15, payroll tax cuts are postponed (though achieved through a reduction in the unemployment tax post-2025), and the fund grows in such a way that deeper cuts can be realized. However, the payroll tax cuts are small because INEM contributions are relatively small. As the previous chapter highlighted, this is one of the trade-offs faced in deciding the "right size" of the fund. Cutting payroll taxes early will result in a smaller fund (further limiting payroll tax cuts), in a longer transition, or both, whereas postponing the payroll tax cut can have the opposite long-term effect. Moreover, a smaller fund may be beneficial if capital markets are impacted.

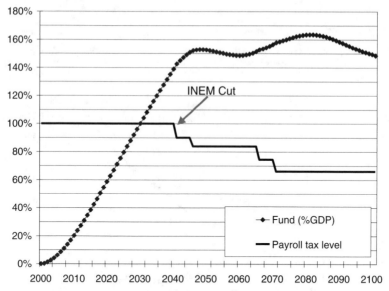

Figure 6.16. Potential path for payroll tax level with the implementation of a flexible retirement age and adding INEM surpluses until 2040. Source: Sainz de Baranda (2001).

Figure 6.16 illustrates a potential path for the payroll tax for the baseline demographic scenario and the introduction of the combination of reforms described at the beginning of this section with the exception of extending the number of years used to calculate the PRB. The cuts are aimed at keeping the fund's assets around 150 percent of GDP.

The "payroll tax level" curve in Figure 6.16 shows the evolution of the required payroll tax in relation to current levels. Both the INEM (unemployment) and the social security portions of the payroll tax were used to calculate this ratio. That is, cuts in the unemployment or social security portions of the payroll tax result in a drop in the "payroll tax level" curve.

The tax remains unchanged until 2040 when the first cut is introduced to reflect the lower INEM expenses (in other words, the INEM surplus is no longer added to the pension fund). By implementing a late cut, the fund grows to around 150 percent of GDP, and subsequent cuts are possible. The payroll tax level can be reduced later on by as much as 33 percent. As indicated in Chapter 5, this introduces intergenerational equity issues.

Figure 6.17 extends Figure 6.16 and, in addition, the years to calculate the PRB are extended from 15 to 35, with an increase in the pension-to-PRB ratio to compensate partially for the effective decrease in the replacement rate. Payroll tax cuts can start earlier than in the previous case and can be deeper given the lower expenses of the

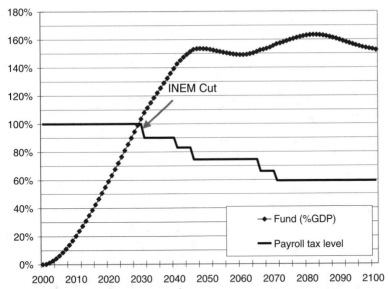

Figure 6.17. Potential path for payroll tax level for the case illustrated in Figure 6.15. Source: Sainz de Baranda (2001).

pension system that result from the extension in the number of years used to calculate the PRB. Payroll taxes are reduced by as much as 40 percent by the end of the projected period. This has important implications for the competitiveness of Spain.

Finally, Figure 6.18 shows an alternative path for the same reform package in which the first payroll tax cuts are implemented earlier and the fund is kept at a smaller size. As expected, this limits the possibility of deeper tax cuts later.

As explained in Chapter 5, each of these scenarios raises issues relating to inter-generational equity, which need to be addressed by the reformers.

RESULTS OF DIFFERENT PROPOSALS

The financial impact of the various reform options described in this section is summarized to emphasize the implications for the payroll tax borne by the workers. The analysis focuses on 3 specific years: 2001 and 2050, which represents the worst period projected in our models; and 2085, which is more representative of a potential long-run steady state. The figures are presented as a percentage of wages and not GDP. Wages are approximately 50 percent of GDP in the national accounts. This ratio remains constant in our model, for we assume that salaries grow at the rate of productivity growth. Therefore, the conversion to ratios relative to GDP is achieved simply by multiplying these ratios by two.

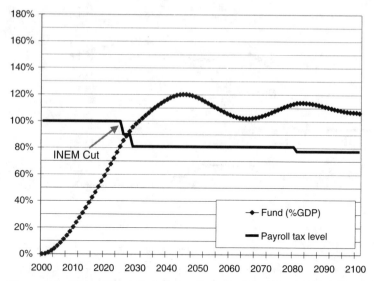

Figure 6.18. Alternative path for payroll tax level for the case illustrated in Figure 6.15.
Source: Sainz de Baranda (2001).

The income and expenses of the social security and INEM programs are merged
in this section, giving a fuller representation of the potential impact of the increase
in expenses in the contributive programs of social security and the decrease expected
in unemployment programs. The expenses for contributive programs in the social
security system and for INEM programs (unemployment subsidies and programs to
foster employability) are lumped together. Income is separated into two key sources:
contributions (payroll taxes) and the return on the SPF's assets, which will be nonzero
only for reform packages that include the creation of the pension fund.

Reform options have been grouped into six possibilities:

A. Baseline scenario in which no reform is implemented. The population and
   macroeconomic variables follow our baseline paths.
B. Option A plus the introduction of a flexible retirement age.
C. Option B plus extending the number of years used to calculate the PRB from 15
   years to 35 years. This reform is coupled with a change in the pension-to-PRB
   ratio to compensate partially for the effective decrease in the replacement rate.
   This is done in such a way that the decline in the effective replacement rate is
   gradual.
D. Option B plus creating a pension fund. Current and future surpluses from
   the social security system are contributed to the SPF together with the INEM

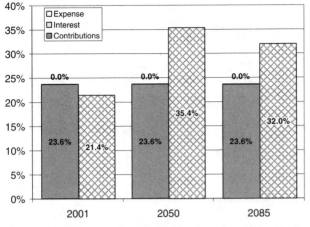

Figure 6.19. Summary financial projections for reform Option A (in percent of wages). Source: Sainz de Baranda (2001).

surpluses until 2040. Payroll tax cuts are aimed at keeping the fund's assets at around 1.5 times of GDP. (This is demonstrated in Figure 6.16.)

E. Option C plus creating a pension fund. Current and future surpluses from the social security system are contributed to the fund together with the INEM surpluses until 2030. Payroll tax cuts are aimed at keeping the fund's assets at around 1.5 times of GDP. (This is demonstrated in Figure 6.17.)

F. Option E plus introducing earlier payroll tax cuts that lead to a smaller fund with assets of around 100 percent of GDP. (This is demonstrated in Figure 6.18.)

Figure 6.19 summarizes the projections for Option A (interest is 0 percent). The small surpluses of approximately 2.2 percent of wages in 2001 (note that this does not include the complements for minimum pensions as a contributive expense in our calculations) turn into a large deficit of 11.8 percent of wages by 2050. The deficit is still large (8.4 percent of wages) in 2085. As discussed earlier, given the difficulty in running large fiscal deficits within the EMU, these deficits would likely be trimmed by decreasing pensions because increasing the payroll tax over the high current level would harm the competitiveness of the country.

Figure 6.20 presents a similar projection for reform Option B. The introduction of the flexible retirement package reduces contributions slightly because workers aged 65 and over who choose to stay in the labor force are exempt from contributions. However, the impact on expenses is even higher because the pension payments are also postponed. Overall, this reasonable reform improves the financial outlook of

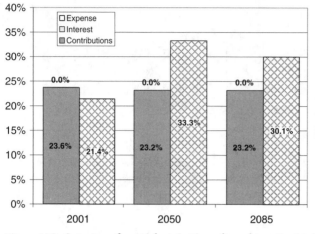

Figure 6.20. Summary financial projections for reform Option B (in percent of wages). Source: Sainz de Baranda (2001).

the system slightly but does not ensure its viability. Large deficits (about 10 percent of wages) are still anticipated in the year 2050.

As illustrated in Figure 6.21 for reform Option C, the effect of adding the extension in the period used to calculate the PRB (from 15 years to 35 years) is that the contributions are unaltered from Option B, whereas the expenses drop further. However, even these two reforms combined fail to ensure the viability of the system. Rather large deficits (8 percent of wages) are still projected for 2050. It should also

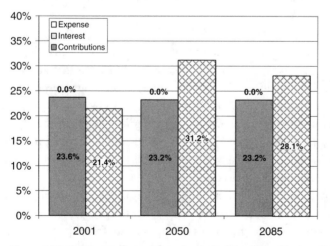

Figure 6.21. Summary financial projections for reform Option C (in percent of wages). Source: Sainz de Baranda (2001).

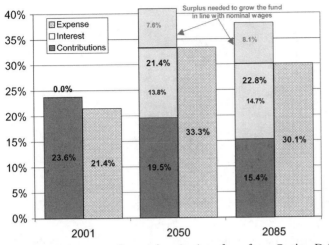

Figure 6.22. Summary financial projections for reform Option D (in percent of wages). Source: Sainz de Baranda (2001).

be noted that this reform may be more difficult to implement politically, for it can be perceived as an effective cut in the pension benefit.

Figures 6.22 and 6.23 present the projections for reform Options D and E, respectively. Both include the introduction of a pension fund (with a 5-percent real rate of return), which can grow to around 150 percent of GDP, or three times that of wages. The situation changes dramatically. The interest earned by the SPF becomes

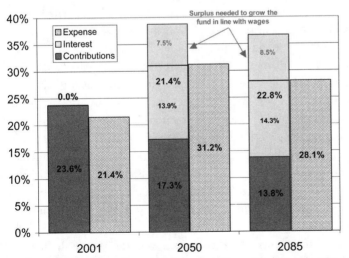

Figure 6.23. Summary financial projections for reform Option E (in percent of wages). Source: Sainz de Baranda (2001).

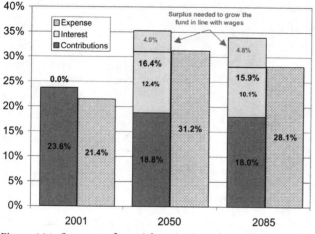

Figure 6.24. Summary financial projections for reform Option F (in percent of wages). Source: Sainz de Baranda (2001).

the larger source of income and allows for the progressive reduction in the payroll tax, as reflected by a declining contribution income. The system maintains current surpluses that are needed to keep the fund growing in line with nominal GDP (and wages). Also note that this is achieved without reducing the expenses relative to options B and C, respectively. Reform Option E, which includes extending the number of years used to calculate PRB, and therefore a reduction in expenses, permits the implementation of earlier and deeper payroll tax cuts relative to reform option D.

Finally, Figure 6.24 presents similar projections for reform package F. The expenses do not change relative to package E. However, for this package, earlier payroll tax cuts are implemented to maintain the fund at a lower level (100 to 120 percent of GDP or double that of wages). As a result, the interest income is smaller and payroll tax cuts that can be realized later are not as deep, as shown by the larger weight of the contribution income as a percentage of wages. Again, the surpluses are needed to keep the fund growing approximately with nominal GDP and wages.

Table 6.6 summarizes the payroll tax (as a percentage of wages) required to keep the system balanced under the different reform scenarios for the years 2050 and 2085. Note that the current payroll tax collections are about 23.6 percent of wages. Without reforms, the tax on wages required to maintain the current level of benefits would have to increase by more than 12 percent in 2050. The other option would be to cut pensions to reduce expenses. The next two sets of reform options in Table 6.6 are modifications of the current PAYGO system and can reduce the required contributions in 2050 by about 2 to 4 percent of wages by reducing expenditures. The last three reform packages in Table 6.6 include the creation of a pension fund

TABLE 6.6 Impact of the different reforms on the payroll tax (as a percent of wages)

Reform package	2050	2085	Comment
A- No reform	35.4%	32.0%	Baseline
B- Flexible retirement	33.3%	30.1%	Reduction in expenses by postponing some pension payments
C- Option B plus using 35 years to calculate pension (plus adjusting pensions)	31.2%	28.1%	Further reduction in expenses by decreasing the replacement rates for some pensions
D- Option B plus creating a fund	19.5%	15.4%	The interest from the fund permits an additional large decrease over and above reform package B
E- Option C plus creating a fund	17.3%	13.8%	The interest from the fund permits an additional large decrease over and above reform package C
F- Option E but with earlier cuts and a smaller fund	18.8%	18.0%	The interest from the fund permits a decrease over and above reform package C but not as large as in the previous package because of the smaller size of the fund

Source: Sainz de Baranda (2001).

to which current and future surpluses of social security and INEM would be added and invested. For reform packages D and E, the fund grows to approximately 150 percent of GDP (or thrice that of wages). The returns from this fund permit a large additional drop in the payroll tax level. This drop is about 14 percent of wages by 2050 (over and above the reductions resulting from PAYGO reforms), and over the long run (2085) these packages can reduce the payroll tax level to less than half that required to balance the system without reform.

As suggested in Chapter 5, we demonstrate the impact of earlier payroll tax cuts. This limits the growth of the fund to about double that of wages. As a result, the interest income is lower and the reduction in payroll taxes that can be realized later on is limited when compared with Option E. The cuts can be about 16.6 percent of wages by 2050 and 14 percent by 2085. Of these cuts, 4 percent can be attributed to the reform of the PAYGO rules and the rest to the interest income provided by the fund.

SUMMARY

With the exception of 3 years in the mid-1990s, the contributive segment of the social security system in Spain has enjoyed increasing surpluses – an outcome of the expansive economic cycle of the second half of the 1990s and implementation of some of the reforms after the Pacto de Toledo.

The current PAYGO system will run small current surpluses over the next two decades, according to our baseline simulations, and will begin to generate increasing current deficits, which peak at about 7 percent of GDP in 2045. This change will be driven mainly by demographic factors. In particular, the old-age dependency ratio will more than double by 2045 as a result of increased life expectancy and the dramatic reduction in fertility rates experienced in Spain since 1975.

Left unchanged, demographic factors will result in an alarming financial deterioration of the contributive portion of the social security system beyond 2020. The restriction on fiscal deficits imposed by the European Monetary Union will make it very difficult to finance a deficit of about 7 percent of GDP, if nothing is done before 2020, the most likely consequence will be a reduction in benefits or an increase in the payroll tax. Given the already high payroll tax, the most likely adjustment mechanism will be a reduction in benefits to the pensioner population, which is clearly an undesirable scenario – particularly for Spaniards currently under 40.

Despite this somewhat gloomy outlook, Spain is in a relatively advantageous position compared with other Western European countries because its baby boom occurred later. Therefore, the deterioration in the old-age dependency ratio will also occur later. This is the key to the expected surpluses in social security over the next two decades, which in turn opens a window of opportunity for social security reform. The longer the delay, the greater the cost of reform.

A permanent solution for the prospective financial problems of the Spanish social security lies in implementing one or a combination of the following three proposals:

- The creation of a Spanish pension fund (SPF) with a formal investment policy and a swap contract. The current and future surpluses of social security – including the complements for minimum pensions currently paid out of contributions – will be transferred to this fund. The return on the fund would complement the payroll tax as a second major source of income for social security.

- The contribution of prospective surpluses from INEM to the fund, at least for a transitory period. For these to be significant, unemployment would have to fall from its current level of around 15 percent to a more reasonable level of around 5 percent. Labor market reforms and the expected shortage of working age people in upcoming cohorts would contribute to a reduction in the unemployment rate.

- Reforms in the pension-calculating procedures would foster participation in the labor force, reduce pension costs, and eliminate some of the distortions introduced by the current system. Two possibilities are implementing a more flexible retirement age policy aimed at promoting later, not earlier, retirement and extending the years used to calculate the base pension from 15 years to 35 years. The latter would result in a larger decrease in pension expenses but would effectively entail a decrease in retirement pension benefits of over 20 percent. Our simulations suggest that this last reform is unnecessary if the other three are implemented. Alternatively, if the change in years for benefit calculations is implemented, the reduction in benefits could be partially compensated by changing the rules used to calculate the pension. Should an extension in the calculation years be introduced, it could be accompanied by a further reduction in the payroll tax.

This reform would effectively turn the public pension system in Spain into a mixed PAYGO-funded DB system that would combine several advantages of PAYGO and funded systems:

- Lower payroll tax for the same benefits. Our estimates suggest a long-term reduction in the payroll tax of about 30 to 40 percent relative to current levels. This, in turn, is expected to reduce some of the labor market distortions induced by high payroll taxes.

- A savings rate increase that would result in higher output per capita and economic welfare (consumption per capita).

- Decreased sensitivity of the financial health of the pension system to demographic and productivity changes.

- Continuation of current redistribution mechanisms under the PAYGO DB scheme.

- Preservation of the "defined benefit" character, thus limiting individual risk.

- Low administration costs compared with systems based on individual accounts.

- Strengthening of local financial markets.

The transition cost would be borne by current workers, and be limited to delaying reductions in the payroll tax that could be implemented immediately and in the near future, to balance the social security and INEM budgets. The benefits of the transition would also accrue to current workers in the form of a guarantee that their retirement benefits would not be reduced. Unless reform is undertaken, a reduction in retirement benefits is highly likely. Future generations would also benefit from the reform because equivalent pension benefits would accrue to them with a lower payroll tax.

One of the key parameters yet to be determined is the optimum size of the fund. A fund that is too large could reduce the return on capital and increase the marginal product of labor and, thus, wages. This, in turn, would decrease the welfare enhancement to be derived from the funded system and would favor a PAYGO scheme. Our recommendation is to create the fund and, as it grows, assess its effect on the Spanish economy, return on capital, financial markets, wages, and corporate governance. The decision on the "right size" of the fund can be made more intelligently based on this impact. The two general options are as follows:

- Target a large fund, of about 150 percent of GDP, so as to permit a large cut in payroll taxes. These would come at the expense of a delay in potential cuts made possible by declining unemployment. This means creating a mixed system with a larger funded component.

- Limit the fund to about 100 percent of GDP or lower mainly as a means of getting past the peak in pension expenses (expected around 2045 as a result of the peculiar demographics of Spain) without raising the payroll tax or decreasing the benefits. This means creating a mixed system with a larger PAYGO component.

Should the creation of a large fund in Spain reduce the return on capital significantly, the option would be to invest the SPF's assets abroad. Some investment abroad is recommended for portfolio diversification and because savings should earn a global return on capital. It also makes sense to secure future pensions through claims on assets in geographical areas with the potential (labor) to see higher rates of growth than Spain, where labor shortages may restrict output growth in the next decade. Finally, it is worth noting, although the forecasts presented in this chapter foresee no financial problems with social security in the next two decades, the window of opportunity to implement these permanent solutions will close soon. Current surpluses, and those expected in the near future, are needed as the foundation for the pension fund in order to generate the second source of income (besides contributions) that will make the system financially viable without increasing payroll taxes or cutting benefits. Moreover, the longer the delay, the greater the cost.

APPENDIX 6.1. Modification of the PAYGO Rules

IMPLEMENTING A MORE FLEXIBLE RETIREMENT AGE POLICY

There appears to be ample consensus among employers, workers, and the government about the desirability of implementing a more flexible retirement age policy. We do not have the details of the policy; however, the press has published some of the guidelines. To estimate the impact of this policy on the finances of the social security system, we have made the following assumptions:

- Contributions remain unchanged from the baseline scenario, because those who choose to continue in the labor force after 65 will be exempt from contributing.

- The participation rate at ages 65–69 is half of that observed at 64 (50 percent of the people active at 64 choose to retire).

- Those who choose to continue in the labor force do so on a part-time basis, devoting only 50 percent of their time to work (50-percent occupation rate).

- The pension paid to active workers of ages 65–69 is proportionate to what they would have received had they retired at 65 multiplied by (1 minus the occupation rate). The pension received at age 70 and over is not affected.

The result is an increase in the total available labor force, which has a positive impact on GDP and reduces the pensions paid to those workers ages 65–69 who remain active. Table A6.1.1 summarizes the results.

This estimate suggests such a policy would have a positive effect on the finances of the social security system. This effect grows during the projected period – from 0.2 percent of GDP in 2010 to almost 1 percent of GDP around 2045 – but the overall trend towards large deficits near the end of the projection period is not reversed. This policy, although clearly a step in the right direction, will by itself be insufficient to ensure the financial viability of the social security system.

Note that the projection period for this and other simulations in this section was extended beyond 2050 using the same demographic and macroeconomic criteria used before 2050. The confidence in the projections beyond 2050 is even lower than those before 2050. However, the extended projections will be useful for the discussions.

EXTENDING THE CONTRIBUTION YEARS USED TO CALCULATE THE PENSION

Another proposal currently under debate is to extend the number of years used to calculate the pension from the current 15 years to 35 years. The supporters of this reform typically argue that indexing the pension to the complete contributive history of the pensioner is a fairer and more logical thing to do and that it would eliminate the incentive to report lower salaries in earlier years and higher salaries closer to the retirement age. This is implicit in our recommendation in the Ideal Model (Chapter 2). However, we would guarantee a return on all contributions if our recommendation were adopted, whereas the traditional defined benefit formula penalizes the worker.

TABLE A6.1.1 Financial Projections. Estimations with flexible retirement age (percent of GDP)

Year	Contrib.	Permanent Disability	Retirement	Spouse	Children	Temp. disability	Mat. leave	Manag.	Comp. minimum	Total expense	Balance
2000	9.8	1.00	5.6	1.5	0.12	0.61	0.12	0.34	0.62	8.8	1.1
2005	9.8	1.07	4.9	1.5	0.09	0.58	0.14	0.32	0.48	8.1	1.7
2010	9.8	1.11	4.6	1.5	0.08	0.55	0.14	0.30	0.36	7.9	1.9
2015	9.7	1.13	4.7	1.5	0.07	0.53	0.13	0.30	0.27	8.2	1.6
2020	9.7	1.14	5.1	1.6	0.08	0.52	0.11	0.31	0.18	8.7	1.0
2025	9.7	1.10	5.9	1.6	0.08	0.51	0.10	0.32	0.11	9.6	0.1
2030	9.6	1.02	7.0	1.8	0.07	0.50	0.10	0.34	0.07	10.7	−1.1
2035	9.6	0.97	8.2	2.0	0.07	0.49	0.10	0.37	0.04	12.1	−2.5
2040	9.6	0.91	9.5	2.2	0.06	0.48	0.10	0.40	0.02	13.7	−4.1
2045	9.6	0.82	10.9	2.4	0.07	0.48	0.10	0.43	0.01	15.2	−5.7
2050	9.6	0.78	11.4	2.6	0.07	0.47	0.09	0.44	0.00	15.9	−6.3

Contrib. = contribution; Temp. = temporary; Mat. = maternity; Manag. = management cost; Comp. = compensation.

Source: Sainz de Baranda (2001).

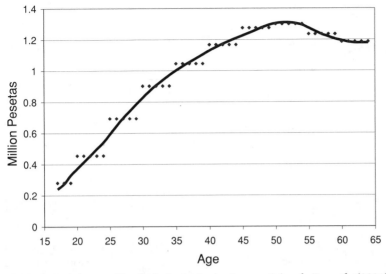

Figure A6.1.1. Age profile of salaries in Spain. Source: Sainz de Baranda (2001).

Opposition to the measure is likely to stem from the fact that this policy represents a significant decrease in average benefits.

To estimate the financial impact of this reform on the social security system, we proceeded as follows:

- We estimated the changes of the salary levels with age using data published by INE (www.ine.es). The changes are illustrated in Figure A6.1.1.

- We assumed the shape of this distribution to be constant. That is, salaries increase in real terms at the rate of productivity growth across the age spectrum.

- We increased the number of contributive years used to calculate the base pension by 1 year for the 35 years from 2006 to 2025. It was kept constant beyond that point.

- We defined the replacement rate as the ratio between the last salary and the first pension. This rate was estimated as follows:

$$R_r^i = \frac{S^i + S^{i-1} + \sum_{j=i-2}^{n} S^j \frac{CPI^{i-2}}{CPI^j}}{nS^i}, \tag{A6.1.1}$$

where R_r^i is the replacement rate for those retired in year i, S^i is the salary in year i, and n is the number of years used to calculate the pension. The salaries, beginning with year three and earlier, are adjusted for inflation (CPI). The results

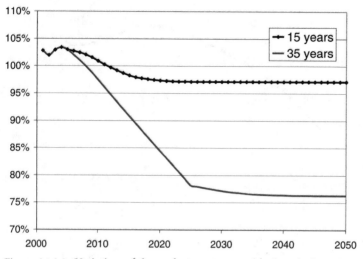

Figure A6.1.2. Variation of the replacement rate with time (using 15 years to calculate the pension benefit and changing to 35 years starting in 2006). Source: Sainz de Baranda (2001).

for the replacement rates, with the current policy of 15 years maintained and a gradual increase to 35 starting in 2006, are reported in Figure A6.1.2. Historical data for inflation and wage increase are used up to 2000 and the projections from our baseline scenario beyond that time.

- The reduction in retirement pensions triggers a decline in the surviving spouse pensions derived from pensioners. Our model is adjusted to prevent this. In effect, this is equivalent to increasing the replacement rate for surviving spouse pensions from 45 percent today to about 60 percent by 2035 to maintain the same coverage for widows and widowers as they would have had with a 15-year calculation base for the pension.

Figure A6.1.3 shows the impact of this reform on the finances of social security over the projection period.

The impact of an increase in the contribution years used for the calculation of the retirement pension is substantial – particularly after 2025, when the transition is complete. Although this reform alone will be insufficient to ensure the financial viability of the pension system, it would significantly reduce the projected deficits by roughly 2 percent of GDP beyond 2045.

However, this reform entails a substantial cut in benefits of about 20 percent compared with the current calculation method. Therefore, it may be politically difficult to implement – particularly while the system is running surpluses.

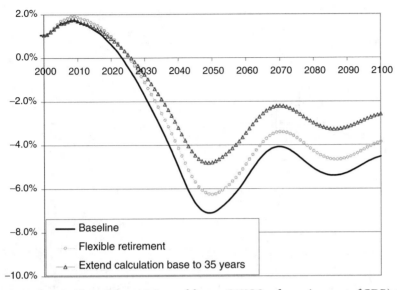

Figure A6.1.3. Financial projections of the two PAYGO reforms (percent of GDP). Source: Sainz de Baranda (2001).

On the positive side, the increase in the number of years used to calculate the PRB improves the equity of the system. Workers who become unemployed toward the end of their careers will see a smaller effect on their pensions because their active years have a higher weight in the PRB. Also, highly educated (and paid) workers tend to see a steeper increase in their salaries with increasing experience than their less skilled counterparts. Therefore, the extension of the calculation period will affect the higher paid workers the most. An alternative could be to extend the number of years used to calculate the PRB and thus to make the system more equitable and to increase the replacement rate to partially compensate for the decrease resulting from such an extension.

APPENDIX 6.2. The Real Rate of Return Earned by the SPF

A key factor in the success of the proposed reforms is to achieve a "good" return on the investment of the fund's assets. We have used a real rate of return of 5 percent for the simulations described in this chapter. This is slightly lower than the rate of 5.2 percent used in Chapter 5 for the United States. This appendix offers some data about the historical performance of the Spanish stock exchange as well as the returns on government and corporate debt.

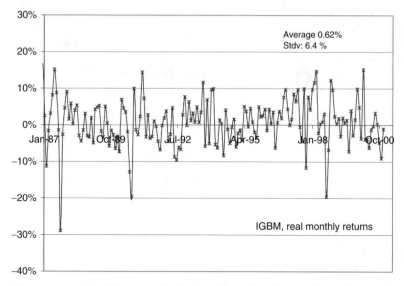

Figure A6.2.1. Monthly returns in the Spanish stock exchange adjusted by the CPI change. Source: Sainz de Baranda (2001).

STOCK MARKET

Figure A6.2.1 shows the monthly changes for Spain's broad index, the Indice General de la Bolsa de Madrid (IGBM), adjusted for changes in the CPI over the same month. The average real return in the last 14 years has been 0.62 percent per month, which would compound to a yearly real return of 7.71 percent.

GOVERNMENT DEBT

Figure A6.2.2 shows the return on the 10-year "risk-free" government bond. Real returns have fallen from levels typically between 4 and 6 percent before 1997 to below 2 percent in 2000. The low returns in the last year of this figure may be a result of the increase in inflation in 2000. This rate is unlikely to be sustainable within the EMU. Figure A6.2.3 compares the real return on Spanish 10-year bonds and German long-term public debt. The real return on the German bond is higher (about 3 percent). This supports the hypothesis that the real returns on the Spanish bond in 2000 were abnormally low, for the spread in government securities has typically favored Germany. It can be reasonable to expect a real rate of return of about 2.5–3 percent in the "risk-free" government debt market.

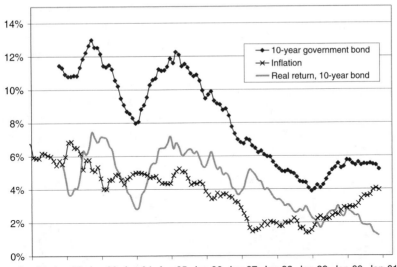

Figure A6.2.2. Return on government debt in the secondary markets. Source: Sainz de Baranda (2001).

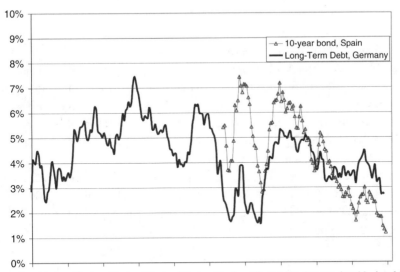

Figure A6.2.3. Real returns for Spanish and German government bonds. Source: Sainz de Baranda (2001).

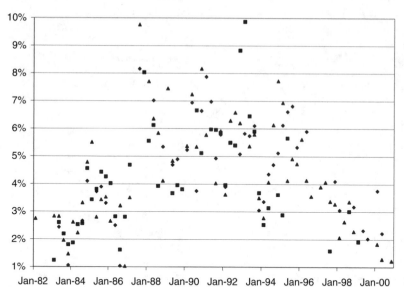

Figure A6.2.4. Real returns on Spanish corporate bonds. Source: Sainz de Baranda (2001).

CORPORATE DEBT

The market for corporate fixed income securities is very underdeveloped in Spain. In 1999, less than 10 percent of corporate financing took the form of corporate bonds in Spain compared with 30 percent in the United States. Figure A6.2.4 shows the available data on Spanish corporate bond returns (from www.ine.es). The real returns follow a pattern somewhat similar to that of public debt and have declined significantly in recent years. It is hard to get a good read on the trends of corporate bond returns from the data in Figure A6.2.4; however, it is reasonable to expect a spread over the "risk free" government bonds. Therefore, a real return of 3 percent on fixed income securities is not unreasonable.

A real return of 7 percent on equities and 7 percent on debt is precisely what was used in Chapter 5 to conclude that the pretax return on capital in the United States is 8 to 8.5 percent. This would leave a spread of 3 to 3.5 percent to reward the guarantor of a real return of 5 percent.

7

The "Two-Pension Fund" Theorem

HELPING RETIREES ACHIEVE RETIREMENT OBJECTIVES

The entire pension reform debate and the previous chapters have focused on whether countries that move to funding pension systems should adopt defined benefit (DB) or defined contribution (DC) plans, whether arrangements should be based on individual accounts or pooled arrangements, whether assets should be publicly or privately managed, and whether asset management fees are appropriate or too high. In addition, in the previous chapters we have discussed and debated whether pension systems should be fully funded or partially funded and whether the transition cost is worth bearing and, if so, who should bear it. However, little has been done to help individuals in DC plans, or governments with DB plans, invest monies (in a macro sense) to achieve retirement goals.[1]

Experts urge investors to consider portfolios that (i) are well-diversified, (ii) follow some pattern of asset-risk allocation to reflect the aging of the individual (so-called life-cycle funds), and (iii) choose asset-risk allocations based on an asset-liability analysis (Muralidhar 2001). Regulators in those developing countries where pension reform has leaned toward privately managed DC accounts, have been under pressure to approve equity (domestic or international) investments to allow investors to diversify their portfolios. Even in Japan, regulators had imposed constraints on how funds can be invested (e.g., a minimum of 50 percent in government bonds). These restrictions are now being targeted as the reason for the severe underfunding of corporate pension plans in Japan. The goal behind these recommendations is to

---

[1] For example, Leibowitz et al. (2002) have demonstrated how participants can measure their progress if the asset-to-salary ratio is below an optimal path. However, this chapter is unable to provide individuals with recommendations on how they should alter their contribution or investment policy on a dynamic basis. See Usuki (2002) for a good overview of recommendations for Japan.

allow diverse groups of individuals achieve their varied retirement objectives with the least possible risk.

In classic portfolio management, individuals are told to hold a proportion of their wealth in risk-free (with or without leverage) and risky assets to achieve their respective investment objectives. This simple paradigm is independent of whether these products are provided through external fund managers or not and is called the Two-Fund Separation theorem. Unfortunately, the pension reform debate has been so caught up in topics related to external fund management that little has been done to examine whether similar risk-free and risky "assets" are available in the pension fund world. Instead, the focus of the debate has been on PAYGO versus funding or DB versus DC but not on the pension choices that individuals require to achieve their varied retirement objectives. For example, two individuals with identical salary and contribution histories may have widely divergent objectives for the annuity or the risk they are willing to bear. How are they to achieve their objectives? Clearly, life-cycle funds are not useful in such a situation.

This chapter seeks to bridge the gap between theory and practice and proposes a radical direction for helping individuals achieve retirement security. We attempt to provide a high-level framework to achieve this goal and then demonstrate which pension systems are needed and what investment products must be developed to facilitate this process.

We argue that the likelihood of pension reform success in developed and developing countries can be improved if (a) individuals have access to DB and DC plans, and (b) even if DB plans are not available, that guaranteed real rate of return products (GRRPs) are made available to allow DC plans to mimic DB outcomes. The time horizon of these guarantees is a key issue, but we demonstrate some interesting results using a simple model. It is inappropriate to expose an individual participant's pension annuities to the vagaries of "diversified portfolios." Hence, new products need to be developed.[2] Some have argued for the introduction of international pension swaps (e.g., Bodie and Merton 2002, Reisen and Williamson 1997) to allow investors to achieve global diversification; however, many of these alternatives are theoretically attractive but cannot be easily implemented.[3] At the end of the day, one needs to first understand the participant's final objective and then product design must follow

---

[2] See Solnik (1973) and Olienyk, Schwebach, and Zumwalt (2000).

[3] Among the problems of pension swaps are that (i) they tend to be over-the-counter and hence are stylized and illiquid, (ii) they are difficult to use if the investor would like to make tactical asset allocation shifts, and (iii) the reference benchmarks for two investors in the same market could be very different (e.g., American investors benchmark themselves to the S&P 500 or the Russell 3000, whereas foreign investors generally benchmark themselves to the MSCI U.S. Equity Index). Where the third situation exists, and this is quite prevalent globally, it will be extremely difficult

from that perspective. Because the goal of pension reform is to ensure retirement wealth with minimal risk, products that achieve this objective directly rather than indirectly (e.g., through the creation of a diversified or life-cycle portfolio) are likely to be more effective and more desirable for participants.

In a pensions context, and as highlighted briefly in Chapters 3, 4, and 5, a guaranteed real rate of return product or GRRP (achieved in our reform proposals through a swap contract wherein the Treasury guarantees a rate of return for a finite horizon to ensure a replacement rate) provides a risk-free accumulation of retirement wealth over the lifetime of the participant. In other words, to ensure a defined pension benefit (or minimize the probability of offering a pension lower than the target), a guaranteed return on fixed contributions was used to achieve this goal. Merton (1983) and Bodie and Merton (1992) would probably argue that guaranteeing the real return is not enough because it may be important to link the benefit adjustment not to a cost of living but to a per capita consumption index to maintain a reasonable link to the national standard of living. However, this is a variation on the same theme: that the purpose of social security is to guarantee the relative quality of life of retirees.

We briefly review the case for why DB plans, where the guaranteed benefit is ensured through a guaranteed return on fixed contributions (or GRRP), are optimal for social security programs. Although we have made this case from a macroeconomic perspective, we demonstrate this conclusion from the point of view of helping individuals achieve optimal pensions consistent with their individual resources and risk tolerance. But then, social security programs are generally just one pillar in a multipillar retirement system. We argue that having a two-pillar system is adequate (and combinations of mandatory DB and voluntary DC funds are preferable to any one fund), whereas institutions like the World Bank argue for a three-pillar system on the basis that different systems diversify risk. We examine how the availability of both schemes allow individuals to achieve optimal pension outcomes. We demonstrate that, even for countries with only (private) DC schemes, there is a role for the type of structure outlined in the Ideal Model and look at how it can be achieved through capital market instruments.

We provide a brief review of the theory of optimal asset selection under uncertainty and then transpose this theory into its application for pension finance. As a result, we are able to demonstrate how GRRPs are critical to the success of pure DC plans. The analysis is also conducted for mixed DB and DC pension plans, and capital market issues for the creation of such products are discussed as well. In summary,

---

to find two offsetting clients to enter into the contract without the clients paying unreasonable amounts for the transaction. See Muralidhar (2001, Chap. 6).

we examine the Two-Fund Separation theorem and demonstrate its logical extension in the pension world – the Two-Pension Fund theorem.

THE OPTIMALITY OF GRRP DB PLANS FOR SOCIAL SECURITY

Chapter 3 suggests, in steady state and under certain conditions, fully funded schemes are preferred to PAYGO for social security, because long-term contributions (a) are lower due to the interest flow (and principal) created by accumulated assets, with which pensions can be paid, (b) are less susceptible to changes in population or productivity growth, and (c) contribute to savings. However, when social security programs are mandatory, government-sponsored DB programs minimize the cost to countries of ensuring that people do not retire poor on account of capital market developments. This result follows because DB schemes are insurance schemes, and the intra- and intertemporal pooling of risks minimizes the cost to the government.[4] Chapter 4 demonstrates the cost to countries if they ignore such attractive risk sharing by using a stylized DB plan in which the defined benefit is achieved through a guaranteed real return on a fixed contribution rate.

Traditional DB plans have been rejected for being too complex for social security.[5] Increasingly, there is a desire to link contributions to benefits and make pension schemes transparent. We argue that a fully funded, contributory, funded, defined benefit (CFDB) plan would achieve these design objectives. In a pure CFDB plan like our Ideal Model, individuals contribute to their individual accounts, but achieve the defined benefit through a guaranteed return on contributions, which can be achieved on the pooled assets through a swap (government-provided GRRP) or a market-based GRRP. This would have all the positive externalities of DC plans (individuals accounts, potential borrowings, less evasion, less political risk, and less dependence on population growth) while ensuring that individuals receive a targeted annuity or replacement rate consistent with the salary growth path achieved. This plan takes care of the fundamental flaws of DC plans for social security, namely (a) that individuals are exposed to the volatility of investment returns and therefore the ex ante probability of retiring with a replacement rate less than the target is 50 percent (on the assumption that the portfolio has the appropriate expected return

---

[4]   The analogy is that health insurance premiums are lowest when all employees of a company are forced to participate and higher when individuals want a minimum level of service but a choice of provider.

[5]   In a pension plan, contributions, investments, and the number of years of contributions and retirement life determine retirement wealth. Traditional DB formulas are complicated and are of the form: pension annuity = number of years of service*accrual factor*final or average salary.

with normally distributed outcomes), and (b) that DC schemes are unfair because two people with the same salary history can have very different pensions, making these schemes particularly unsuitable for developing countries and for poor and unsophisticated participants. Bateman et al. (2001) suggest the use of puts, calls, and collars to mitigate the risk of poor asset performance, but the use of options is only second best to achieving these outcomes directly through a well-designed DB plan. Options are expensive to purchase, require sophistication to use, and could imply a view on the volatility of asset markets that is not intended (Muralidhar 2001, Chapter 6).

In addition, a publicly provided CFDB plan allows for optimal risk sharing and risk taking, because the institution best positioned to provide intertemporal smoothing of returns and benefits (i.e., the government) is the one that provides the plan. Chapter 4 demonstrated how the cost of offering a guaranteed pension can be minimized through a CFDB plan. In fact, a variation of this plan is being adopted increasingly by corporate pension plans in the United States as "cash-balance plans," and participants receive periodic statements of the wealth accumulating in their individual accounts.

This scheme is transparent, and the investment of assets is greatly simplified, because a clear return target is established (i.e., the guaranteed real return). Further, this plan involves a lower cost of investment management, which has not been achieved in Latin America (Chapter 3) inasmuch as the assets may be pooled. Alternatively, individuals can opt out of social security schemes, as in the United Kingdom (or possibly even Germany), for a private fund that offers an equal or a higher guarantee. The final advantage of the CFDB plan is that it would be ideal for regional plans such as in Euroland, the Pacific, and the Caribbean islands. These regions would benefit from economies of scale and international diversification of assets; more important, pooling diverse groups of people in an insurance scheme (i.e., the CFDB plan) minimizes liability risk, thereby lowering the cost of such explicit or implicit guarantees. These advantages cannot be captured under any of the DC options that have been proposed so far.

THE THEORY OF CHOICE UNDER UNCERTAINTY IN FINANCE

A brief review of some basic finance principles, namely the Two-Fund Separation theorem, is provided before we discuss the use of GRRPs in DC plans.

Let us assume (a) preferences are defined by a desire for greater wealth and an aversion to volatility (i.e., mean-variance preferences), (b) a risk-free asset exists with no variance of returns, (c) markets, with many risky assets, are complete, (d) a market portfolio exists, characterized by the capitalization-weighted composite

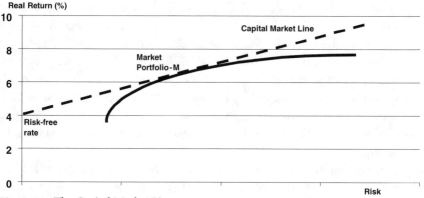

Figure 7.1. The Capital Market Line.

of all risky assets, and (e) asset returns are normally distributed. Then, for a given investment horizon, it is optimal for all investors to hold a combination of the risk-free asset and the market portfolio, although different investors can hold different proportions of the two. This is known as Two-Fund Separation (Tobin 1958, Sharpe 1964). In practice, one assumes that the risk-free rate is the default-free government treasury security for the given time horizon and the market portfolio is the underlying equity index. The choice of optimal portfolio (a combination of risk-free asset and risky asset) is made by selecting a point on the Capital Market Line in Figure 7.1 that corresponds to the desired risk allocation of the client. Each point corresponds to a different mix of the two assets, and points closer to the risk-free asset heavily favor that asset for risk-averse investors, whereas points beyond the market portfolio suggest that the investor may want to leverage the allocation to the market portfolio for a higher degree of risk tolerance.

APPLICATIONS TO PENSION FINANCE

The pensions situation is a little more complicated because it is a multiperiod problem in which individuals make monthly and yearly contributions to the pension fund. These contributions have to be invested while taking into account previous investments and future contingencies. Further, at retirement, accumulated wealth is converted into an annuity; hence, it runs the risk that wealth will be too meager or too uncertain. How well would the Two Fund model work in this multiperiod framework?

The market portfolio would not change as long as the distribution remained static over time. The risk-free rate would have to be stable over the working life of the participant hence, the currently available individual Treasury securities would be unable to achieve a risk-free pension (though a portfolio of Treasury securities could, theoretically, achieve such a result). In addition, the greatest risk to one's pension is the erosion of real wealth. Therefore, to apply this paradigm to pensions, one must equate the risk-free rate to an investment in a multiperiod, guaranteed, real return. However, does this suit the utility function of a potential pensioner, given other complications such as the possibility that contributions could change over time?

We postulate that, in the pension context, individuals can be described as having mean-variance preferences in that they desire greater wealth at retirement but are averse to uncertainty in this retirement wealth – or the probability of retiring poor). One way to achieve a risk-free, real replacement rate is to invest all contributions in an "asset" that provides a real, fixed, annualized return with zero volatility until retirement. By definition, investing in a GRRP achieves this. Alternatively, access to a DB pension fund (either funded or PAYGO) with inflation indexation is equally acceptable, for the sponsor of the pension plan guarantees the real annuity.[6] One can achieve a higher expected replacement rate, with greater uncertainty, through a DC plan invested in the market portfolio of risky assets. Graphically, this is represented in Figure 7.2.

To simplify this section, let us first assume the contribution rate is fixed over time, and we address this in Chapter 8. Therefore, given (i) individual preferences, (ii) returns that are normally distributed over multiple time periods, and (iii) the existence of a market portfolio and a DB–GRRP, the Two-Pension Fund theorem is expected to hold as well. All investors, given complete choice, will decide to invest a fraction of their total savings, devoted to retirement, partly in the market portfolio (or a diversified, defined contribution fund based on voluntary contributions) and partly in the DB–GRRP fund, and their decision, reflecting the individual's degree of risk aversion, will determine their placement on the "Capital Market Line." An individual who prefers a sure, low replacement rate will place all of his or her funds in the DB–GRRP (where the Capital Market Line intersects the y-axis in Figure 7.2); an individual who is more willing to bear uncertainty of the final outcome will choose the market portfolio (point M) cognisant of the higher probability of not meeting the expected higher replacement rate. Others may choose different mixes of the two

---

[6] Pension plans in Europe provide indexed annuities but, in the United States, pension plans do not provide mandatory inflation adjustment of pensions. Also, if the DB plan is underfunded, there is a small risk that the real annuity will not be guaranteed should the plan have insufficient insurance when the sponsor becomes bankrupt. In the case of countries, one can ignore this likelihood.

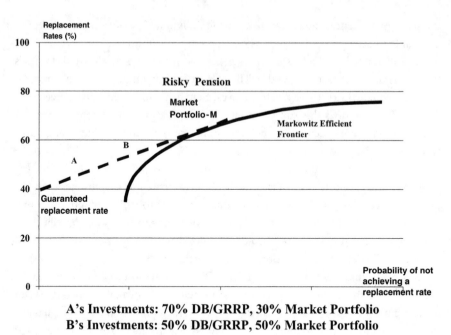

A's Investments: 70% DB/GRRP, 30% Market Portfolio
B's Investments: 50% DB/GRRP, 50% Market Portfolio

Figure 7.2. Two-Pension Fund theorem.

portfolios as in the case of investors A (more risk-averse) and B (less risk-averse) in Figure 7.2. Therefore, the available choices represent a trade-off between greater expected pension wealth and a higher uncertainty of the expected pension described by the Capital Market Line. Dutta, Kapur, and Orszag (1999) have made a similar assessment of the proportion of funding in optimal social security schemes as well as the proportion invested in equities in the partially funded scheme using a portfolio optimization technique. However, they treat the low-risk asset as a government bond, whereas we suggest that the true zero-risk asset is either a DB or, if it is market-based, a GRRP – the type of product suggested by Merton (1983).

APPLICATION TO PURE DC PLANS

The case in which countries have abandoned all existing DB funds and converted completely to DC systems is the clearest form of investment choice under uncertainty. Without a DB plan, it would appear that there is no risk-free asset. In most markets, products offered to investors are a conflation of bond and equity funds. There has been some discussion of creating investment funds with inflation-protected bonds, but even these are likely to have fluctuating real rates of return over time as in

Switzerland or Germany. Further, in many emerging markets, fund managers are demanding the freedom to offer equity and international investments, but regulators are exercising caution.

The three fundamental problems for countries with DC plans only are (i) the nonexistence of the GRRPs, (ii) the selection of the market portfolio (national or international), and (iii) the absence of sufficient tools to help investors invest their funds (i.e., tools to help them determine how much to save and how to allocate these savings to different products).

The challenge of creating privately offered guaranteed returns (POGRs) is that the provider must be able to offer the same fixed rate over long horizons given the volatility of asset markets. Some examples of GRRPs are the 4-percent real guaranteed recognition bonds that were given to Chileans in compensation for their accrued benefits under the old PAYGO scheme and the bonds offered to Israeli pension funds by the Israeli government. Increasingly, other countries have begun to recognize the benefit of such products, and Belgium requires many of its pension funds to provide such insurance. In the case of Belgium, the guaranteed rate is nominal. However, Belgium (and Switzerland) are under pressure to lower the guaranteed rate for future contributions because interest rates have declined and equity markets have experienced negative performance. In Chile, future contributions cannot be made to these products, whereas in Israel these bonds have been discontinued. The World Bank's pension fund is one of the few pension funds that offers staff the choice of a 3-percent real return guaranteed investment (in U.S. dollars) or other risky portfolios (S&P 500 Index fund, a bond fund, and a non–U.S. equity fund). However, the World Bank pension department manages the risk between the return offered to participants and that earned through market instruments (or effectively, they provide the swap).

The following needs to happen in markets that have DC plans only: (a) private institutions offer POGRs, (b) a market portfolio of risky assets is identified, and (c) a mechanism is made available to participants that allows them to select replacement rates optimally and, in turn, allocations to investment alternatives. The absence of POGRs means that individuals select portfolios below the Capital Market Line, which is clearly suboptimal because higher replacement rates can be achieved for the same level of risk with POGRs. The absence of a clearly specified market portfolio creates similar problems, because it runs the risk of investment in suboptimal portfolios. The third requirement is necessary to allow investors to achieve their desired replacement rate; its absence causes investors to select portfolios inconsistent with their appetite for risk.

The following section discusses POGRs and market portfolios, and provides a simple model that helps individuals to achieve their retirement objectives.

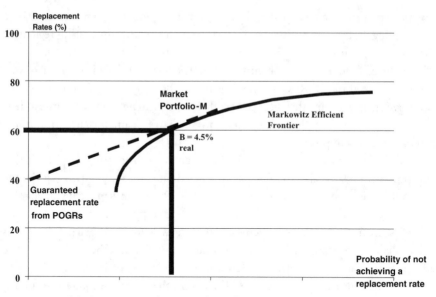

Figure 7.3. Achieving pension objectives through POGRs.

THE OPTIMAL INVESTMENT CHOICE MODEL

On the assumption of a fixed contribution rate throughout working life, wealth at retirement is equal to contributions during working life compounded at the investment return until retirement. Further, we assume that demographic profiles (life expectancy, retirement date, etc.), initial wealth and salaries, salary growth, and inflation are given. Then, for a given contribution rate and target real replacement rate (or retirement wealth), there is a unique expected real rate of return that must be targeted by the investor. This is a simple identity, and models have been developed to demonstrate this (we have provided one in the appendix to Chapter 1). Assume further that a POGR is available and the market portfolio (M) is uniquely determined. Then, the relevant portfolio for the individual is the portfolio specified by the corresponding target "expected return" or expected replacement rate on the Capital Market Line (Figure 7.3).[7] Hence, shares of POGRs and M are uniquely determined, and all contributions must be invested in this proportion. However, accompanying this expected real return or annuity is the volatility of such a portfolio

---

[7] Assume the GRRP yields a 3-percent real return and the real return on equities is 6 percent; then, portfolio B, which is a 50–50 mix of the two, yields 4.5 percent. For an individual who works 40 years, lives 20 years postretirement, and has a salary that grows at an annual 3 percent, a 60-percent replacement rate of average lifetime salary can be earned by contributing 8.8 percent annually if these contributions earn an annual 4.5 percent real rate.

and that of pension outcomes, and the individual has to decide whether the level of risk is acceptable. If the risk is too high, then the individual must lower the expected annuity target (i.e., investment in M) and re-do the foregoing procedure. This process is repeated until the individual is satisfied with the expected wealth–risk trade-off at a particular point on the Capital Market Line. If targets change over time as risk aversion changes, then the portfolio will need to be rebalanced to the new optimal shares for POGRs and M.[8]

THE CASE FOR MIXED PENSION SCHEMES

The notion of a three-pillar pension scheme was formalized in a World Bank report (World Bank 1994) in which it was suggested that countries (a) offer mandatory PAYGO schemes (first pillar), (b) force individuals to participate in a funded and privately managed DC scheme (second pillar), and (c) encourage voluntary savings (third pillar). Our recommendation is for countries to offer a mandatory CFDB – because the PAYGO and mandatory DC (first and second pillars) can be replaced by a better CFDB – and encourage individuals to save voluntarily. This is in effect a two-pillar scheme. The DB portion offers the risk-free replacement rate and may be either partially or fully funded. Because participation in the first pillar is mandatory and contribution rates are fixed, individuals could be constrained from achieving their optimal mix (i.e., the proportions invested in GRRPs and M, respectively). Therefore, participants should have access to other POGRs or have the ability to contribute more to their CFDB accounts. It is possible to propose that individuals be permitted to contribute up to an additional 5 percent (a randomly selected figure that could be changed) of their mandated contributions to the national pension scheme.[9] This would be particularly helpful for poor or unsophisticated participants who would like to save more but are afraid to set up new accounts with financial institutions and who pick the default option, as in Australia and Sweden. The absence of CFDBs or the inability to add to mandatory contributions in pension design will lead to suboptimal asset allocation and wealth–risk trade-offs. In effect, under this paradigm Two-Pension Fund separation holds whereby voluntary contributions and contributions to guaranteed real return products ensure that the affiliate achieves the desired replacement rate for the degree of uncertainty he or she is willing to bear.

---

[8] This practical approach is an extreme simplification of the correct approach of choosing (a) between current and retirement consumption and (b) between risk-free and risky pension outcomes.

[9] Tax implications of voluntary contributions are ignored. If the scheme is fair and the GRRP is set at an appropriate level, this will pose few problems to the national CFDB scheme.

CAPITAL MARKET AND INVESTMENT MANAGEMENT ISSUES

We now examine (a) how a market portfolio might be determined, (b) issues relating to the creation and offering of GRRPs for DB or POGRs for DC plans, and (c) what needs to be done to hedge the risks of postretirement annuity indexation (inflation or decline in the real standard of living).

With respect to the market portfolio, there is no dearth of research that tries to estimate a market portfolio for an international Capital Asset Pricing Model (CAPM). For simplicity, the World Bank's pension fund offered participants the choice of the following risky assets: an S&P 500 index fund, a non–U.S. equity fund, and a bond fund. The problem of mixing bonds with equities in the realm of risky assets is, What proportion of each should be held in the market portfolio? We recommend using capitalization-weighted portfolios (Chapter 5) except that, in the paradigm articulated here, we extend the market portfolio over time to include international assets. However, each country needs to make decisions on permissible investments based on its own constraints. Investing abroad requires additional oversight, because many countries (especially developing countries) are not comfortable exporting their capital; moreover, the act of purchasing foreign assets tends to weaken local currency. Equally important, investing abroad engenders currency risk because currency movements can cause returns in local currencies to be dramatically different from returns in foreign currency, and this risk has to be managed (Muralidhar 2001, Chapter 5).

Given that guaranteed real return products are not currently provided by private vendors, one must ask whether this is purely a neat theoretical construct. GRRPs can be implemented for a public, compulsory DB plan as long as the plan sponsor (a) sets a reasonable guaranteed return target and (b) can make up intrayear deficits from the stabilization (or sinking) fund. Under these conditions, it has been shown that one can apply asset-liability management principles to maintain such a fund because mandatory participation pools liabilities and minimizes liability risk (of life expectancy and inflation).[10] The simulations in Chapters 5 and 6 demonstrate

---

[10] There is growing literature on asset-liability management of DB and DC pension funds. See, for example, Dert (1995). In a pension framework, individuals are exposed to the risk that they will live beyond the average life expectancy for the country or that inflation will erode their pension. Because national DB is a mandatory insurance scheme with a large number of participants, it is able to offer life, inflation-indexed annuities at the lowest cost, thereby providing a hedge for participants against longevity and inflation. Countries moving to DC plans will impose a significant cost on participants to achieve these annuities because of the classic adverse selection problem.

how such an offering can be made in the context of the U.S. and the Spanish social security systems.

With DC pension schemes, participation in a particular fund is not mandated, and this creates numerous problems. Participants can enter and exit a fund at will because they have complete choice. For a private vendor to provide a POGR, the provider must have access to inflation-proof securities of different maturities that together provide a return in excess of the guaranteed rate. This follows because the vendor must hedge against participation risk (i.e., against adverse selection, which means that people will participate when market rates are below the guaranteed rate and vice versa), maturity risk (i.e., the maturity of the instruments will be different from the investment horizon of any investor), and inflation risk (i.e., that inflation-adjusted payments will be made at the same frequency as exit is permitted from the funds). In the United States, Treasury Inflation-Proof securities (TIPs) are of long maturities (10–30 years) and currently yield between 2 and 2.5 percent real rate of return. Vendors are likely to be willing to provide mutual fund POGRs at slightly less than the TIPs' real yield (for the aforementioned risks and practical difficulties in liquidating small portfolios) on condition that they are able to revise the guaranteed level for future contributions should rates decline substantially.[11] The difference between the DC POGRs' and the TIPs' yield will depend on the market's perception of the aforementioned risks. One would expect, if these securities are issued with different maturities, the maturity risk is somewhat reduced; conversely, shorter maturity securities will, on average, have lower real yields as well. In effect, the private market would have to offer laddered POGRs – namely, different rates for different maturities – thereby complicating the analysis for participants.

However, when participation is mandatory and a sponsor exists, it is feasible to offer GRRPs at a national level through a CFDB system with significant advantages over other private schemes. The guaranteed rate is likely to be much higher in a DB scheme than in any DC scheme. This is a trivial result, for the government has a greater ability to manage intertemporal risk when participation is mandated. Hence, the Capital Market Line in pure DC schemes will be steeper, and the risk to achieving any replacement rate will be higher (Figure 7.4). The difference between the DB-sustainable GRRP and the pure DC-sustainable POGR is the reduced replacement rate that an individual must incur for the same degree of risk (or greater risk for the same replacement rate) to have the freedom to select an optimal portfolio (and

---

[11] This comment is based on conversations with investment banks and insurance companies on their willingness to provide such products.

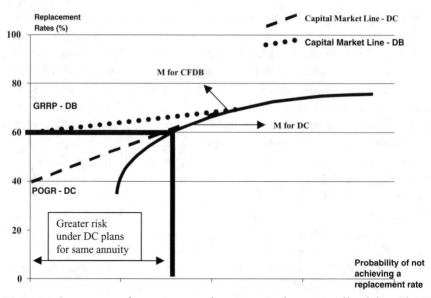

Figure 7.4. Impact on replacement rates when guaranteed rates are offered through DB plans or the private sector (DC plans).

to enter into and exit from funds). In short, there is a trade-off between risk or lower replacement rates (i.e., the cost of choice) and choice that previous analysts have ignored. The greater risk is shown in Figure 7.4 because in our hypothetical example a 60-percent replacement rate has no risk under the CFDB plan but a more meaningful non-zero risk under a pure DC scheme.[12] In the CFDB plan, individuals get higher expected replacement rates for a given risk and could have some choice relating to borrowing and voluntary contributions.

The final risk to investors arises from the issue of whether using consumer price inflation (CPI) indices is adequate for all inflation adjustments and whether these indices protect against a decline in the relative standard-of-living of retirees (relative to the working population). In short, is the current range of investment products adequate to protect real spending of retirees? Unfortunately, TIPs are presently offered only on CPI. If beneficiaries receive pensions that are indexed to CPI, individuals will still bear some risk if the standard-of-living of the working population increases. As a result, some experts propose that the government offer standard-of-living adjusted bonds (i.e., where the real component is indexed to per capita consumption) rather

---

[12] Notice that the market portfolio under CFDB and pure DC plans is very different when we apply the idea of selecting the market portfolio based on tangency of the line drawn from the risk-free asset to the efficient frontier.

than just price-inflation adjusted bonds (Merton 1983). We have shown in Chapter 3 that such an indexation would require a higher long-term contribution.

SUMMARY

The chapter has demonstrated from a micro-economic perspective that it is critical to the success of pension reform for individuals to have access to (a) DB and DC plans and (b) GRRPs, regardless of the range of plans. These may come in the form of mandated DB social security accounts or may be provided by the market. However, the real rate of the former is likely to be higher than that of the latter. Participants should also have the freedom to increase their allocations to these GRRPs. The existence of such products ensures that individuals will receive targeted annuities by optimally allocating their contributions between the "risk-free" and the risky asset. Therefore, we recommend that countries considering pension reform should offer a CFDB plan in which the benefit takes the form of a guaranteed replacement rate (ensured through a guaranteed real rate of return on fixed contributions) and encourage the issuance of such guaranteed "real" return bonds by the Treasury and corporations alike. In addition, such products allow for efficient achievement of retirement objectives – of both the target replacement rate and acceptable levels of risk – through the principle of Two-Pension Fund separation.

8

The Case for Mixed Systems and Variable Contributions: Improving the Performance of Pension Systems

With Ronald van der Wouden

We have successfully disproved the World Bank's notion that pension reform should incorporate three pillars and have demonstrated that the World Bank's first two pillars can be integrated into one well-designed DB scheme with the "third" pillar being a voluntary DC plan. We now extend this approach to show how the first pillar can be optimally designed.

We examine two issues that we have ignored so far: (i) mixing PAYGO and funding and (ii) variable contributions. We demonstrated (in Chapter 2) how the best features of DB and DC schemes can be captured in one well-designed DB scheme – the Ideal Model. We continue to prove in this chapter that the advantages of combining PAYGO and funded DB schemes can also be assimilated into one scheme. However, in a departure from previous research, we demonstrate how this should be achieved, not just to secure the benefit of diversification (i.e., asset returns not highly correlated to wage growth) but also to limit the impact that a funded system might have on capital market efficiency.

In our scheme, individuals in a country are guaranteed pensions and the government is responsible for collecting contributions and making payments. We have also discussed how a swap contract can be used to guarantee a rate of return on fixed contributions and how the risks that returns will deviate from the guaranteed rate in the shortrun can be managed through a "sinking fund." However, eventually, any persistent imbalance will have to be covered by the government (and, ultimately, participants). We demonstrate that a technique employed in the management of corporate pension funds – variable contributions – can be used very effectively to manage the risk to the guarantor or government that the accumulation will fall short of obligations. Two key investment risks of our funded system are (i) the variability of short-term asset returns and (ii) the possibility that the long-term guaranteed rate of return is overestimated. In effect, we are able to show that, with variable contributions, the guaranteed replacement rate is now achieved through levying contributions appropriate for the long-term realized average asset return. This technique could also lead to a lowering of the average contribution. Therefore, if the long-term average return of our portfolio is the same as the guaranteed rate, then there may be, at worst, small intertemporal transfers (if, for example, the early years' returns are below the guaranteed rate). But, if the guaranteed rate of return was severely overestimated, then, with the traditional fixed contribution, there would be a large deficit to be borne by the government guaranteeing the benefit and hence, in the final analysis, by the population through higher taxes or by future generations through the government deficit. By contrast, a system with variable contributions can be managed so as to minimize the burden transferred to future generations. The contribution rate for the realized return is achieved through the dynamic rule governing the variable contribution; thus, the average contribution rate need not be known in advance. However, the adjustment mechanism must be clearly articulated, and we consider some simulations to demonstrate the sensitivity of the results to these parameters.

COMBINING PAYGO AND FUNDING THROUGH PARTIAL FUNDING

Several commentators have noted that having a pure PAYGO system, or a pure funded system for the combined first and second pillar, may be somewhat risky for the participants or for the economy. Those in favor of DC schemes (for the second pillar) feel the benefit of the PAYGO scheme (for the first pillar) is that it provides some insurance against harmful outcomes in the DC schemes (Feldstein and Ranguelova 2001). Others have argued that because returns from assets are not highly correlated or even negatively correlated to earnings and GDP growth, combining the two schemes is likely to yield the benefits of diversification. This suggestion is implicit in the recommendation of the World Bank (1994) and Boldrin et al. (1999) but is also reflected in the work of Bodie et al. (1988) and Dutta et al. (1999). The last paper highlights the fact that partial funding allows retirees to hold shares in the earnings growth of the working population. Sinn (1999) has argued that partial transition to a funded system may be a way to overcome the demographic crises that caused the social security crisis. In effect, because the current generation has "not played ball" by producing enough children, the partially funded system, achieved through compulsory additional saving, is required to replace missing human capital with real capital.

However, low to negative correlation between wage growth and asset returns may not necessarily suffice to justify a mixing, for the expected rates of return need to be examined to ensure that the combination of the two systems will provide an adequate rate of return for the combined system. For example, a sufficiently low forecast of growth of wages could lead to situations in which the optimal mix may not include any PAYGO component (Dutta et al. 1999) or in which the mix could imply a higher long-term contribution. More important, though, the creation of two massive public schemes is likely to lead to unnecessary administrative costs and unwieldy systems. If one considers the costs indicated in Baker and Kar (2002) of regulatory bodies overseeing these pillars (an estimate of over a percentage in annual contributions), the more integrated and simple the structure, the lower the cost.

Although others have argued that mixing PAYGO with funding is advantageous because it diversifies risk, we take a different path. Clearly, diversification makes sense only if it is possible to create portfolios whereby combining assets can either provide higher returns per unit of risk or lower risk per unit of return. This is not a simple mean-variance optimization problem, for there are institutional constraints that also come to bear on the issue. It is insufficient to look only at the correlation of wage growth to financial returns. Data provided in Boldrin et al. (1999) and summarized in Appendix 8.1 suggest a good case for such diversification in France, Germany, Italy, and Japan but not necessarily in the United States. These data are generally reported from 1961 to 1996 and, in the case of the United States, the return on assets outstrip growth. We take a longer data history for the United States (1951–2000) in the simulations later in the chapter to evaluate the potential benefit of a mixed system. Data from Blake (1994) suggest that diversification might not work for Australia, Germany, the Netherlands, and United Kingdom. As a result, the case for mixing systems based on diversification, it appears, is very data– and time–sensitive with no clear pattern emerging.

We suggest that a broader case for mixing the two systems is to be found in limitations in the acceptable size of the asset-to-wage ratio in a funded system. We use this ratio as a proxy for the impact of a funded system on the financial markets. The higher this ratio, the larger the proportion of outstanding securities held in the public social security system reserves. There are multiple combinations of contributions and rates of return that will provide adequate funds to service a target replacement rate, and the appropriate combination is determined on the basis of the pension promise that needs to be funded. However, the higher the rate of return, the lower the contribution and, potentially, the lower the asset to wage ratio and vice versa. As a result, preventing the funded portion of the pension system from overwhelming the financial system provides a good justification for the balance of the system to be financed through PAYGO. One of the key reasons for our recommendation of a combination of PAYGO and funding in Chapter 5 is driven by considerations of maintaining a strong, private capital market in the United States.

To determine the proportions of PAYGO and funding requires an additional level of analysis. As shown in Chapters 5 and 6, a funded system may result in an asset-to-wage ratio that can eventually dominate an economy. Therefore, in Chapter 5, we demonstrated a transition for the United States whereby a partially funded system is created and for which the asset-to-wage ratio was at such a level (1.6 times) that pension reserves did not dominate the capital markets. A fully funded system was expected to have an asset-to-wage ratio in excess of 3. Even if resources were available to change to full funding, such a high ratio would threaten to generate distortions in capital markets. The case will be more dramatic in systems in Europe, where the benefits are very generous. To limit the ratio, we have proposed, for the United States, a partially funded DB system that can be broken down into a fully funded component and a PAYGO component. The difference between the contribution rate under the partially funded system and the fully funded system can be seen as the PAYGO component of social security.

By creating this mixed system under the partial funding umbrella, a combination of the two pillars can easily be achieved under one pillar – a case we have been making since Chapter 1. In effect, this creates a partially funded system, as reflected in Dutta et al. (1999), but effectively imposes a constraint on the proportion that can be invested in the funded system driven by a constraint on the asset-to-wage ratio.

In Chapter 3, we developed the Golden SS Rule – in steady state, pensions will be paid from contributions and returns from assets (equation 3.4), that is,

$$p = c + A_{t-1}(r - \rho). \tag{8.1}$$

We now allow for contributions and pensions to be broken up into subcategories such that

$$p = p_f + p_{PG}, \tag{8.2}$$

where p_f is the pension financed by a funded scheme and p_{PG} is the pension financed by PAYGO. Further, the same can be done for contributions,

$$c = c_f + c_{PG}, \tag{8.3}$$

where c_f is the contribution to the funded scheme and c_{PG} is the contribution to a PAYGO scheme. Under a pure PAYGO plan,

$$c_{PG} = p_{PG}. \tag{8.4}$$

As a result, we know, under steady state, for a fully funded pension scheme with guaranteed rates of return,

$$p_f = c_{f+} + A'_{t-1}(r - \rho). \tag{8.5}$$

We apply this analysis, of splitting a partially funded system into a PAYGO and a fully funded component to the transition we proposed for the American case in Chapter 5. The cost ratio in the United States is expected to reach 19–20 percent, and our steady state contribution was 13.5 percent. A contribution of 1.65 percent to a fully funded system with a net of growth return of 4 percent results in a 1.6 asset-to-wage ratio and a 16-percent replacement rate on average salary. Therefore, the funded system would generate resources of 8 percent (1.65 percent + 1.6*4 percent) for pensions, with the balance of approximately 11.9 percent coming from PAYGO to satisfy a cost ratio of 20 percent. Consistency is ensured, for the total contribution of approximately 13.5 percent = 11.9 percent PAYGO and 1.6 percent for funding. Note that the 1.65 percent contribution to the funded system is close to the 2 percent diversion advocated by proponents of privatization.

By breaking the system into the two components of fully funded and PAYGO, what we know is the variability in contributions is a function of the variability of the contribution under the two systems. Variability in growth affects both systems. Under the PAYGO scheme, faster growth in the wage bill implies lower long-term contributions, but in the funded scheme, faster growth requires higher long-term contributions as shown in Chapter 3, Table 3.1.

An important feature of the dynamic contribution rate is its variability, which is a function of the longrun variability of the weighted sum of asset returns, the growth of the (real) wage bill, and hence of their variances and covariance. We conducted several simulations to demonstrate how variable contributions can be incorporated into our proposed reform and to show how this can reduce risks to governments. These are described in greater detail in the next section.

THE CASE FOR VARIABLE CONTRIBUTIONS

In a DB scheme, the risk of collections or accumulations falling short of obligations is borne by the sponsor. We argue that individuals should receive defined benefits and governments should offer a DB social security because the government is best able to bear the risk of poor pension outcomes and can ensure inter- and intragenerational pooling of risk. However, even with pooling of risks, there are significant risks that are borne by the sponsor. For example, how does one deal with the difficulty of projecting the future rates of return on assets, GDP and productivity growth, and population growth? In addition to forecasting expected long-term future values for these variables, over time their possible variability has to be managed. To deal with the short-term variability and to ensure robust pension outcomes requires certain variables such as the contribution rate not be fixed forever. Another possibility is to have variable benefits, as in the case of Sweden (Werding 2003), but as shown in the Ideal Model we favor variable contributions (i.e., predictable benefits from the social security component of one's pension) over variable benefits.

The key strategy emphasized in the Ideal Model was for the pension system to enter into a swap with the Treasury to hedge against the variability of short-term asset returns and still offer defined benefits. The government would enter into a swap with social security and set up a sinking fund. The one issue, which we addressed partially, was how the government would deal with the risk of a secular decline in the return on assets; our response was to establish a blue-ribbon board to lower the guaranteed rate and to compensate for the loss of revenue by raising the fixed contribution rate. This response is necessary to avoid taxing future generations to pay for the benefits of the current one – resulting in an intergenerational redistribution of cost. Allowing a variable contribution rate should make it possible to share the burden more equitably across generations – especially if the formula for making such variable contributions is transparent and allows for smoothing of short-term imbalances.

This measure has been used extensively in the corporate pension fund world.[1] Up to this point in the book, we have attempted to create a steady-state equilibrium whereby the long-term contribution, after the transition, can be set at the steady-state level. But the hypothesis of perpetual fixity cannot be maintained if unanticipated long-term changes in the trend of productivity (salary growth), population growth, or asset returns occur and may necessitate lowering or raising the long-term contribution rate (or if the volatility of the underlying pension parameters can be diffused through better design). As suggested earlier, contributions should change only in response to perceived "permanent" changes in the trend. It is difficult to distinguish whether certain changes are temporary or secular, but this can be a decision for the blue-ribbon board; they can achieve desired policy by adjusting parameters that dictate the variable contribution. We highlight these parameters in the next section.

Research demonstrates, for corporate pension plans, the variability of contributions, in reaction to short-term variability in asset returns, permits more aggressive risk-taking for the fund, resulting in higher expected rates of return, which in turn allows for a lower average contribution rate (Muralidhar 2001). The more surprising result from research on variable contributions is that corporate funds are able to lower the volatility in the asset to liability ratio (or lower funded status risk). On further investigation, this result is more obvious because flexible contributions serve as a hedge against poor investment performance, thereby resulting in a more stable overall pension system. In Bodie, Merton, and Samuelson (1992), a similar case is made for DC plans in the argument that those who have greater variability in labor

---

[1] Typically, in corporate plans, the employee portion is fixed and the employer's contribution may vary. In the Ideal Model, the employee is the sole contributor.

supply are able to bear more asset risk. The labor supply decision acts as a hedge against asset risk (because of the flexibility to substitute labor for leisure). In addition, a flexible labor supply permits more aggressive accumulation early in life (i.e., covering less-than-average performance or salary growth with contributions), thereby gaining the full benefit of accumulation over a long cycle. Muralidhar (2001) has argued that this analog is directly applicable to the corporate DB pension world, where variability in labor supply can easily be transposed to variability of contributions (because, implicitly, changes in labor supply can be used to offset or complement changes in contributions).

In the case of a mixed system, there are two key exogenous parameters that control accumulation and the retirement target: growth of wages and return on assets. The more ambiguous impact is that of wage growth on the system and required contributions. If, through the PAYGO component, countries can hedge against high growth rates (and potentially profit from them) while participating in the market through the funded portion, then it is possible that the overall system is less volatile (than either a fully funded system or a PAYGO system in isolation) in achieving its objectives of ensuring acceptable pension outcomes. Alternatively, it can be shown that the costs to the sponsor, namely, the government in our case, of ensuring such outcomes are lowered in a system with variable contributions.

If the risk to the government is that the sinking fund might experience a significant deficit, can the impact of the sinking fund on government finances be minimized? In the simulations in the next section, we demonstrate how a dynamic contribution policy lowers the risk to the government. We demonstrate the trade-off between less risk, higher contributions, and a higher "nuisance factor" (i.e., the inconvenience of periodic, large changes in contributions). In effect, we are able to show that with variable contributions, the guaranteed replacement rate is now achieved through levying contributions appropriate for the long-term realized average asset return.

SIMULATIONS FOR SYSTEMS WITH VARIABLE CONTRIBUTIONS

DESCRIPTION OF THE SIMULATION TECHNIQUE

All the parameters are simulated for the life of an individual for one path, and then 1,000 simulations are conducted to give 1,000 paths. The greater the number of paths, the more robust the results. This individual can be seen as one cohort in a DB plan. From Chapter 4 we know that adding cohorts will lower the risk to the sponsor. The individual or cohort is guaranteed a pension benefit by the government, evaluated on a prescribed path based on initial ex ante expectations of various parameters (real salary growth, inflation, etc.).

At the end of each year, the funded ratio of the system (in our simulation a person or cohort) is assessed against the target-funded ratio. The target-funded ratio is the ratio between the target accumulation (contributions plus interest) and target liabilities and is set at 100 percent every year.[2] The next step is to calculate the realized funded ratio of the system at the end of the year. The numerator is accumulated assets until that point. On the other hand, the target liability for a particular preretirement date is the value on the date that allows the individual or cohort to be on a prespecified path (specified and computed at the start of his or her working life) to meet the target retirement goal – in our case, the 50-percent replacement rate of average salary – when the person or cohort retires. This target liability is calculated by using the initially expected future salary growth, expected investment return, and basic contribution rate. This is similar to the technique in Leibowitz et al. (2002).

The Blue Ribbon Board sets upper and lower bounds on the realized funded ratio. If the realized funded ratio at year-end (i.e., ratio of year-end accumulation to target liabilities) falls within the lower and upper funded ratio trigger, no action is taken. The contribution rate for the next year will be the base contribution. If the funded ratio is lower than the lower trigger, the contribution of the next year will be increased (taking the maximum increase from one year to the next into account and the maximum allowable contribution rate) such that the funded ratio is 100 percent. The procedure is somewhat similar if the funded ratio is above the upper trigger. However, in this case the contribution rate decreases. In effect, there is a one-shot change in the contribution rate to "top up" deficiencies caused by either poor investment performance or poor salary growth (for both are stochastic).

This method implies that the gap between the target liabilities and intermediate wealth of the person is made up within a year (if we take into account the permissible constraints on maximum and minimum increases and decreases and maximum and minimum contributions). Allowing amortization of this gap over multiple years gives similar results and will smooth the contribution rate. The method followed in the simulation is the most conservative approach and does not allow any ambiguity or subjectivity for the government or Board to establish the terms over which the gap is financed.

Note that if the realized investment return is equal to the expected investment return (this is the projected return the asset allocation will give), the contribution rate has to be exactly the base contribution rate (if there is no uncertainty about

---

[2] This need not be the case for two reasons: (i) corporate plans tend to target a ratio higher than 100 percent to ensure that they can maintain contribution holidays with a high probability, and (ii) if there are other guarantees to ensure that full pensions can be paid, the target can be set at less than 100 percent. We keep the assumptions simple in our simulation.

TABLE 8.1 Data assumptions (nominal rates of return for assets and rates of growth for GDP and wages)

		50 years (1951–2000), in percent				
		S&P 500	20-yr Treas.	CPI	GDP	Wages
Return		14.02%	6.50%	4.00%	7.31%	7.27%
Volatility		16.77%	11.01%	3.11%	2.96%	3.00%
		Used in simulation				
		S&P 500	20-yr Treas.	CPI	GDP	Wages
Return		10.50%	7.50%	4.00%	7.50%	6.00%
Volatility		16.77%	11.01%	3.11%	2.96%	3.00%
		Correlation over 1951–2000				
		S&P 500	20-yr Treas.	CPI	GDP	Wages
	S&P 500	1.00	0.18	−0.30	−0.31	−0.38
	20-yr Treas.		1.00	−0.17	−0.23	−0.24
	CPI			1.00	0.59	0.56
	GDP				1.00	0.90
	Wages					1.00

Sources: Ibbotson Associates and Bureau for Economic Analysis.

salary growth) because this contribution rate is constructed so that it gives the target wealth upon retirement.

DATA ASSUMPTIONS

We first describe data assumptions before highlighting the simulations and the key parameters by which we evaluate the advantages of variable contributions. Historical data on the asset returns of the S&P 500 equity index and returns from investing in a portfolio of 20-year Treasuries were obtained for the United States for 50 years (1951–2000) (Ibbotson Associates data). In addition, data from the Bureau of Economic Analysis were gathered for GDP growth, CPI, and income growth. Table 8.1 summarizes the historical data for each of these variables (i.e., on the assumption that wages are an asset) as well as the volatility of these series. Moreover, this table provides correlation information across these variables. For ease of exposition, information is provided on a nominal basis.

The techniques employed for the forward-looking simulation are identical to those in Chapter 4. We conduct Monte Carlo simulations (assuming 1,000 paths) for a single participant or cohort, assuming different systems (both in terms of degree of funding and contribution policy), and then evaluate their outcome at retirement in terms of the average pension achieved and the risk of not achieving targeted pension outcomes.[3] To make the forward-looking simulation more reasonable, we adjusted the "expected returns" and assumed a 4-percent inflation, a 3.5-percent real-bond yield for an investment in 20-year Treasuries, and a 3-percent equity premium over the Treasury portfolio return, thereby delivering a 7.5-percent nominal return for bonds and a 10.5-percent nominal return for equities. A portfolio investing two-third in stocks and one-third in bonds (approximately 70:30) would have a real return of 5.5 percent (Feldstein and Samwick 1997). For real growth in wages or the PAYGO internal rate of return, we assume a real rate of 2 percent, which is marginally higher than that assumed in the Trustee Report (SSA 2002). We use the historical correlation data for the simulations. Reduction in the PAYGO internal rate of return still leads to the inclusion of PAYGO systems, but results in greater funding for a given contribution rate and replacement rate. However, this section focuses on the value of variable contributions for both fully funded and partially funded systems, rather than determine allocations across PAYGO and funding.

To effect this analysis, we make an extremely simplified assumption – we treat wage growth as the return on an asset and assume that contributions invested in wage growth truly accumulate like those invested in stocks and bonds; this is not the case in reality. The "investment" in wage growth is fictitious (as though taking place through the PAYGO component), but it allows us to explain and compare all the simulations (e.g., comparing funded with partially funded systems) on the same basis.

For example, in a fully funded system with a 5.5-percent real return and a 3.2-percent contribution (with the replacement rate on average salary at 50 percent and on the assumption that the growth of real wages is 2 percent and postretirement real return is 3.5 percent), the asset-to-wage ratio is 2.7. If we simulate a system that is "50-percent funded" – namely, a system wherein the return from funding and the PAYGO internal rate of return are mixed 50–50 – then the total expected real return falls from 5.5 percent to 3.5 percent. Therefore, additional contributions are needed to achieve the same ex ante target replacement rate (or cost ratio of 12.1 percent). However, the magnitude of the contribution from the true PAYGO in the 50-percent funded case is much larger (approximately 6 percent) than we would obtain by this extreme assumption (approximately 3.1 percent) of treating wage growth as the return on assets. This means the results in our simulations need to be viewed relative to one another (i.e., the overall simulation is biased but not the comparison across different variations for the same amount of funding). In the simulations, the parameters are set to ensure that we achieve the guaranteed replacement rate on average.

---

[3] More simulations may change the magnitude of results but not the ordering of the systems, for we assume the same 1,000 paths for all variations in the pension system in Table 8.2.

DEMOGRAPHIC AND PENSION ASSUMPTIONS

We ignore population growth, for we simulate the experience of a single individual or cohort. The growth of wages of the population in a system with many participants depends on real productivity growth and population growth. We have conducted simulations with additional participants or cohorts (as in Chapter 4) and have found that the primary conclusions are unchanged though the exact values are affected. These simulations are not reported here. For the individual, we assume an ex ante target replacement rate of 50 percent of average salary, 40 years of working life, and 18 years of postretirement life expectancy. For this calculation, we assume that the expected return and inflation after retirement will be 7.5 percent and 4 percent (this is for the annuity calculation), respectively, and that this pension will be paid from the accumulation upon retirement at age 65.

We assume the expected nominal salary of the individual grows at the rate of 6 percent (or 2 percent real). With static contributions and an expected real return of 5.5 percent (9.5 percent nominal) guaranteed, annual contributions will be 3.23 percent. The average contribution is affected by the variability of contributions when annual changes in the contribution rate are permitted. The individual receives the guaranteed return, but the Treasury bears the risk of the volatility of the parameters through the swap. However, in the long term, such costs are transferred to citizens and, therefore, when we evaluate the risk of each type of strategy, we effectively examine the potential cost and volatility of the cost (range of outcomes) of the system to the participants.

VARIABLE CONTRIBUTIONS – ESTABLISHING FORMAL RULES

At year-end, a comparison between the realized and target-funded ratios will determine whether the contribution needs to be left unchanged or modified. Typically, there are rules to govern actions, and they require three key parameters to be articulated in the "reaction function" to determine the annual change in the dynamic contribution policy: (a) minimum and maximum range of the funded ratio before increases and decreases are triggered, respectively, (b) minimum and maximum annual contribution, and (c) maximum permissible *increase* or *decrease* in contributions from one year to the next. These parameters can be implemented to mitigate the nuisance of many large and small changes during one's working life. Setting a range for the funded ratio before a new contribution rate is implemented prevents frequent changes in the contribution policy. We have made the simple assumptions that all shortfalls are made up in one year, but these can also be amortized to smooth the contribution volatility. Moreover, with multiple cohorts there can be smoothing at a system level because some cohorts experiencing deficits can be offset by those with surpluses. The range can be widened to prevent unnecessary, small changes every year. The minimum and maximum annual contribution levels set absolute levels that participants can experience and are required for long-term stability of the system (i.e., if the absolute maximum is too high, there will be less confidence in the system and a belief that the guaranteed rate has been set at much too optimistic a level). Limits on annual changes allow participants to budget their after-tax income more effectively than if no limits existed.

The way this all comes together is, once these parameters are set, the funded ratio is examined at year-end to see whether any action is required. Say, the lower funded ratio range is breached, then the actuary needs to establish a reasonable new contribution that will immediately ensure full funding given the guaranteed rate of return, target replacement rate, and current funded status. This "new" contribution rate needs to be examined to see if it breaches the parameters selected in (b) and (c). To the extent it is constrained by certain choices, the applicable contribution will be below the desired level. As is obvious, the less constrained the contribution policy, the better off the fund will be, but there are financial and often emotional implications in permitting high levels and ranges or frequent changes.

For example, in the corporate world, institutions with severe budget constraints may not want to have large annual changes in contributions inasmuch as they affect planning and other parts of the organization; thus, these institutions may want to restrict parameters (b) and (c). In addition, participants may prefer to ensure against a decline of the funded status below a certain level, thereby threatening the security of their pensions, and they may insist on a relatively high lower threshold (i.e., closer to 100 percent); moreover, sponsors may choose to have excess funds returned (i.e., contribution holidays, in the corporate world) once the funded status is reasonably above full funding (e.g., 110 percent). Participants and sponsors in our system are no different and are sensitive to similar impacts. The final selection of these parameters requires a keen understanding of the sensitivity of contributors and sponsors to change, and the desired outcome in lowering the risk to the government. In the simulations, we examine the implications of changing the parameters for the average contribution, the "nuisance factor," and the downside risk of poor pension outcomes.

KEY PARAMETERS

For each simulation, in Table 8.2 we report the investment policy (i.e., the allocation to equities, bonds, and wage growth in columns 2, 3 and 4, respectively), the contribution policy (initial or base contribution, the lower funded ratio below which

TABLE 8.2 Simulations assuming static and variable contributions in funded and mixed DB systems

Simulation number (1)	Description (funding and contribution policy) (1)	Investment policy Equity (2)	Bonds (3)	PAYGO (4)	Base cont. (5)	Lower funded ratio trigger (6)	Upper funded ratio trigger (7)	Min cont. limit (8)
1	100% Funded − Static Cont.	66.7%	33.3%	0.0%	3.23%	NA	NA	NA
2	100% Funded + Dynamic	66.7%	33.3%	0.0%	3.23%	90%	110%	−100
3	100% Funded + Dynamic	66.7%	33.3%	0.0%	3.23%	90%	110%	−25
4	60% Funded − Static Cont.	40.0%	20.0%	40.0%	4.40%	NA	NA	NA
5	60% Funded – Dynamic	40.0%	20.0%	40.0%	4.40%	90%	110%	−100
6	50% Funded – Static Cont.	33.3%	16.7%	50.0%	4.74%	NA	NA	NA
7	50% Funded + Dynamic	33.3%	16.7%	50.0%	4.74%	90%	110%	−25
8	50% Funded + Dynamic	33.3%	16.7%	50.0%	4.74%	90%	110%	−25
9	50% Funded + Dynamic	33.3%	16.7%	50.0%	4.74%	90%	110%	0
10	50% Funded + Dynamic	33.3%	16.7%	50.0%	4.74%	80%	120%	0
11	50% Funded + Dynamic	33.3%	16.7%	50.0%	4.74%	75%	125%	0
12	50% Funded + Dynamic	33.3%	16.7%	50.0%	4.74%	75%	125%	−25
13	50% Funded + Dynamic	33.3%	16.7%	50.0%	4.74%	75%	125%	−10

a top-up contribution is needed, the upper funded ratio above which a reduction can be made in the contribution rate, the minimum annual contribution, the maximum annual contribution, the maximum year-on-year increase in contributions, and the maximum year-on-year decrease in contributions in columns 5 through 11, respectively), and the key parameters by which to gauge the success of the simulation – the average contribution (column 12), standard deviations or volatility of contributions (column 13), average number of changes that the cohort experiences (column 14), the average change in contribution (column 15), average return (column 16), the standard deviation of returns (column 17), and a risk measure of the simulation (i.e., downside risk of pension below the target level or column 18), respectively. The risk measure is similar to the one used in Chapter 4 except that here the pension is guaranteed and the government bears the risk of covering shortfalls. The "nuisance factor" encompasses the standard deviation of contributions, the number of changes in the contributions out of a possible 39 (or the frequency of change), and the average change in annual contributions (or the magnitude of change); these are shown in columns 13–15, respectively. Clearly, the goal is to lower all three parameters to whatever extent possible.

Under these simulations, if no additional funds were available from the government, a funded status below 100 percent suggests that participants would receive a

LE 8.2 (*continued*)

					Simulation results				
Max cont. limit (9)	Max inc. YR to YR (10)	Max dec. YR to YR (11)	Average cont. (% of wages) (12)	Cont. volatility (%) (13)	Average number of changes in years (out of 39) (14)	Average change (absolute) in contribution (15)	Avg. invest. return (16)	Invest. return volatility (17)	Downside risk of not meeting target (DsD) (18)
NA	NA	NA	3.23%	0.00%	0	0	9.50%	12.37%	20.75%
100%	100%	100%	2.11%	44.18%	36	64.34%	9.50%	12.37%	9.94%
25%	10%	10%	3.17%	5.58%	33	7.99%	9.50%	12.37%	10.90%
NA	NA	NA	4.40%	0.00%	0	0.00%	8.10%	7.01%	13.13%
100%	100%	100%	3.75%	44.88%	35	65.60%	8.10%	7.01%	7.25%
NA	NA	NA	4.74%	0.00%	0	0.00%	7.75%	5.73%	11.26%
25%	10%	10%	4.68%	16.65%	28	7.74%	7.75%	5.73%	6.62%
25%	5%	5%	4.68%	2.58%	29	4.19%	7.75%	5.73%	7.05%
25%	3%	3%	4.70%	1.53%	27	2.26%	7.75%	5.73%	7.47%
25%	5%	5%	4.61%	1.85%	19	3.86%	7.75%	5.73%	9.26%
25%	5%	5%	4.56%	1.56%	14	3.74%	7.75%	5.73%	10.37%
25%	5%	5%	4.57%	1.54%	13	4.01%	7.75%	5.73%	10.34%
25%	5%	5%	4.57%	1.53%	13	4.01%	7.75%	5.73%	10.34%

: Cont. = contribution; Inc. = increase; Dec. = decrease; Invest. = investment; YR = year.

replacement rate below the 50 percent average salary target. We do not report the final funded ratio because the simulations are set up to achieve, on average, the target replacement rate.[4] Further, if the only variable parameter had been investment returns, given the distribution assumptions, the probability of falling below the target replacement rate would be 50 percent for all simulations and, hence, not a risk that distinguishes one simulation from the next. With stochasticity permitted for multiple variables, and different systems mixing different elements (e.g., full funding and partial funding have different reactions to changes in growth), the critical risk parameter is downside risk, a measure of how poor pension outcomes will be when accumulations by the sponsor of the fund are below the target level (i.e., the risk to the government of having to provide benefits from the general budget). In the country-level DB plan, the government benefits when accumulations for some cohorts are short of the target, for they could be offset by other cohorts that are ahead of the target. The goal of the system should be to achieve the target pension for all cohorts with the lowest possible contribution, lowest volatility of contribution (with potentially few

[4] There is a small risk that the absolute level of the pension is much too low owing to poor salary growth and because, in such a system, the participant bears the risk unless means testing or minimum pensions are offered.

changes), and low downside risk of a shortfall in pensions. However, the different simulations demonstrate the trade-offs that must be made between the average contribution, volatility of contributions (and other nuisance parameters), and the risk of pension outcomes.

RESULTS

We consider several different simulations to explore the benefit of adding "wage growth" as an asset, or creating a mixed system, and the impact of variable contributions. The basic descriptions of the simulations are summarized in Table 8.2 in column 1, and changes in assumptions from one simulation to the next are highlighted in bold.

- Simulation 1 assumes a fully funded system with static contributions. This is the base case of a fully funded system. Assets are invested 66.7 percent in equity and 33.3 percent in fixed income, which (under the assumptions stated before) provide an expected return of 9.5 percent or 5.5 percent real; the volatility of the return is 12.4 percent. The average contribution – given that it is a static system – is 3.23 percent, and the downside risk is 20.8 percent. The goal of any system, relative to this system, should be to lower the average contribution (note that this is not time weighted but a simple average) and the downside risk.

- Simulation 2 examines a variation in this base case by first permitting variable contributions to the fully funded system. This simulation tops up contributions when the funded status falls below 90 percent and reduces contributions when the funded status rises above 110 percent. The increments and decrements are largely unlimited. This variation provides a lower downside risk parameter of 9.9 percent because any "less than average returns" in a particular year or series of years do not lose out on the benefit of compounding, thereby lowering downside risk (the work of Bodie et al. 1992 offers a similar result). In other words, the contribution rate acts as a hedge for asset return volatility (i.e., following a period of bad asset returns, contributions are raised for the next period to top up the pension fund) and, hence, changes the distribution of outcomes to be less risky. However, this occurs even though the asset portfolio volatility remains unchanged. Also, by virtue of taking advantage of favorable funding occurrences and the hedging effect, the average contribution is lowered to 2.1 percent. However, the contribution volatility is extremely high (44 percent), changes are much too frequent (36 out of 39 years), and the average change is high (64 percent).

- Since Simulation 2 could have many large contribution changes, Simulation 3 extends Simulation 2 by reducing the minimum and maximum contributions, and the maximum increase and decrease in contributions to contain the "nuisance" factor. Although the contribution volatility drops to 5.6 percent (as do other "nuisance" parameters), the average contribution and downside risk increase.

   The key conclusion from the first three simulations is that variable contributions lower risk. However, all else being equal, reducing the nuisance factor typically comes at the cost of a higher average contribution, a higher downside risk to the government, or both.

- Simulation 4 is a partial funding outcome with a static contribution rate in which 40 percent of the system is PAYGO with a proportional reduction in the allocation to bonds (20 percent) and equity (40 percent), resulting in a 8.1 percent nominal return. As a consequence of diversification between assets and wage growth, the volatility of the portfolio drops to 7.01 percent. This occurs because there are diversification gains from "investing" in wage growth, but the required contribution rises to 4.4 percent (as shown in Chapter 5). The downside risk measure rises above that of Simulations 2 and 3 to 13 percent.

- Simulation 5 allows variable contribution in the partial funding outcome in Simulation 4. This simulation tops up contributions when the funded status falls below 90 percent and reduces contributions when the funded status rises above 110 percent. The increments and decrements are largely unlimited. The purpose is to show, in some simulations, contributions under partial funding with dynamic contributions may approach the level of a static, fully funded case. The average contribution is now 3.75 percent and the downside risk is 7.25 percent. Although, at face value, a fully funded system with variable contributions (simulation 3) may be preferred to a static mixed system, because the average contribution is lower (especially if we treat wage growth as the PAYGO internal rate of return), the mixed system has lower downside risk and will have a lower asset-to-wage ratio. *Hence, the mixed system may dominate on the basis of impact to capital markets or risk to the government.* The result will be country specific, and each country will need to trade off between lower contributions, lower risk, and potentially higher asset-to-wage ratios for the respective country parameters, if they prefer full funding.

- Simulation 6 reports the impact of an increase in PAYGO to 50 percent, dropping the expected return to 7.7 percent with a volatility of 5.7 percent. The equity allocation drops to 33.3 percent, and the bond allocation declines to 16.7 percent.

Simulation 6 shows, as we increase the PAYGO component, the contribution rate rises to 4.74 percent but the downside risk parameter falls to 11.3 percent (relative to Simulation 1, with a downside risk of 20 percent, and Simulation 4, with a downside risk of 13 percent) because of the negative correlation between asset returns and wage growth.

- Simulations 7 through 13 allow for dynamic contributions around 50-percent funding with changes to the contribution policy, to show how the "nuisance" factor can be minimized. For example, Simulation 7 has a −25 percent to +25 percent corridor for the contribution rate. Because the volatility of contributions is high (16 percent), as are the number of changes, we modify the three key parameters in the contribution policy. Simulation 8 restricts the maximum annual increase or decrease to only 5 percent (and Simulation 9 narrows it to 3 percent). Simulations 10–13 vary the lower funded ratio and upper funded ratio threshold to trigger increases or decreases in contributions (with changes to other parameters as well). In short, it is possible to lower (a) the contribution volatility quite dramatically (as in Simulations 8 through 13), (b) the number of changes in contributions (especially Simulations 10 through 13), and (c) average change in contributions (as in Simulations 8 through 13). These changes come with some marginal lowering of contributions relative to the static case and with some possible improvement in downside risk.

In effect, these simulations demonstrate the following:

a. Designing a good social security system, which incorporates variable contributions, can help governments contain the risk of not having sufficient funds to meet obligations;

b. A funded system with variable contributions can potentially outperform a mixed funded and PAYGO system with fixed contributions on the basis of average contributions and downside risk (Simulation 2 versus 4);

c. A mixed system with variable contributions, however, has the most attractive properties, but this is predicated on the requirement that the returns on assets, growth, and covariance factors are such that both financing approaches provide a reasonable expected return; and

d. The benefit from variable contributions depends on the rules imposed – the greater the latitude, the greater the hedging of "asset" risk and the greater the overall benefit; however, any benefit from lowering the nuisance factor can only come at the price of a potentially higher average contribution rate, a higher downside risk, or both. Each country needs to make its own trade-off on these parameters in accordance with its objectives. Moreover, with multiple cohorts, the same conclusions apply, except the magnitude is different.

SUMMARY

Throughout this book, we have discussed the importance of mixed systems and variable contributions in the context of delivering a DB scheme through a guaranteed replacement rate (initially through a guaranteed rate in a swap agreement). The traditional case for mixing funded and PAYGO systems was driven by the notion that it diversifies risk. In this chapter, we demonstrate the impact of such diversification. Clearly, these benefits depend critically on key parameters (expected future growth and its correlation to asset returns). The potential benefit of diversification is a lower cost to governments of offering a guaranteed return DB. We have also emphasized the need to create a new system that will not interfere with the smooth functioning of capital markets. In many cases, the extremely generous benefits in existing social security schemes make such mixing, or creation of partially funded systems, critical. As a result, some countries may truly reap the gains of such diversification, whereas others may have to settle for higher average contributions as a result of partial funding.

The more important result is that it is impossible to design a system in which all parameters are held constant through the future, for we live in a dynamic world. Many parameters are changing, including asset markets, demographics, prospective economic and productivity growth, and inflation. In earlier chapters, we have argued that a blue-ribbon board should have the authority to lower or raise the guaranteed rate, starting many years in the future (to reduce political risks) and as determined by the condition of the "sinking fund" and future asset market prospects.

This chapter goes a step further to demonstrate that a key policy tool available to overseers of corporate pension funds – the contribution rate – should be made variable. There are many advantages to keeping contributions variable. At the most basic level, doing so allows a fully funded scheme to achieve the benefit of diversification that accrues to a mixed system (in terms of lower downside risk) even though the volatility of asset returns is not reduced. Moreover, we achieve this with lower average contributions. This may be appealing to developing countries that have committed to full funding but for which the asset market volatility can be very high. At a more sophisticated level, we are able to show, with variable contributions, the guaranteed replacement rate is now achieved through levying contributions appropriate for the long-term realized average asset return. This prevents intertemporal problems of burden sharing had the guaranteed rate been set at an incorrect level.

Moreover, regardless of whether the primary system is funded or mixed, variable contributions help to lower the risk and potentially the cost to governments of implementing such systems. However, each country needs to make an optimal trade-off between lower average contributions and lower volatility of contributions. The tolerance of governments, employers, and employees for such changes needs to be gauged and issues of intergenerational equity have to be addressed. But it is important to isolate these because there are significant welfare benefits and finalizing such rules depoliticizes the process.

CONCLUSION

In an attempt to ensure retirement safety, many countries have created, or are considering, multipillar systems that depart from the basic principles of social security. In many cases, the reforms that emphasize three-pillar systems (with a funded, mandatory DC relying on individual accounts as a second pillar anchor) will lead to an enormous waste of resources and run the risk of leaving individuals with poor balances in their DC accounts while enriching asset managers. Often, the transition to these systems has not been effected through additional savings necessary to accumulate the required funding but instead by using government debt, which threatens to create serious future problems. Finally, although reformers have convinced themselves that these arrangements have minimized political risk and offered participants choice, they have failed to recognize the true political risk that governments continue to threaten retirement safety because of insufficient focus on target replacement rates and ensuring basic after-fee returns on investments. Moreover, offering an extensive choice of investments to participants is irrelevant when the individuals are not financially sophisticated or interested in choice as in Sweden or Australia.

We have attempted to demonstrate a more appealing structure that favors a two-pillar system in which the first pillar is a mandatory DB system (our Ideal Model) and the second is a voluntary DC system. The DB system may be either partially or fully funded but, more important, it ensures a defined benefit through pooling of assets and the government guarantees a rate of return on contributions through an innovative swap contract. This contract greatly minimizes the political risk of the government being able to manipulate funds. We recommend that a blue-ribbon board oversee the management of such assets to clear and transparent benchmarks. Further, the risks to governments of offering DBs can be minimized through variable contributions (i.e., contributions that can be changed over time to reflect the changing conditions that are unavoidable in a dynamic economy). Although countries have a tendency to want to reduce contributions only, requiring prescribed rules (such as those highlighted in the simulations) can once again minimize political risk.

The gains from our proposal are clear:

a. Creating two pillars, of which only one is mandatory, as opposed to three, will result in an enormous saving of resources;
b. There will at least be transparency as to accruals in the individual accounts and some safety in retirement;
c. The costs of ensuring such safety are minimized through the "collectivization of risks" in a pooled asset structure and variable contributions;
d. The costs of managing assets are minimized, as are political risks, leading to better after-fee replacement rates; and
e. Individuals will have access to a "risk-free" and a "risky" pension, and each person can choose a desired mix, thereby giving citizens the true and only choices they need.

We have also demonstrated how the transition can be effected in our system in the United States and Spain. The message, though, is clear for all countries. Unless immediate and thoughtful action is taken, countries are likely to encounter growing problems, forcing people to take unnecessary and unfair burdens and risks to achieve pension outcomes. And, for the sake of avoiding controversy today, they will bequeath to future citizens the harrowing experience of having to reform pension reforms!

APPENDIX 8.1. Asset Returns, Growth and Earnings (1961–96): Averages, Standard Deviations and Correlations

1961–96	United States		Germany		United Kingdom		France		Italy		Japan	
	Avg%	Std.Dev.	Avg%	Std.Dev.	Avg%	Std.Dev.	Avg%	Std.Dev.	Avg%	Std.Dev.	Avg%	Std.Dev.
GDP growth	2.90%	2.02%	3.10%	2.66%	2.30%	1.99%	3.20%	1.96%	3.30%	2.35%	5.40%	3.53%
Earnings	2.80%	1.74%	3.00%	2.89%	2.30%	2.11%	3%	2.19%	3%	2.48%	3%	2.48%
Long-term bonds	2.70%	2.48%	3.60%	1.45%	2.40%	3.51%	3.00%	2.47%	1.90%	4.41%	2.60%	4.01%
Equity	7.40%	16.70%	0.80%	16.25%	2.50%	16.25%	0.90%	18.73%	-1.80%	38.82%	5.50%	19.08%
Portfolio (60EQ/40FI)	5.52%	10.45%	1.92%	9.93%	2.46%	10.22%	1.74%	11.49%	-0.32%	23.76%	4.34%	34.62%

Correlations

United States

	GDP Growth	Earnings	Bonds	Equity
GDP growth	1			
Earnings	0.85	1		
Long-term bonds	-0.01	-0.02	1	
Equity	-0.18	-0.35	0.39	1

Germany

	GDP Growth	Earnings	Bonds	Equity
GDP growth	1			
Earnings	0.89	1		
Long-term bonds	-0.1	-0.31	1	
Equity	-0.07	-0.37	0.28	1

United Kingdom

	GDP Growth	Earnings	Bonds	Equity
GDP growth	1			
Earnings	0.61	1		
Long-term bonds	0.35	0.09	1	
Equity	0.35	-0.09	0.27	1

France

	GDP Growth	Earnings	Bonds	Equity
GDP growth	1			
Earnings	0.8	1		
Long-term bonds	-0.33	-0.63	1	
Equity	-0.11	-0.39	0.21	1

Italy

	GDP Growth	Earnings	Bonds	Equity
GDP growth	1			
Earnings	0.7	1		
Long-term bonds	-0.27	-0.39	1	
Equity	0.14	-0.16	0.23	1

Japan

	GDP Growth	Earnings	Bonds	Equity
GDP growth	1			
Earnings	0.69	1		
Long-term bonds	0.12	-0.34	1	
Equity	0.2	-0.08	29	1

Notes: Japan data 1971 = 1996; Italy data 1971 = 1996.
Reprinted with permission from Boldrin, Dolado, Jimeno, and Peracchi 1999.

References

Aaron, Henry J. 1966. The Social Insurance Paradox. *Canadian Journal of Economics*, 32:371–374.

Aaron, Henry. 1997. Privatizing Social Security: A Bad Idea Whose Time Will Never Come. *Brookings Review*, 15(3):17–23.

Aaron, Henry J. and Robert D. Reischauer. 1998. *Countdown to Reform: The Great Social Security Debate*. New York: The Century Foundation Press.

Advisory Council on Social Security [ACSS]. 1997. *Report of the 1994–1996 Advisory Council on Social Security. Volume I: Findings and Recommendations*. Washington, DC.

Ambarish, Ramasastry, and Lester Siegel. 1996. Time Is the Essence. *Risk*, August 1996, 9:41–42.

Angelis, Theodore. 1998. Investing Public Money in Private Markets: What Are the Right Questions? In R. Douglas Arnold, Michael J. Graetz, and Alicia Munnell (eds.), *Framing the Social Security Debate: Values, Politics, and Economics*. Washington, DC: Brookings Institution Press.

Archer, Bill, and Clay Shaw. 1999. The Social Security Guarantee Plan: Saving and Strengthening Social Security Without Raising Taxes or Cutting Benefits (http://www.house.gov/shaw/pr_1997_2001/pr_042899_ssbillintro.html), April 28, 1999.

Asad-Syed, Kemal, Arun Muralidhar, and Ronald J. P. van der Wouden. 1998. Determination of Replacement Rates for Savings Schemes. *Investment Management Department, Model Development Paper 1*, The World Bank.

Asher, Mukul. 1998. Social Security Systems in Southeast Asia: Are They Sustainable? Unpublished working paper.

Auerbach, Alan J. 1997. Comment on Macroeconomic Aspects of Social Security Reform by Peter A. Diamond. *Brookings Papers on Economic Activity*, 2:67–73.

Bader, Lawrence N. 1995. The Financial Executive's Guide to Pension Plans – 1995 Edition. *Salomon Brothers United States Investment Research – Pension Services*. New York.

Baker, Dean. 1999. Saving Social Security in Three Steps. *Economic Policy Institute briefing paper*, Washington, DC.

Baker, Dean, and Debayani Kar. 2002. Defined Contributions from Workers, Guaranteed Benefits for Bankers: The World Bank's Approach to Social Security Reform. *Center for Economic Policy Research*, Washington, DC, 16 July 2002.

Ball, Robert M. 1978. *Social Security Today and Tomorrow*. New York: Columbia University Press.

Ball, Robert M., and Thomas N. Bethel. 1997. Bridging the Centuries: The Case for Traditional Social Security. In Eric R. Kingson and James H. Schulz (eds.), *Social Security in the 21st Century*. New York: Oxford University Press, pp. 259–294.

Barr, Nicholas. 2000. Reforming Pensions: Myths, Truth, and Policy Choices. *IMF working paper*, Washington DC.

Bateman, Hazel, Geoffrey Kingston, and John Piggott. 2001. *Forced Saving: Mandating Private Retirement Incomes*. Cambridge, UK: Cambridge University Press, 2001.

Bateman, Hazel, and John Piggott. 1997. Mandatory Retirement Saving: Australia and Malaysia Compared. In S. Valdes-Prieto (ed.), *The Economics of Pensions*. Cambridge, UK: Cambridge University Press, pp. 318–349.

Blahous, Charles P. III. 2000. *Reforming Social Security: For Ourselves and Our Posterity*, Foreword by Senator Alan K. Simpson. Published in cooperation with the Center for Strategic and International Studies, Washington, D.C. Westport, CT: Praeger Publishers.

Blake, David. 1995. *Pension Schemes and Pension Funds in the United Kingdom*. Oxford University Press.

Blake, David. 2000. Does It Matter What Type of Pension Plan You Have? *The Economic Journal*, February 2000, 110(461):46–81.

Bodie, Zvi. 2001. Financial Engineering and Social Security Reform. Chapter 8 in *Risk Aspects of Investment-Based Social Security Reform*, Campbell and Feldstein (eds.), Chicago: University of Chicago Press, pp. 291–320.

Bodie, Zvi, and Robert C. Merton. 1992. Pension Reform and Privatization in International Perspective: The Case of Israel. *The Economics Quarterly*, Number 152, August 1992.

Bodie, Zvi, and Robert C. Merton 2002. International Pension Swaps. *Journal of Pension Economics and Finance*, January 2002.

Bodie, Zvi, A. J. Marcus, and Robert C. Merton. 1988. Defined Benefit versus Defined Contribution Pension Plans: What Are the Real Trade-offs, Z. Bodie, J. B. Shoven and D. A. Wise. (eds.), *Pensions in the U.S. Economy*. Chicago: University of Chicago Press, pp. 139–162.

Bodie, Zvi, Robert C. Merton, and W. F. Samuelson. 1992. Labor Supply Flexibility and Portfolio Choice in a Life Cycle Model. *Journal of Economic Dynamics and Control*, 16:427–449.

Boender, Guus C. E., and Fred Heemskerk. 1995. A Static Scenario Optimization Model for Asset/Liability Management of Defined Benefit Plans. *Report 9512/A Econometric Institute*, Erasmus University Rotterdam.

Boender, Guus C. E., Fred Heemskerk, and Sacha van Hoogdalem. 1996. Asset/Liability Management: de indexeringsafspraken. *Het verzekeringsarchief*, third quarter, 1996, pp. 98–102.

Boender, Guus C. E., P. C. van Aalst, and Fred Heemskerk. 1997. Modeling and Management of Assets and Liabilities of Pension Plans in the Netherlands. *World Wide Asset and Liability Modeling*, Ziemba, W. T. and J. M. Mulvey (eds.). Cambridge, UK: Cambridge University Press.

Boldrin, Michele, Juan J. Dolado, Juan Jimeno, and Franco Peracchi. 1999. The Future of Pension Systems in Europe. A Re-appraisal. *FEDEA Working Paper 99–08*. Madrid, Spain.

Boletin Oficial de la Cortes Generales. Congreso de los Diputados. 1995. Aprobación por el Pleno del Congreso de los Diputados del texto aprovado por la Comisión de Presupuestos en relación con el informe de la ponencia para el análisis de los problemas estructurales del sistema de la Seguridad Social y de las principales reformas que deberán acometerse. Serie E: Otros Textos. Num. 134, 12 April 1995.

Bosworth, Barry. 1996. Fund Accumulation: How Much? How Managed? In Peter Diamond, David Lindeman, and Howard Young (eds.), *Social Security: What Role for the Future?* National Academy of Social Insurance, Washington, DC, pp. 172–180.

Brinson, G. P, B. D. Singer, and G. L. Beebower. 1991. Determinants of Portfolio Performance II: An Update. *Financial Analysts Journal*, May–June: 40–48.

Burtless, Gary. 1998. Testimony before the Committee on Ways and Means, Subcommittee on Social Security, U.S. House of Representatives, June 18.

Cavanaugh, Francis. 1996. *The Truth about the National Debt.* Boston: Harvard Business School Press.

Cerda, Luis, and Gloria Grandolini. 1997. Mexico: The 1997 Pension Reform. *Unpublished World Bank working paper.*

Chand, Sheetal K., and Albert Jaeger. 1996. *Aging Populations and Public Pension Schemes.* Washington, DC: International Monetary Fund.

Chinoy, Ira, and Charles Babington. 1998. Low Income Players Feed Lottery Cash Cow. *Washington Post*, 3 May 1998.

Ciampi, Thomas V. 2002. Argentine Pension Funds Moving into Attack Mode. *Pensions and Investments*, 15 April 2002.

Corsetti, Giancarlo, and Klaus Schmidt-Hebbel. 1997. Pension Reform and Growth. In S. Valdes-Prieto (ed.), *The Economics of Pensions.* Cambridge, UK: Cambridge University Press, pp. 127–159.

Davis, E. Philip. 1995. *Pension Funds, Retirement-Income Security and Capital Markets – an International Perspective.* Oxford University Press.

Dert, Cees L. 1995. *Asset Liability Management for Pension Funds.* Ph.D. Thesis, Erasmus University Rotterdam.

Diamond, Peter A. 1994. Privatization of Social Security: Lessons from Chile. *Revista de Analisis Economico,* 9(1):21–33.

Diamond, Peter A. 1995. Government Provision and Regulation of Economic Support in Old Age. In Bruno, M. and Pleskovic, B. (eds.), *Proceedings of the Seventh Annual World Bank Conference on Development Economics, 1995*, pp. 83–103.

Diamond, Peter, A. 1996a. The Future of Social Security. In Peter Diamond, David Lindeman, and Howard Young (eds.), *Social Security: What Role for the Future?* National Academy of Social Insurance, Washington, D.C., pp. 172–180.

Diamond, Peter, A. 1996b. Proposals to Restructure Social Security. *Journal of Economic Perspectives,* 10(3): 67–88.

Diamond Peter, A. 1997a. Macroeconomic Aspects of Social Security Reform. *Brookings Papers on Economic Activity.* 2:1–66.

Diamond Peter A. 1997b. Insulation of Pensions from Political Risk. In S. Valdes-Prieto (ed.). *The Economics of Pensions.* Cambridge, UK: Cambridge University Press, pp. 33–57.

Diamond Peter A. 1998. The Economics of Social Security Reform. In R. Douglas Arnold, Michael J. Graetz, and Alicia Munnell (eds.), *Framing the Social Security Debate: Values, Politics and Economics.* Washington, D.C.: Brookings Institute Press.

Diamond, Peter A. 1999. Investing in Equities – The Linear Case. *Center for Retirement Research working paper.*

Diamond, Peter A., and Peter R. Orszag. 2002. Reducing Benefits and Subsidizing Individual Accounts: An Analysis of the Plans Proposed by the President's Commission to Strengthen Social Security. *Center on Budget Policy Priorities and The Century Foundation paper.* Washington, D.C.

Diamond, Peter A., and Salvador Valdes-Prieto. 1994. Social Security Reforms. In Barry Bosworth, Rudiger Dornbusch, and Raul Laban (eds.), *The Chilean Economy: Policy Lessons and Challenges.* Washington, D.C.: Brookings Institution Press.

Disney, Richard. 1998. Social Security Reform in the UK: A Voluntary Privatization, *Queen Mary and Westfield College working paper* (for conference on Social Security Reform: International Comparisons, Rome), March 1998.

Dutta, Jayasri, Sandeep Kapur, and J. Michael Orszag. 1999. A Portfolio Approach to the Optimal Funding of Pensions. *Unpublished working paper, Birkbeck College,* University of London.

East Asia and Pacific Region. 1997. Philippines Contractual Savings Reform: Improving Fiscal Sustainability and Allocative Efficiency. *World Bank,* June 1997, Appendix I.

Economist, The. 2002. Pensions – Time to Grow Up. A Survey of Pensions. 16 February 2002.

Feldstein, Martin. 1975. Towards a Reform of Social Security. *Public Interest,* 40:75–95.

Feldstein, Martin. 1995. Would Privatizing Social Security Raise Economic Wellbeing? *National Bureau of Economic Research Working Paper No. 5281,* National Bureau of Economic Research, Inc, Cambridge, MA.

Feldstein, Martin. 1996. The Missing Piece in Policy Analysis, Social Security Reform. *NBER Working Paper No. 4513.*

Feldstein, Martin. 1997. Transition to a Fully Funded Pension System: Five Economic Issues. *NBER Working Paper No. 6149.*

Feldstein, Martin. 1999. Prefunding Medicare. *American Economic Review,* 89(2):222–227.

Feldstein, Martin, and Elena Ranguelova. 2001. Individual Risk in an Investment-Based Social Security System. *American Economic Review,* 91:1116–1125 (available as *NBER Working Paper No. 8074*).

Feldstein, Martin, and Andrew Samwick. 1997. The Transition Path in Privatizing Social Security. In M. Feldstein (ed.), *Privatizing Social Security.* Chicago: University of Chicago Press, pp. 215–260.

Feldstein, Martin, and Andrew Samwick. 1998. Potential Effects of Two Percent Personal Retirement Accounts. *Tax Notes,* 79(5):615–620.

Ferrara, Peter J. 1982. *Social Security: Averting the Crisis,* Cato Institute, Washington DC.

Ferrara, Peter J. 1997. *A Plan for Privatizing Social Security.* SSP No. 8, April 30, Cato Institute, Washington, D.C.

Fontaine, Juan Andres. 1997. Are There (Good) Macroeconomic Reasons for Limiting External Investments by Pension Funds? The Chilean Experience. In S. Valdes-Prieto (ed.), *The Economics of Pensions.* Cambridge, UK: Cambridge University Press, pp. 251–275.

García, Miguel Angel. 2000. El sistema de seguridad social español en el año 2000. *Confederación Sindical de Comisiones Obreras.* Madrid, June 2000.

Garrido, Paulo. 2003. Spain Says It Postpones Pension Reform. *Investments and Pensions – Europe,* ipe.com (article 14755), May 30, 2003.

Geneakoplos, John, Olivia Mitchell, and Stephen Zeldes. 1999. Social Security's Money's Worth. In Olivia Mitchell, Robert J. Myers and Howard Young (eds.), *Prospects for Social Security Reform.* Philadelphia: Pension Research Council and University of Pennsylvania Press.

Godoy, Oscar, and Salvador Valdes-Prieto. 1997. Democracy and Pensions in Chile: Experience with Two Systems. In S. Valdes-Prieto (ed.), *The Economics of Pensions.* Cambridge, UK: Cambridge University Press, pp. 58–91.

Greenspan, Alan. 1996. Remarks at the Abraham Lincoln Award Ceremony of the Union League of Philadelphia, Philadelphia, Pennsylvania, 6 December 1996.

Greenstein, Robert. 1999. The Archer–Shaw Social Security Proposal. Center on Budget and Policy Priorities, May 1999.

Guerrard, Yves. 1998. Presentation at World Bank EDI Conference on China-Pension Reform, Hang Zhou, China, May 1998.

Heller, Peter. 1998. Rethinking Public Pension Initiatives. *International Monetary Fund Working Paper 98/61*, April 1998.

Hemming, Richard. 1998. Should Public Pension Funds Be Funded? *International Monetary Fund Working Paper 98/35*, March 1998.

Herce, José A., and Javier Alonso Meseguer. 2000. La Reforma de las Pensiones ante la Revisión del Pacto de Toledo. La Caixa; *Colección de Estudios económicos*, Num. 19. Barcelona.

Herce, Jose A. 2001. Privatization of the Spanish pension system. *Foundacion de Estudios de Economia Aplicada (FEDEA) Working Paper 2001–01*.

Ibbotson Associates. 2001. *2001 Stocks, Bonds, Bills and Inflation*. Chicago.

International Monetary Fund [IMF]. 2000. Spain: Selected Issues. IMF Staff Country Report No. 00/156. November 2000.

James, Estelle. 1998. New Models for Old Age Security: Experiments, Evidence and Unanswered Questions. *Choices in Financing Health Care and Old Age Security, World Bank Discussion Paper No. 392.*

James, Estelle, and Dimitri Vittas. 1995. Mandatory Saving Schemes: Are They an Answer to the Old Age Security Problem? In Zvi Bodie, Olivia S. Mitchell, and John Turner (eds.), *Securing Employer-Based Pensions: An International Perspective.* Philadelphia: Pension Research Council Publications.

Jimeno, Juan F. 2000. El Sistema de Pensiones Contributivas en España: Cuestiones Básicas y Perspectivas a Medio Plazo. *FEDEA Documento de Trabajo* 2000–15, May 2000.

Kaban, Elif. 2002. Diversify. It's How Rich Got Even Richer Last Year. *The Star Ledger*, 18 June 2002, p. 29.

Kelley, Jonathan M., Luis F. Martins, and John H. Carlson. 1998. The Relationship between Bonds and Stocks in Emerging Countries. *The Journal of Portfolio Management*, Spring 1998, 24(3):110–122.

Kotlikoff, Laurence, J. 1996. Privatizing Social Security: How It Works and Why It Matters. In James Poterba (ed.), *Tax Policy and the Economy 10*. Cambridge, MA: MIT Press, pp. 1–32.

Kotlikoff, Laurence. and Jeffrey Sachs. 1998. The Personal Security System: A Framework for Reforming Social Security. *Federal Reserve Bank of St. Louis Review*, 80(2):11–13.

Kotlikoff, Laurence J., Kent A. Smetters and Jan Walliser. 1998. Opting Out of Social Security and Adverse Selection. *National Bureau of Economic Research Working Paper No. 6430,* National Bureau of Economic Research, Inc., Cambridge, MA.

Krishnamurthi Sudhir, Arun Muralidhar, and Ronald Jan Pieter van der Wouden. 1998a. Pension Investment Decisions. *Investment Management Department working paper*, World Bank.

Krishnamurthi Sudhir, Arun Muralidhar, and Ronald Jan Pieter van der Wouden. 1998b. Asset Liability Management of Pension Funds. *Investment Management Department working paper*, World Bank.

Lachance, Marie-Eve, and Olivia S. Mitchell. 2002. Understanding Individual Account Guarantees. *Working Paper presented at the Risk Transfers and Retirement Income Security Conference –* Pension Research Council, Philadelphia, April 2002.

Leibowitz, Martin L., J. Benson Durham, P. Brett Hammond, and Michael Heller. 2002. Retirement Planning and the Asset/Salary Ratio. In O. S. Mitchell, Z. Bodie, P. B. Hammond, and S. Zeldes (eds.), *Innovations in Retirement Financing,* Pension Research Council. Philadelphia: University of Pennsylvania Press.

Leibowitz, Martin L., Stanley Kogelman, and N. Bader. 1994. Funding Ratio Return. *Journal of Portfolio Management,* Fall 1994, 21(1):39–48.

Lindbeck, Assar, and Mats Perrson. 2001. The Gains from Pension Reform. *Institute for International Studies (working paper),* Stockholm University, Stockholm Sweden.

Logue, D. E., and J. S. Rader. 1997. *Managing Pension Plans: A Comprehensive Guide to Improving Plan Performance* (Financial Management Association Survey and Synthesis Series). Cambridge, MA: Harvard Business School Press.

Mantel, Jan and David Bowers. 1999. *European Pension Reforms: Three Fundamental Questions.* Merrill Lynch Europe Strategy, Global Securities Research and Economics Group, London, UK.

Markowitz, Harry. 1952. Portfolio Selection, *Journal of Finance,* March 1952, 7:77–91.

Mehrling, P. 1998. The Social Mutual Fund: A Proposal for Social Security Reform. *Unpublished working paper.*

Merton, Robert C. 1983. On Consumption-Indexed Public Pension Plans. Chapter 10 in Bodie and Shoven (eds.), *Financial Aspects of the U.S. Pension System.* Chicago: University of Chicago Press, 1983.

Ministerio de Economía. 2001. Actualización del Programa de Estabilidad del Reino de España. 2000–2004. Madrid, Spain.

Ministerio de Trabajo y Asuntos Sociales. 2000. Presupuestos de la Seguridad Social. Año 2000. Madrid, Spain.

Ministerio de Trabajo y Asuntos Sociales. 2000. Guía Laboral. Madrid, Spain.

Minns, Richard. 1996. The Political Economy of Pensions. *New Political Economy,* 1(3).

Mitchell, Olivia S. 1996a. Administrative Costs in Public and Private Retirement Systems, *NBER Working Paper 5734,* Cambridge, MA.

Mitchell, Olivia S., and Flavio Ataliba Barreto. 1997. After Chile, What? Second-Round Pension Reforms in Latin America, *NBER Working Paper 6316,* Cambridge, MA.

Mitchell, Olivia S., and Roderick Carr. 1996. State and Local Pension Plans. In J. Rosenbloom (ed.), *Handbook of Employee Benefits.* Chicago: Irwin, pp. 1207–1221.

Mitchell, Olivia S., and Ping-Lung Hsin. 1997. Public Pension Governance and Performance. In S. Valdes-Prieto (ed.), *The Economics of Pensions.* Cambridge, UK: Cambridge University Press, pp. 92–126.

Modigliani Franco. 1966. The Life Cycle Hypothesis of Saving, the Demand for Wealth and the Supply of Capital. *Social Research* 33:160–217.

Modigliani, Franco, and A. Ando. 1963. The Lifecycle Hypothesis of Savings: Aggregated Implications and Tests. *American Economic Review,* 53:55–84.

Modigliani, Franco and Richard Brumberg. 1980. Utility Analysis and the Aggregate Consumption Function: An Attempt at Integration. Unpublished manuscript 1954, published in Abel, A (ed.) *The Collected Papers of Franco Modigliani,* vol. 12. Cambridge, MA: MIT Press.

Modigliani, Franco, and Maria Luisa Ceprini. 1998. Social Security Reform: A Proposal for Italy. *Review of Economic Conditions in Italy. Ed. Bank of Rome,* No. 2.

Modigliani, Franco, Maria Luisa Ceprini, and Arun Muralidhar. 2001. A Better Solution to the Social Security Problem: Funding with a Common Portfolio. *MIT Sloan School working paper.*

Modigliani, Franco, and Merton Miller. 1958. The Cost of Capital, Corporate Finance and The Theory of Investment. *American Economic Review*, 48:261–297.

Modigliani, Franco, and Andre Modigliani. 1987. The Growth of the Federal Deficit and the Role of Public Attitudes. *Public Opinion Quarterly*, 51: 459–480.

Modigliani, Franco, and Arun Muralidhar. 1998. Taxonomy of Pension Reform Issues: The Case of Social Security. *MIT Sloan School working paper*.

Munnell, Alicia. H. 1977. *The Future of Social Security*, Brookings Institute, Washington, D.C.

Munnell, Alicia H. 1999. Reforming Social Security: The Case against Individual Accounts. *Draft for National Tax Journal*.

Munnell, Alicia. H., and Annika Sunden. 2000. Investment Practices of State and Local Pension Funds: Implications for Social Security Reform. In Olivia S. Mitchell, Brett Hammond, and Anna Rappaport (eds.), *Forecasting Retirement Needs and Retirement Wealth*. Philadelphia: University of Pennsylvania Press.

Muralidhar, Arun. 2001. *Innovations in Pension Fund Management*. Stanford: Stanford University Press.

Muralidhar, Arun, and Khin Mala U. 1997. Establishing a Peer Comparator Universe for an Institutional Investor. *Journal of Pension Plan Investing*, 1(4):52–74.

Muralidhar, Arun, and Ronald Jan Pieter van der Wouden. 1998a. Reforming Pension Reform – The Case for Contributory Defined Benefit Second Pillars. *Investment Management Department, working paper*, World Bank.

Muralidhar, Arun, and Ronald Jan Pieter van der Wouden. 1998b. Welfare Costs of Defined Contribution Plans – The Case for an Alternative Pension Scheme. *Investment Management Department working paper*, World Bank.

Muralidhar, Arun, and Shaila Muralidhar. 2001. Manager Selection: The Importance of Skill. In Muralidhar, A, *Innovations in Pension Fund Management*. Stanford: Stanford University Press.

National Academy of Social Insurance [NASI]. 1999. *Issues in Privatizing Social Security: Report of an Expert Panel of the National Academy of Social Insurance*, Peter A. Diamond (ed.). Cambridge, MA: MIT Press.

National Commission on Retirement Policy (NCRP). 1998. *The 21st Century Retirement Security Plan*. Center for Strategic and International Studies. Washington, D.C.

Olienyk, John P., Robert G. Schwebach, and J. Kenton Zumwalt. 2000. The Impact of Financial Crises on International Diversification. *Colorado State University working paper*.

Orszag, Peter, and Joseph Stiglitz. 2001. Rethinking Social Security: Ten Myths about Social Security Systems. In Robert Holzman and Joseph Stiglitz (eds.), *New Ideas About Old Age Security*. The World Bank, Washington, D.C., pp. 17–56.

Parniczky, Tibor A. 1998. Private Pension Funds in Hungary – Regulation and Institutional Arrangements. *Unpublished working paper*.

Payne, Beatrix. 2002. Belgian Plan Participants Will Get Guaranteed Returns on Investments. *Pensions & Investments*, March 18:241.

Pennachi, George. 1997. Government Guarantees for Old-Age Income. *Pension Research Council Working Paper 97–10*, The Wharton School.

Penn-World Tables, http://www.nber.org/pwt56.html.

Pinera, Jose. 1997. Empowering People. Testimony before Senate Committee on Banking, Housing and Urban Affairs Subcommittee on Securities, 26 June 1997.

Poterba, James. 1998. The Rate of Return to Corporate Capital and Factor Shares. *Carnegie-Rochester Conference on Public Policy*, No. 48. (1998):211–246.

Reisen, Helmut, and John Williamson. 1997. Pension Funds, Capital Controls, and Macroeconomic Stability. In S. Valdes-Prieto (ed.), *The Economics of Pensions*. Cambridge, UK: Cambridge University Press, pp. 227–250.

Sainz de Baranda, Pedro. 2001. Social Security Reform in Spain. Unpublished thesis, MIT Sloan School of Management, Cambridge, MA.

Sales-Sarrapy, Carlos, Fernando Solis-Soberon, and Alejandro Villagomes-Amezcua. 1996. Pension System Reform: The Mexican Case, *NBER Working Paper 5780*, Cambridge, MA.

Samuelson, Paul A. 1975. Optimum Social Security in a Life-Cycle Growth. *International Economic Review*, 16:539–544.

Scheiwe, Dan. 2001. Why Australia's Pension System Is Not a Good International Model. *Unpublished working paper.*

Schieber, Sylvester J. and John B. Shoven. 1999. *The Real Deal: The History and Future of Social Security*. New Haven: Yale University Press.

Seidman, Laurence S. 1999. *Funding Social Security: A Strategic Alternative*. New York: Cambridge University Press.

Shah, Hemant. 1997. Toward Better Regulation of Private Pension Fund. *World Bank Policy Research Working Paper 1791*, June 1997.

Sharpe, William. 1964. Capital Asset Prices. *Journal of Finance*. 19:425–442.

Siegel, Jeremy, J. 1994. *Stocks for the Long Run*. Irwin, IL: Burr Ridge.

Siegel, Jeremy, J. 1999. The Shrinking Equity Premium: Historical Facts and Future Forecasts. *Unpublished working paper*. University of Pennsylvania.

Sinn, Hans-Werner. 1999. Pension Reform and Demographic Crisis: Why a Funded System Is Needed and Why It Is Not Needed. *Paper presented at the 55th IIPF Congress in Moscow*, 23–26 August 1999.

Social Security Administration (SSA). 2002. *SSA Trustees Report 2002*. Washington, D.C.

Solnik, Bruno H. 1973. *European Capital Markets: Towards a General Theory of International Investment*. Lexington, MA: Lexington Books, D.C. Heath and Company.

Sortino, Frank A., and Robert van der Meer. 1991. Downside Risk. *The Journal of Portfolio Management*, 17(4):27–32.

Srinivas, P. S., and J. Yermo. 1999. Do Investment Regulations Compromise Pension Fund Performance? Evidence from Latin America. *Revista de Análisis Económico*, 14(1): 67–120.

Thillainathan, R. 2002. Adequacy and Performance of Malaysia's Employees Provident Fund and Its Governance – A Critical Review. *Presentation at the Conference on Financial Sector Governance – World Bank, IMF, and Brookings Institute*, New York, 17–19 April 2002.

Tobin, James. 1958. Liquidity Preference as a Behavior towards Risk. *Review of Economic Studies*, 67:65–86.

Turner, John, and David Rajnes. 2002. Rate of Return Guarantees for Voluntary DC Plans. *Working paper presented at the Risk Transfers and Retirement Income Security Conference– Pension Research Council*, Philadelphia, April 2002.

United Nations, 1995. World Population Prospects – The 1994 Revision.

Usuki, Masaharu. 2002. The New Investment Management Scheme for Japan's Public Pension Fund. *Nippon Life Insurance Research Institute Working Paper No. 163*, Tokyo, April 2002.

Valdes-Prieto, Salvador. 1997. Financing a Pension Reform towards Private Funded Pensions. In S. Valdes-Prieto (ed.), *The Economics of Pensions*. Cambridge, UK: Cambridge University Press, pp. 33–57.

Vittas, Dimitri. 1996. Designing Mandatory Pension Schemes. *Viewpoint*, (72).

Walliser, Jan. 2002. Retirement Guarantees around the World: What Can They Really Promise. *Working paper presented at the Risk Transfers and Retirement Income Security Conference–* Pension Research Council, Philadelphia, April 2002.

Werding, Martin. 2003. After Another Decade of Reform: Do Pension Systems in Europe Converge? CESifo DICE Reports, *Journal of Institutional Comparisons,* (1).

Wolff, Edward N. 2002. *Retirement Insecurity: The Income Shortfalls Awaiting the Soon to Retire,* Economic Policy Institute, Washington, D.C.

World Bank. 1994. *Averting the Old Age Crisis: Policies to Protect the Old and Promote Growth.* World Bank Policy Research Report. New York: Oxford University Press.

Index

accumulation. *See also* capital formation
  advantages of, 28, 29
  in DC schemes, 4
  in defined benefit (DB) funded schemes,
    4, 28
  in Ideal Model, 34–35
  in PAYGO systems, 28–29
  contribution to national stock of capital,
    46
accumulation at retirement, formulas,
    14–15
active *vs.* passive management, 36,
    43
Advisory Council on Social Security
    (ACSS), 18
AFPs, in Chilean model, 10, 66–67
age pyramid effect, 48, 50–51. *See also*
    demographic changes
annuities. *See also* DB pension plans
  benefit of pooling in, 29–30
  benefit payment formulas for, 13–14
  contribution and replacement rate
    formulas in, 13–16
  in Ideal Model, 35–36
  from 401K plans and IRAs, 10
Argentina
  adoption of Chilean model variant in,
    42
  attempt to lower debt by, 20
  impact of manager fees on replacement
    rates in, 64
  management fees in, 63
  pension system in, 10
  risk of equity markets in, 57

asset management. *See* management
    arrangements; portfolios
asset-to-wage ratio dynamics
  equilibrium ratio, 108–109, 116, 142–144
  in funded systems, 47
  growth rate and, 53
  in PAYGO with partial funding, 206–207
  population growth and, 50–51
  in transition to funded systems, 108–109,
    142–144
Australia
  diversification of risk in partial funding,
    206
  impact of management fees on
    replacement rate in, 64
  lack of product choice in, 26
  mandated savings in, 8
  pension reforms in, ix
  superannuation schemes, 11
  tax incentives in, 31
  testing the viability of pension systems in,
    24

Belgium
  guaranteed rate of return in, 72, 197
benchmarks, importance of, 42–43, 60–61,
    67, 119
benefit payment formulas, 13–14
Blue Ribbon board, 118, 209, 221
borrowing from pension systems. *See also*
    liquidity features
  by individuals in Ideal Model, 38
  by individuals from provident funds, 11,
    26

235